KitchenAid®
Recipe Collection

pil

Publications International, Ltd.

Pictured on the front cover *(left to right, top to bottom):* Sun-Dried Tomato Cucumber Rolls *(page 88),* Papaya Berry Blend *(page 41),* Crispy Potato Latkes *(page 22),* Appetizer Cream Puffs *(page 66),* Fresh Fruit Tart with Vanilla Shortbread Crust *(page 482),* Vanilla Buttermilk Biscuits with Strawberries and Whipped Cream *(page 480)* and Fresh Tomatillo Salsa *(page 87).*

Pictured on the back cover *(left to right, top to bottom):* Vegan Sloppy Joes *(page 302),* Sunset Berry Juice *(page 52),* Grilled Prosciutto, Brie and Fig Sandwiches *(page 150),* Vietnamese Vegetarian Spring Rolls *(page 78),* Spicy Italian Sausage and Penne Pasta *(page 171),* Chipotle Lamb Chops with Crispy Potatoes *(page 197),* Mocha Dots *(page 399),* Crusty Pizza Dough *(page 166)* and Caramel Bacon Nut Brownies *(page 414).*

ISBN: 978-1-68022-020-9

Library of Congress Control Number: 2015941364

Manufactured in China.

8 7 6 5 4 3 2 1

Contents

NOTES

Basic Recipes

EGG PASTA DOUGH

MAKES ABOUT 1 POUND

3 eggs

2 tablespoons water

1 tablespoon extra virgin olive oil

1 teaspoon salt

2¼ cups all-purpose flour

1. Attach flat beater to stand mixer; beat eggs, water, olive oil and salt in mixer bowl at low speed to combine. In three additions, add flour to make dough that clumps together. Stop mixer and press a few tablespoons of dough into a small ball; dough should feel tacky, moist and pliable. If too wet, beat in flour, 1 tablespoon at a time. If too dry, beat in water, 1 tablespoon at a time. Gather dough into a ball.

2. Replace beater with dough hook; knead on low 5 minutes or until dough is smooth and elastic. Shape dough into a ball and wrap in plastic wrap; let rest at room temperature 20 minutes or refrigerate until ready to use.

3. Cut dough into quarters. Flatten one piece of dough; dust with flour. Rewrap remaining pieces to prevent drying out. Attach Pasta Sheet Roller to mixer and set to thickness setting 1. Turn mixer to medium speed; feed dough through rollers three or more times, folding and turning each time until smooth. If dough feels sticky, dust with flour. Adjust rollers to setting 2 and feed dough sheet through rollers twice. Feed dough through once at settings 3 and 4; roll to suggested roller setting. Let dough sheets rest on floured surface 10 minutes. Replace roller with desired Pasta Cutter. Feed dough sheets through cutter.

4. To cook pasta, bring large saucepan of salted water to a boil. Add pasta; cook 2 minutes or until barely tender, stirring frequently.

Semolina Pasta Dough: Substitute 1¼ cups semolina flour and 1 cup all-purpose flour for the 2¼ cups all-purpose flour.

SPINACH PASTA DOUGH

MAKES ABOUT 1¼ POUNDS

10 ounces fresh spinach*

3 eggs

1 tablespoon extra virgin olive oil

1 teaspoon salt

2¼ cups all-purpose flour

Or substitute 1 package (10 ounces) frozen chopped spinach, thawed, squeezed dry and very finely chopped. Proceed with step 2.

1. Rinse spinach and shake dry; place in large saucepan with water clinging to leaves. Cover and cook over medium heat 5 to 7 minutes or until wilted and tender, stirring occasionally. Rinse under cold water until cool; squeeze all excess liquid from spinach. Finely chop spinach and place in bowl of stand mixer.

2. Attach flat beater to stand mixer. Add eggs, olive oil and salt to spinach in mixer bowl; mix on low speed until blended. Gradually mix in flour until dough clumps together. Dough should feel tacky, moist and pliable. If too wet, add additional flour 1 tablespoon at a time. If too dry, add water 1 tablespoon at a time. Shape dough into a ball.

3. Replace flat beater with dough hook; knead on low speed 5 minutes or until smooth and elastic. Wrap dough in plastic wrap; let rest at room temperature 30 minutes or refrigerate until ready to use.

4. Cut dough into quarters. Flatten one piece of dough; dust with flour. Rewrap remaining pieces to prevent drying out. Remove dough hook; attach Pasta Sheet Roller to mixer and set to thickness setting 1. Turn mixer to medium speed; feed dough through rollers three or more times, folding and turning each time until smooth. If dough feels sticky, dust with flour. Adust rollers to setting 2 and feed dough sheet through rollers twice. Feed dough through once at settings 3 and 4; roll to desired thickness.

5. Let dough sheets rest on floured surface 10 minutes. Replace roller with desired Pasta Cutter. Feed dough sheets through cutter.

6. To cook pasta, bring large saucepan of salted water to a boil. Add pasta; cook 2 minutes or until barely tender, stirring frequently.

Note: The spinach needs to be very finely chopped or the dough will be hard to cut into noodles. For best results, process the spinach in a food processor.

WHOLE WHEAT PASTA DOUGH

MAKES ABOUT 1 POUND

2½ cups wheat berries *or* 3 cups whole wheat flour, sifted

2 eggs, beaten, plus water to equal ¾ cup

½ teaspoon salt

1. Attach Grain Mill to stand mixer. Place wheat berries in hopper and process on fine grind into bowl. Measure 3 cups flour and sift into mixer bowl. Remove Grain Mill; attach flat beater. Add egg mixture and salt to mixer bowl. Mix 30 seconds. Replace beater with dough hook; knead 1 to 2 minutes.

PASTA PREPARED WITH ROLLER AND CUTTERS

2. Cut dough into eight pieces. Flatten one piece of dough; dust with flour. Rewrap remaining pieces to prevent drying out. Attach Pasta Sheet Roller to mixer and set to thickness setting 1. Turn mixer to medium speed; feed dough through rollers three or more times, folding and turning each time until smooth. If dough feels sticky, dust with flour. Adjust rollers to setting 2 and feed dough sheet through rollers twice. Feed dough through once at settings 3 and 4; roll to suggested roller setting. Let dough sheets rest on floured surface 10 minutes. Replace roller with desired Pasta Cutter. Feed dough sheets through cutter.

KitchenAid®

PASTA PREPARED WITH PASTA PRESS

3. Assemble Pasta Press with desired plate; attach to mixer. Feed walnut-sized pieces of dough into hopper and extrude pasta into desired shapes. Immediately separate pasta, dust with flour and spread in single layer on cloth or rack to dry 20 to 30 minutes.

4. To cook pasta, bring large saucepan of salted water to a boil. Add pasta; cook 2 minutes or until barely tender, stirring frequently.

EGGLESS DOUGH FOR PASTA PRESS
MAKES ABOUT 1 POUND

1½ cups all-purpose flour

1½ cups semolina flour

¾ cup water

1. Attach flat beater to stand mixer. Combine all-purpose flour and semolina flour in mixer bowl. Gradually add water on low. Stop when rough dough forms. Dough should stick together when pressed with fingers, but should be fairly dry. Add additional water by teaspoonfuls, if needed.

2. Assemble Pasta Press with desired pasta plate; attach to stand mixer. Feed walnut-size pieces of dough into hopper and extrude pasta to desired shape. Immediately separate pasta, dust with flour and spread in single layer on cloth or rack to dry 20 to 30 minutes.

3. To cook pasta, bring large saucepan of salted water to a boil. Add pasta; cook 2 minutes or until barely tender, stirring frequently.

CHICKEN BROTH
MAKES ABOUT 12 CUPS BROTH

2 medium onions

1 capon (5 pounds),* cut into pieces

2 medium carrots, halved

2 stalks celery including leaves, cut into halves

1 clove garlic, crushed

1 bay leaf

6 sprigs fresh parsley

8 whole black peppercorns

½ teaspoon dried thyme

3 quarts cold water

Capon provides a wonderfully rich flavor, but chicken can be substituted.

1. Trim tops and roots from onions, leaving dried outer skin intact; cut into wedges.

2. Place onions, capon, carrots, celery, garlic, bay leaf, parsley, peppercorns, thyme and water into stockpot or 6-quart Dutch oven. Bring to a boil over high heat. Reduce heat to medium-low; simmer, uncovered, 3 to 4 hours, skimming foam that rises to the surface with large spoon.

3. Remove broth from heat and cool slightly. Remove large bones. Strain broth through large sieve or colander lined with several layers of damp cheesecloth removing all bones and vegetables; discard bones and vegetables. Reserve meat for another use.

4. Use immediately or refrigerate broth in tightly covered container up to 2 days or freeze broth in storage containers for several months.

FISH STOCK

MAKES ABOUT 10 CUPS STOCK

1¾ pounds fish skeletons and heads from lean fish, such as red snapper, cod, halibut or flounder

2 medium onions

3 stalks celery, cut into 2-inch pieces

10 cups cold water

2 lemon slices

¾ teaspoon dried thyme, crushed

8 whole black peppercorns

1 herb bouquet*

Use any combination of herbs and spices, such as parsley stems, thyme sprigs, peppercorns, whole cloves, bay leaves and garlic cloves. Wrap small bundles in cheesecloth or tie with string.

1. Rinse fish; cut out gills and discard.

2. Trim tops and roots from onions, leaving dried outer skin intact; cut into wedges.

3. Combine fish skeletons and heads, onions and celery in stockpot or Dutch oven. Add water, lemon, thyme, peppercorns and Herb Bouquet. Bring to a boil over high heat. Reduce heat to medium-low; simmer, uncovered, 30 minutes, skimming foam that rises to the surface.

4. Remove from heat; cool slightly. Strain stock through large sieve or colander lined with several layers of damp cheesecloth, removing all bones, vegetables and seasonings; discard.

5. Use immediately or refrigerate stock in tightly covered container up to 2 days or freeze for several months.

POACHED CHICKEN

MAKES 1¼ POUNDS COOKED CHICKEN

1¼ pounds boneless skinless chicken breasts

1 teaspoon salt

3 cloves garlic, crushed (optional)

1. Place chicken in single layer in large deep skillet. Sprinkle with salt; add cold water to cover by 1 inch. Add garlic to water, if desired. Bring to a boil over high heat.

2. Reduce heat to maintain a simmer; cover and cook 10 to 15 minutes until chicken is cooked through (165°F). Transfer chicken to cutting board to cool. Shred, dice or cube chicken when cool enough to handle.

PESTO SAUCE

MAKES ½ CUP

1 cup packed fresh basil leaves

½ cup pine nuts, toasted*

1 ounce Parmesan cheese (optional)

2 cloves garlic

½ teaspoon salt

¼ teaspoon freshly ground black pepper

¼ cup plus 1 tablespoon olive oil, divided

Place pine nuts in small saucepan. Heat over low heat 2 minutes or until light brown and fragrant, shaking occasionally.

1. Place basil, pine nuts, cheese, if desired, garlic, salt and pepper in food processor; drizzle with 1 tablespoon olive oil. Process about 10 seconds or until coarsely chopped.

KitchenAid®

2. With motor running, drizzle in remaining ¼ cup olive oil. Process about 30 seconds or until almost smooth. Transfer to jar with tight-fitting lid; store in refrigerator.

Note: This recipe can be doubled.

BASIC CRÊPES

MAKES ABOUT 12 CRÊPES

1½ cups milk

1 cup all-purpose flour

2 eggs

¼ cup butter, melted and cooled, divided

¼ teaspoon salt

1. Combine milk, flour, eggs, 2 tablespoons butter and salt in food processor; pulse until smooth. Let stand at room temperature 30 minutes.

2. Heat ½ teaspoon butter in 7- or 8-inch crêpe pan or skillet over medium heat. Pour ¼ cup batter into hot pan. Immediately swirl batter over entire surface of pan.

3. Cook 1 to 2 minutes or until crêpe is brown around edges and top is dry. Carefully turn with spatula; cook 30 seconds. Transfer crêpe to waxed paper. Repeat with remaining batter, adding remaining butter only as needed to prevent sticking; stack finished crepes between sheets of waxed paper.

Tip: Crepes can be covered and refrigerated up to 1 day or frozen up to 1 month. Thaw before using.

SINGLE-CRUST PIE PASTRY

MAKES PASTRY FOR ONE 9-INCH PIE

1¼ cups all-purpose flour

½ teaspoon salt

6 tablespoons cold butter, cubed

3 to 4 tablespoons ice water

½ teaspoon cider vinegar

1. Combine flour and salt in medium bowl. Cut in butter with pastry blender or two knives until mixture resembles coarse crumbs. Combine 3 tablespoons ice water and vinegar in small bowl. Add to flour mixture; mix with fork until dough forms, adding additional water as needed.

2. Shape dough into disc; wrap in plastic wrap. Refrigerate 30 minutes.

DOUBLE-CRUST PIE PASTRY

MAKES PASTRY FOR ONE 9-INCH PIE

2½ cups all-purpose flour

1 teaspoon salt

1 teaspoon sugar

1 cup (2 sticks) cold butter, cubed

7 tablespoons ice water

1 tablespoon cider vinegar

1. Attach flat beater to stand mixer. Combine flour, salt and sugar in mixer bowl. Add butter; mix on low speed 1 minute or until coarse crumbs form.

2. Combine ice water and vinegar in small bowl. With mixer running on low speed, drizzle in enough water mixture just until dough starts to come together.

3. Turn out dough onto lightly floured surface; press into a ball. Divide in half. Shape each half into a disc; wrap separately in plastic wrap. Refrigerate 30 minutes.

RICH PIE PASTRY

MAKES PASTRY FOR ONE 9-INCH DOUBLE CRUST PIE

> 2 cups all-purpose flour
>
> ¼ teaspoon salt
>
> 6 tablespoons cold butter
>
> 6 tablespoons shortening or lard
>
> 6 to 8 tablespoons ice water

1. Combine flour and salt in medium bowl. Cut in butter and shortening with pastry blender until mixture resembles coarse crumbs. Sprinkle in ice water, 1 tablespoon at a time, mixing until dough forms.

2. Turn out dough onto lightly floured surface; press into a ball. Divide dough in half. Shape each half into a disc; wrap separately in plastic wrap. Refrigerate 30 minutes.

Note: Pie pastry can also be made in a food processor. Pulse flour and salt in food processor. Add butter and shortening; pulse until mixture forms coarse crumbs. With motor running, drizzle water by tablespoons through feed tube until dough forms.

CREAM CHEESE FROSTING

> 1 package (8 ounces) cream cheese, softened
>
> ½ cup (1 stick) butter, softened
>
> 2 tablespoons vanilla
>
> 2 cups powdered sugar
>
> 3 to 5 tablespoons milk

1. Attach flat beater to stand mixer. Beat cream cheese, butter and vanilla in mixer bowl on medium speed 2 minutes or until light and fluffy.

2. Beat in powdered sugar on low speed until well blended. Beat on medium speed 3 minutes or until fluffy. If frosting is too thick, add milk, 1 tablespoon at a time, until desired consistency is reached.

CHOCOLATE FROSTING

> 6 tablespoons butter, softened
>
> 5 cups powdered sugar
>
> ½ cup unsweetened cocoa powder
>
> 1 teaspoon vanilla
>
> 4 to 6 tablespoons milk

1. Attach flat beater to stand mixer. Beat butter in mixer bowl on medium speed 2 minutes or until creamy. Gradually add powdered sugar and cocoa, beating until smooth. Beat in vanilla.

2. Add milk, 1 tablespoon at a time, until desired consistency is reached. Beat 4 to 6 minutes on medium-high speed until fluffy.

KitchenAid®

BUTTERCREAM FROSTING

½ cup (1 stick) butter, softened

3 cups powdered sugar

2 tablespoons milk

½ teaspoon vanilla

Dash of salt

1. Attach flat beater to stand mixer. Beat butter in mixer bowl on medium-high speed until creamy. Gradually add powdered sugar, beating on medium-low speed 2 minutes until creamy and well blended.

2. Beat in milk, vanilla and salt until blended. Beat on medium-high speed 4 to 6 minutes or until fluffy.

ESPRESSO CHOCOLATE FROSTING

½ cup (1 stick) butter, softened

4 cups powdered sugar

5 to 6 tablespoons brewed espresso, divided

3 ounces semisweet chocolate, melted

1 teaspoon vanilla

Dash of salt

1. Attach flat beater to stand mixer. Beat butter in mixer bowl on medium-high speed 1 minute or until creamy. Gradually add powdered sugar, beating on medium-low speed 2 minutes or until creamy. Add 4 tablespoons espresso; beat until smooth.

2. Add melted chocolate, vanilla and salt. Beat on medium-high speed 4 to 6 minutes or until fluffy, adding additional espresso if needed for desired consistency.

LEMON CURD
MAKES ABOUT 1 CUP

2 regular lemons or Meyer lemons

½ cup sugar

6 tablespoons butter

Pinch of salt

2 eggs, beaten

1. Finely grate lemon peel to measure ½ tablespoon. Juice lemons; measure ⅓ cup juice.

2. Combine sugar, butter, salt, lemon juice and lemon peel in medium saucepan over medium heat, stirring until butter is melted and sugar is dissolved. Gradually whisk in eggs in thin steady stream. Cook over medium-low heat 5 minutes or until thickened to the consistency of pudding, whisking constantly.

3. Strain through fine-mesh sieve into medium bowl. Press plastic wrap onto surface; refrigerate until cold. Transfer to jar with tight-fitting lid; store in refrigerator.

SWEETENED WHIPPED CREAM
MAKES ABOUT 3 CUPS

1½ cups heavy cream

¼ cup powdered sugar

½ teaspoon vanilla

1. Place mixer bowl and wire whip in the freezer for 15 minutes to chill. Attach wire whip; pour cold heavy cream into mixer bowl. Begin whipping on low speed and gradually increase speed to high.

2. When cream forms soft peaks, add powdered sugar and vanilla and continue beating until the desired consistency. (Do not overbeat or cream will become grainy.)

CHOCOLATE CURLS

8 ounces semisweet chocolate

1. Melt chocolate in small bowl over hot water, stirring often.

2. Pour melted chocolate onto cold baking sheet and spread out into a 6×4-inch rectangle. Refrigerate 15 minutes or just until set.

3. Pull long edge of a long metal spatula across surface of soft chocolate, letting it curl up in front of the spatula. Place curls on waxed paper to set.

NOTE ON TOASTED NUTS

Many of the recipes in this book call for nuts that are toasted. There are two basic techniques for toasting any kind of nut. Use the oven method if you're baking and already have the oven preheated; use the skillet method if you aren't using the oven.

OVEN METHOD
Preheat oven to 350°F. Spread nuts in single layer on ungreased baking sheet. Bake 8 to

10 minutes or until very lightly browned, stirring frequently.

SKILLET METHOD
Place nuts in nonstick skillet large enough to fit nuts in single layer. Cook over medium-low heat 2 to 5 minutes or until nuts are fragrant and beginning to brown, stirring frequently.

NOTE ON SPINACH

Use the following technique to substitute fresh spinach for frozen chopped spinach in recipes that call for 1 package (10 ounces) thawed frozen chopped spinach.

10 ounces fresh baby spinach or stemmed spinach leaves

1. Rinse spinach and shake dry; place in large saucepan or wok with water clinging to leaves. Cover and cook over medium heat 7 minutes or until wilted and tender, stirring occasionally.

2. Drain and rinse under cold running water until cool. Squeeze all excess liquid from spinach a handful at a time. Finely chop spinach in food processor or with knife.

KitchenAid®

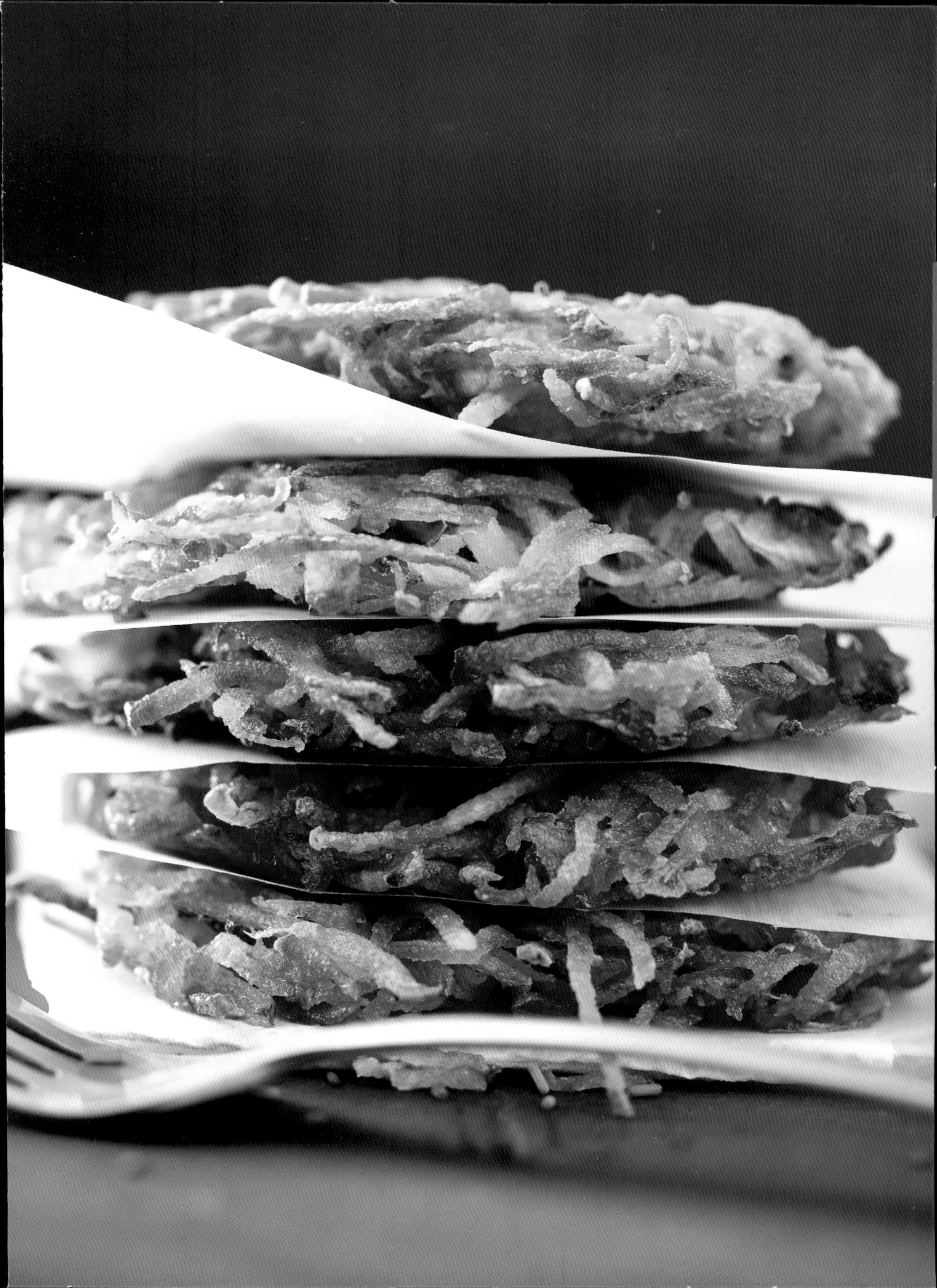

Breakfast and Brunch

BLUEBERRY PANCAKES

MAKES 10 TO 12 PANCAKES

3 tablespoons butter

1¼ cups milk

1 egg, beaten

1¼ cups all-purpose flour

¼ cup packed brown sugar

1 tablespoon baking powder

½ teaspoon salt

½ cup fresh blueberries, plus additional for garnish

Powdered sugar or maple syrup

1. Melt butter in large skillet or griddle over medium heat. Pour into medium bowl, leaving thin film of butter in skillet. Whisk milk and egg into butter in bowl.

2. Combine flour, brown sugar, baking powder and salt in large bowl; mix well. Add milk mixture; stir just until blended. *Do not beat.* Fold in ½ cup blueberries.

3. Heat skillet over medium heat. Pour batter by ¼ cupfuls into skillet. Cook 2 to 3 minutes or until bubbles appear on surface and edges are dull. Turn; cook until golden brown on both sides. Top with additional blueberries, if desired; sprinkle with powdered sugar.

IRISH PORRIDGE WITH BERRY COMPOTE

MAKES 4 SERVINGS

4 cups plus 1 tablespoon
  water, divided

½ teaspoon salt

1 cup steel-cut oats

½ teaspoon ground cinnamon

⅓ cup half-and-half

¼ cup packed brown sugar

1 cup fresh strawberries,
  hulled and quartered

1 container (6 ounces) fresh
  blackberries

1 container (6 ounces) fresh
  blueberries

3 tablespoons granulated
  sugar

1. Bring 4 cups water and salt to a boil in medium saucepan over medium-high heat. Whisk in oats and cinnamon. Reduce heat to medium; simmer, uncovered, about 40 minutes or until water is absorbed and oats are tender. Remove from heat; stir in half-and-half and brown sugar.

2. Meanwhile, combine strawberries, blackberries, blueberries, granulated sugar and remaining 1 tablespoon water in small saucepan; bring to a simmer over medium heat. Cook 8 to 9 minutes or until berries are tender but still hold their shape, stirring occasionally.

3. Serve porridge topped with berry compote.

KitchenAid®

OLD-FASHIONED CAKE DOUGHNUTS

MAKES 12 DOUGHNUTS AND HOLES

3¾ cups all-purpose flour

1 tablespoon baking powder

1 teaspoon ground cinnamon

¾ teaspoon salt

½ teaspoon ground nutmeg

3 eggs

¾ cup granulated sugar

1 cup applesauce

2 tablespoons butter, melted

2 cups sifted powdered sugar

3 tablespoons milk

½ teaspoon vanilla

1 quart vegetable oil

Colored sprinkles (optional)

1. Combine flour, baking powder, cinnamon, salt and nutmeg in medium bowl.

2. Attach flat beater to stand mixer. Beat eggs in mixer bowl on high speed until frothy. Gradually beat in granulated sugar; beat 4 minutes until thick and pale yellow in color. Reduce speed to low; beat in applesauce and butter.

3. Beat in flour mixture until well blended. Divide dough into halves. Place each half on large piece of plastic wrap. Pat each half into 5-inch square; wrap in plastic wrap. Refrigerate 3 hours or until cold.

4. For glaze, whisk powdered sugar, milk and vanilla in small bowl until smooth. Cover and set aside.

5. Roll out half of dough to ¼-inch thickness. Cut dough with floured 3-inch doughnut cutter; repeat with remaining dough. Reserve doughnut holes. Reroll scraps and cut additional doughnuts. Heat oil in Dutch oven over medium heat to 375°F. Adjust heat to maintain temperature.

6. Cook doughnuts and holes in batches 2 minutes or until golden brown, turning often. Remove with slotted spoon; drain on paper towels. Spread glaze over warm doughnuts; decorate with sprinkles, if desired.

HONEY-PECAN COFFEE CAKE

MAKES 12 SERVINGS

⅔ **cup milk**

6 **tablespoons butter, softened**

9 **tablespoons honey, divided**

2½ **to 3½ cups all-purpose flour, divided**

1 **package (¼ ounce) active dry yeast**

¾ **teaspoon salt**

3 **eggs, divided**

1¼ **cups toasted* coarsely chopped pecans, divided**

3 **tablespoons packed brown sugar**

2 **tablespoons butter, melted**

1 **tablespoon ground cinnamon**

1 **teaspoon water**

*See page 12.

1. Heat milk, softened butter and 3 tablespoons honey in small saucepan over low heat until temperature reaches 120° to 130°F.

2. Attach flat beater to stand mixer. Combine 2¼ cups flour, yeast and salt in mixer bowl. Gradually add milk mixture on low speed. Add 2 eggs; beat 2 minutes or until mixture is well blended. Gradually add additional flour until soft dough forms.

3. Replace flat beater with dough hook; knead on low speed 5 to 8 minutes or until dough is smooth and elastic, gradually adding remaining flour to prevent sticking if necessary. Shape dough into a ball. Place in large, lightly greased bowl; turn once to grease surface. Cover and let rise in warm place 35 to 40 minutes or until dough has increased in size by one third.

4. Punch down dough; turn out onto lightly floured surface. Roll out into 14×8-inch rectangle using lightly floured rolling pin.

5. Grease 9-inch cake pan. Combine 1 cup pecans, brown sugar, melted butter, cinnamon and 3 tablespoons honey in small bowl. Spread evenly over dough; press in gently with fingertips. Roll up tightly from one long end; pinch seams lightly to seal. Turn seam side down; flatten slightly. Twist dough six to eight turns.

6. Place dough in prepared pan in loose spiral, starting in center and working to the side. Tuck outside end under dough; pinch to seal. Loosely cover with lightly greased sheet of plastic wrap. Let rise in warm place about 1 hour or until doubled.

7. Preheat oven to 350°F. Place pan on baking sheet. Beat remaining egg with 1 teaspoon water in small bowl; brush over dough. Drizzle remaining 3 tablespoons honey evenly over top; sprinkle with remaining ¼ cup pecans.

8. Bake about 45 minutes or until deep golden brown. Turn pan and tent with sheet of foil halfway through baking time to prevent burning. Remove foil for last 5 minutes of baking. Cool in pan on wire rack 5 minutes. Remove from pan; cool completely on wire rack.

RASPBERRY BREAKFAST RING

MAKES 16 SERVINGS

½ cup warm milk (105° to 115°F)

⅓ cup warm water (105° to 115°F)

1 package (¼ ounce) active dry yeast

3 to 3¼ cups all-purpose flour, divided

1 egg

3 tablespoons butter, melted

3 tablespoons granulated sugar

1 teaspoon salt

¼ cup red raspberry fruit spread

1 teaspoon grated orange peel

⅓ cup powdered sugar

2 teaspoons orange juice

Sliced almonds (optional)

1. Attach dough hook to stand mixer. Combine milk, water and yeast in mixer bowl. Let stand 5 minutes.

2. Add 2¾ cups flour, egg, butter, granulated sugar and salt; beat on medium-low speed until soft dough forms. Knead about 6 minutes or until dough is smooth and elastic, adding remaining flour to prevent sticking if necessary. Place dough in large, lightly greased bowl; turn to grease top. Cover and let rise in warm place 45 to 60 minutes or until doubled.

3. Punch dough down. Cover and let rest in warm place 10 minutes. Line large baking sheet with parchment paper. Combine fruit spread and orange peel in small bowl; mix well.

4. Roll out dough into 16×9-inch rectangle on lightly floured surface. Spread fruit spread mixture evenly over dough. Roll up tightly from long end; pinch seam to seal. Shape dough into ring on prepared baking sheet, seam side down; pinch ends to seal.

5. Use serrated knife to cut slices three fourths of the way through dough every inch. Slightly twist each section of the dough out, forming many rings. Cover loosely with plastic wrap and let rise in warm place 30 to 45 minutes or until doubled. Preheat oven to 350°F.

6. Bake about 25 minutes or until lightly browned. Remove to wire rack to cool completely.

7. Whisk powdered sugar and orange juice in small bowl until well blended. Drizzle over bread. Sprinkle with almonds, if desired.

KitchenAid®

CRISPY POTATO LATKES

MAKES 8 TO 10 LATKES

¼ large white onion

5 russet potatoes, scrubbed
　and peeled

2 eggs

2 tablespoons all-purpose flour

¾ teaspoon salt

½ teaspoon freshly ground
　black pepper

½ cup vegetable or canola oil
　for frying

　Sour cream and/or
　applesauce

1. Assemble KitchenAid® Pro Line® 16-cup Food Processor with large work bowl and adjustable slicing disc; slide to fifth notch. Slice onion on high speed. Transfer to large bowl.

2. Replace slicing disc with medium (4mm) shredding disc. Shred potatoes on high speed. Place potatoes in another large bowl. Cover with water; soak 15 minutes. Drain in colander, squeezing out excess water. Spread potatoes on clean kitchen towel and blot dry. Add potatoes to onion; mix well.

3. Whisk eggs, flour, salt and pepper in small bowl until well blended. Add to potato mixture; mix well.

4. Heat oil in large cast iron or heavy skillet over medium-high heat until small drop of batter sizzles. Drop potato mixture by ¼ cupfuls into skillet; press down lightly with back of measuring cup to flatten. Cook 5 to 7 minutes per side or until golden brown and crispy. Drain on paper towel-lined baking sheet. Serve with sour cream and applesauce.

KitchenAid®

BACON-CHEESE GRITS

MAKES 4 SERVINGS

2 cups milk

½ cup quick-cooking grits

1½ cups (6 ounces) shredded sharp Cheddar cheese *or* 6 slices American cheese, torn into bite-size pieces

2 tablespoons butter

1 teaspoon Worcestershire sauce

½ teaspoon salt

⅛ teaspoon ground red pepper (optional)

4 thick-cut slices bacon, crisp-cooked and chopped

1. Bring milk to a boil in large saucepan over medium-high heat. Slowly stir in grits. Return to a boil. Reduce heat; cover and simmer 5 minutes, stirring frequently.

2. Remove from heat. Stir in cheese, butter, Worcestershire sauce, salt and red pepper, if desired. Cover and let stand 2 minutes or until cheese is melted. Top each serving with bacon.

Variation: For a thinner consistency, add an additional ½ cup milk.

CRISPY SKILLET POTATOES

MAKES 4 SERVINGS

2 tablespoons olive oil

4 red potatoes, cut into thin wedges

½ cup chopped onion

2 tablespoons lemon pepper

½ teaspoon coarse salt

Chopped fresh parsley (optional)

1. Heat olive oil in large skillet over medium heat. Stir in potatoes, onion, lemon pepper and salt. Cover and cook 25 to 30 minutes or until potatoes are tender and browned, turning occasionally.

2. Sprinkle with parsley just before serving.

COUNTRY FRENCH EGGS

MAKES 6 SERVINGS

6 hard-cooked eggs, peeled and sliced in half lengthwise

2 tablespoons milk

1 tablespoon minced fresh tarragon *or* 1 teaspoon dried tarragon

1 clove garlic, minced

⅛ teaspoon salt

⅛ teaspoon freshly ground black pepper

2 teaspoons Dijon mustard

2 teaspoons tarragon vinegar

1 teaspoon honey

Dash salt and freshly ground black pepper

1 tablespoon olive oil

1 tablespoon butter

1. Remove yolks from egg halves. Mash yolks in small bowl. Add milk, minced tarragon, garlic, ⅛ teaspoon salt and ⅛ teaspoon pepper; mix well. Reserve 2 tablespoons yolk mixture. Fill egg halves with remaining yolk mixture, patting firmly into each egg.

2. For dressing, add mustard, vinegar and honey to reserved yolk mixture. Season with dash of salt and pepper. Whisk in olive oil, pouring in thin steady stream; set aside.

3. Heat butter in large skillet over medium-low heat. Place egg halves in skillet, yolk side down. Cook 2 to 3 minutes or until yolk mixture is slightly golden. *Do not overcook.*

4. Pour dressing onto serving plate. Place cooked egg halves on plate over dressing.

Tip: For a more elegant breakfast or brunch entrée, add bits of cooked fish, shellfish, spinach or chopped mushrooms to the mashed yolk mixture before filling the egg halves.

KitchenAid®

FRUIT-FILLED PUFF PANCAKE

MAKES 4 SERVINGS

½ cup all-purpose flour

¼ teaspoon salt

2 eggs

½ cup milk

1 teaspoon vanilla

1 tablespoon butter

2 cups sliced fresh
strawberries

1 teaspoon granulated sugar

Powdered sugar

1. Preheat oven to 400°F.

2. Combine flour and salt in large bowl. Whisk eggs in medium bowl until frothy. Add milk and vanilla; whisk until blended. Add to flour mixture; whisk until blended. (Batter will be slightly lumpy.)

3. Place butter in 9-inch glass pie plate. Heat in oven 1 minute or until butter is bubbly. Remove from oven; swirl pan to coat bottom and sides of pie plate. Pour excess butter into batter; mix well. Pour batter into hot pie plate; bake 20 minutes or until puffed and lightly browned.

4. Meanwhile, combine strawberries and granulated sugar in medium bowl.

5. Cut pancake into wedges; sprinkle with powdered sugar. Top with strawberries.

KitchenAid®

APRICOT NUT PANCAKES

MAKES 12 PANCAKES

⅔ cup whole wheat flour

⅓ cup all-purpose flour

2 teaspoons baking powder

2 tablespoons sugar

¼ teaspoon salt

¾ cup milk

1 egg

2 tablespoons butter, melted

½ cup dried apricots, finely chopped*

½ cup finely chopped walnuts

Vegetable oil

Maple syrup

If apricots are too sticky to chop, dust with flour before chopping.

1. Combine whole wheat flour, all-purpose flour, baking powder, sugar and salt in medium bowl.

2. Attach flat beater to stand mixer. Beat milk, egg and butter in mixer bowl on medium-high speed 30 seconds. With mixer running on low speed, add flour mixture in one addition. Beat 30 seconds; stop and scrape bowl. Beat 30 seconds on medium-high speed. Add apricots and walnuts; mix on low speed until blended.

3. Heat griddle or heavy skillet over medium heat; brush with vegetable oil or melted butter. Drop 2 tablespoons batter onto griddle for each pancake. Cook 2 to 3 minutes or until bubbles appear on surface and edges are dull. Turn; cook until golden brown on both sides. Serve with maple syrup.

LEMON CRÊPES WITH FRESH RASPBERRIES AND CREAM

MAKES 8 TO 9 CRÊPES

½ cup Lemon Curd (page 11)

1½ cups heavy cream

3 tablespoons powdered sugar, plus additional for garnish

2 tablespoons sour cream

1 tablespoon lemon juice

1 teaspoon orange liqueur (optional)

8 Basic Crêpes (page 9)

1 container (6 ounces) fresh raspberries

1. Prepare Lemon Curd.

2. Chill bowl of stand mixer and wire whip. Attach wire whip to stand mixer. Beat heavy cream and 3 tablespoons powdered sugar in chilled mixer bowl on high speed until stiff peaks form. Fold in sour cream, lemon juice and liqueur, if desired. Refrigerate until ready to use.

3. Prepare Basic Crêpes.

4. Spread 1 tablespoon curd evenly over each crêpe; spoon ⅓ cup filling down center. Fold edges to center of crêpe to enclose filling. Sprinkle with fresh raspberries and additional powdered sugar, if desired. Serve immediately.

FRUITED GRANOLA

MAKES ABOUT 20 SERVINGS

3 cups quick oats

1 cup sliced almonds

1 cup honey

½ cup wheat germ or honey wheat germ

3 tablespoons butter, melted

1 teaspoon ground cinnamon

3 cups whole grain cereal flakes

½ cup dried blueberries or golden raisins

½ cup dried cranberries or cherries

½ cup dried banana chips or chopped pitted dates

1. Preheat oven to 325°F.

2. Spread oats and almonds in single layer in 13×9-inch baking pan. Bake 15 minutes or until lightly toasted, stirring frequently.

3. Combine honey, wheat germ, butter and cinnamon in large bowl until well blended. Add oats and almonds; toss to coat completely. Spread mixture in single layer in baking pan. Bake 20 minutes or until golden brown. Cool completely in pan on wire rack. Break mixture into chunks.

4. Combine oat chunks, cereal, blueberries, cranberries and banana chips in large bowl. Store in airtight container at room temperature up to 2 weeks.

GLAZED COFFEE CAKE RING

MAKES 8 SERVINGS

3 cups all-purpose flour

1 package (¼ ounce) active dry yeast

1 teaspoon salt

1 cup warm water (120°F)

2 tablespoons butter, melted

¼ cup raisins or dried cranberries

½ cup water

3 tablespoons butter, softened

2 tablespoons sugar

1 teaspoon ground cinnamon

¼ teaspoon ground nutmeg

2 tablespoons apricot fruit spread

1 ounce sliced almonds or pecan chips, toasted*

*See page 12.

1. Attach dough hook to stand mixer. Combine flour, yeast and salt in mixer bowl. Stir in warm water and butter to form rough dough. Knead on low speed 5 to 7 minutes or until dough is smooth and elastic.

2. Shape dough into a ball. Place in large, lightly greased bowl; turn once to grease surface. Cover and let rise in warm place 45 minutes or until doubled.

3. Preheat oven to 350°F. Place raisins in small microwavable bowl; cover with ½ cup water. Microwave on HIGH 2 minutes.

4. Roll out dough into 12×8-inch rectangle on lightly floured surface. Spread 3 tablespoons softened butter over dough. Combine sugar, cinnamon and nutmeg in small bowl; sprinkle mixture evenly over dough.

5. Drain raisins; sprinkle evenly over cinnamon-sugar mixture. Roll up dough, starting at wide end.

6. Spray nonstick baking sheet with nonstick cooking spray. Place dough on baking sheet. Join ends to make ring. Pinch dough tightly to seal. Using serrated knife, make 5 to 6 diagonal slits into top of dough.

7. Bake 23 minutes or until golden. Remove to wire rack; let cool 5 minutes.

8. Place fruit spread in small microwavable bowl. Microwave on HIGH 15 seconds or until melted. Stir. Brush evenly over top and sides of coffee cake. Sprinkle with almonds. Cut into slices. Serve warm or at room temperature.

KitchenAid®

FRENCH TOAST STICKS

MAKES 4 SERVINGS

4 eggs

⅓ cup milk

1 teaspoon ground cinnamon

1 teaspoon vanilla

1 round loaf unsliced peasant-style whole grain bread

4 teaspoons butter, divided

1 teaspoon powdered sugar

Maple syrup

1. Whisk eggs, milk, cinnamon and vanilla in large bowl.

2. Cut bread into 12 (4×1×1-inch) pieces.

3. Melt 2 teaspoons butter on large nonstick griddle or in skillet over medium-high heat. Dip bread sticks, one at a time, in egg mixture to coat. Immediately place on griddle; cook until golden brown on all sides. Sprinkle with powdered sugar and serve with maple syrup.

CARAMELIZED BACON

MAKES 6 SERVINGS

12 slices (about 12 ounces) applewood-smoked bacon

½ cup packed brown sugar

2 tablespoons water

¼ to ½ teaspoon ground red pepper

1. Preheat oven to 375°F. Line 15×10-inch jelly-roll pan with heavy-duty foil. Spray wire rack with nonstick cooking spray; place in prepared pan.

2. Cut bacon in half crosswise, if desired; arrange in single layer on prepared wire rack. Combine brown sugar, water and red pepper in small bowl; mix well. Brush generously over bacon.

3. Bake 20 to 25 minutes or until bacon is well browned. Immediately remove to serving platter; cool completely.

Note: Bacon can be prepared up to 3 days ahead and stored in the refrigerator between sheets of waxed paper in a resealable food storage bag. Let stand at room temperature at least 30 minutes before serving.

APPLE PANCAKES

MAKES 10 TO 12 PANCAKES

2 tablespoons plus
2 teaspoons butter

1¼ cups milk

2 eggs

1¼ cups all-purpose flour

¼ cup finely chopped dried
apple

¼ cup golden raisins

3 tablespoons sugar

1 tablespoon baking powder

1 teaspoon ground cinnamon

½ teaspoon salt

Maple syrup and additional
butter

1. Melt butter in large skillet or griddle over medium heat. Pour into medium bowl, leaving thin film of butter in skillet. Whisk milk and eggs into butter in bowl until well blended.

2. Combine flour, apple, raisins, sugar, baking powder, cinnamon and salt in large bowl. Add milk mixture; stir to combine.

3. Pour ¼ cup batter into skillet for each pancake. Cook over medium heat 2 to 3 minutes on each side or until golden. Serve with maple syrup and additional butter.

Variation: Substitute ¼ cup chopped pecans for the raisins.

KitchenAid®

HAM AND CHEESE BREAD PUDDING

MAKES 8 SERVINGS

1 small loaf (8 ounces)
   sourdough, country French
   or Italian bread, cut into
   1-inch-thick slices

3 tablespoons butter, softened

8 ounces ham or smoked ham,
   cubed

1 cup (4 ounces) shredded
   Cheddar cheese

3 eggs

2 cups milk

1 teaspoon ground mustard

½ teaspoon salt

⅛ teaspoon freshly ground
   white pepper

1. Grease 11×7-inch baking dish. Spread one side of each bread slice with butter. Cut into 1-inch cubes; place on bottom of prepared dish. Top with ham; sprinkle with cheese.

2. Whisk eggs in medium bowl. Whisk in milk, mustard, salt and pepper. Pour evenly over bread mixture. Cover; refrigerate at least 6 hours or overnight.

3. Preheat oven to 350°F. Bake, uncovered, 45 to 50 minutes or until puffed and golden brown and knife inserted into center comes out clean. Serve immediately.

KitchenAid®

Juices and Smoothies

PAPAYA BERRY BLEND

MAKES 4 SERVINGS

1½ **cups fresh raspberries**

⅛ **papaya, peeled and seeded**

½ **grapefruit, peeled, seeded and separated into sections**

1. Assemble juicer for desired amount of pulp.

2. Juice raspberries, papaya and grapefruit; stir. Serve immediately.

BLACK FOREST SMOOTHIE

MAKES 2 SERVINGS

1 container (6 ounces) dark cherry yogurt

½ cup frozen dark sweet cherries

¼ cup milk

2 tablespoons sugar

2 tablespoons unsweetened cocoa powder

¼ teaspoon almond extract

1 to 2 ice cubes

1. Combine yogurt, cherries, milk, sugar, cocoa, almond extract and ice in blender; blend until smooth.

2. Pour into two glasses; serve immediately.

MORNING GLORY CREAM FIZZ

MAKES 3 SERVINGS

1 banana, cut into chunks

1 cup cubed and peeled papaya or mango

1 container (6 ounces) vanilla yogurt

3 tablespoons milk

1 tablespoon honey

½ cup cold club soda or sparkling water

Ground nutmeg

1. Combine banana, papaya cubes, yogurt, milk and honey in blender. Process until fruit is pureed and mixture is nearly smooth.

2. Gently stir club soda into fruit mixture. Pour into three glasses. Sprinkle with nutmeg. Serve immediately.

KitchenAid®

BERRY MORNING MEDLEY

MAKES 2 SERVINGS

1 cup frozen mixed berries

1½ cups milk

½ cup plain yogurt

1 tablespoon sugar

¼ teaspoon vanilla

¼ cup granola

1. Combine berries and milk in blender; blend until smooth.

2. Add yogurt, sugar and vanilla; blend until smooth. Add granola; pulse 15 to 20 seconds.

3. Pour into two glasses; serve immediately.

KitchenAid®

BLUEBERRY BANANA SMOOTHIE

MAKES 4 SERVINGS

2 cups frozen blueberries

1 cup milk

1 cup vanilla frozen yogurt

1 medium banana

½ cup ice cubes

1 tablespoon honey

1. Combine blueberries, milk, yogurt, banana, ice and honey in blender; blend until smooth.

2. Pour into four glasses; serve immediately.

APPLE, SWEET POTATO AND CARROT JUICE

MAKES 4 SERVINGS

4 apples

1 sweet potato

1 carrot

1. Assemble juicer for desired amount of pulp.

2. Juice apples, sweet potato and carrot; stir. Serve immediately.

KitchenAid®

PINEAPPLE CRUSH

MAKES 2 SERVINGS

2 ice cubes

1½ cups frozen pineapple
chunks

½ cup coconut milk

½ cup milk

½ cup plain yogurt

2 teaspoons sugar

1 teaspoon vanilla

1. Crush ice in blender. Add pineapple, coconut milk, milk, yogurt, sugar and vanilla; blend until smooth.

2. Pour into two glasses; serve immediately.

CHERRY MELON JUICE

MAKES 3 SERVINGS

⅛ small watermelon, rind removed

¼ cantaloupe, rind removed

¾ cup cherries

1. Assemble juicer for desired amount of pulp.

2. Juice watermelon, cantaloupe and cherries; stir. Serve immediately.

KitchenAid®

TROPICAL SUNRISE

MAKES 4 SERVINGS

1 frozen banana

1 cup frozen mango chunks

1 cup fresh pineapple chunks

⅓ cup coconut milk

⅓ cup orange juice, plus additional if needed

1¾ cups plain yogurt

1. Combine banana, mango, pineapple, coconut milk and ⅓ cup orange juice in blender; blend until combined.

2. Add yogurt; blend until smooth. Add additional orange juice to thin smoothie to desired consistency.

3. Pour into four glasses; serve immediately.

ISLAND ORANGE JUICE

MAKES 2 SERVINGS

2 oranges, peeled

2 guavas

½ cup strawberries

1. Assemble juicer for desired amount of pulp.

2. Juice oranges, guavas and strawberries; stir. Serve immediately.

KitchenAid®

PURPLEBERRY JUICE

MAKES 2 SERVINGS

2 cups red seedless grapes

1 apple

½ cup blackberries

½ inch fresh ginger, peeled

1. Assemble juicer for desired amount of pulp.

2. Juice grapes, apple, blackberries and ginger; stir. Serve immediately.

KitchenAid®

SUNSET BERRY JUICE

MAKES 2 SERVINGS

1 cup strawberries

1 orange, peeled

½ lime, peeled

1. Assemble juicer for desired amount of pulp.

2. Juice strawberries, orange and lime; stir. Serve immediately.

KitchenAid®

MANGO CITRUS JUICE

MAKES 2 SERVINGS

1 mango, peeled

1 lime, peeled

½ lemon, peeled

Ice cubes

1. Assemble juicer for desired amount of pulp.

2. Juice mango, lime and lemon; stir. Serve over ice.

COOL PEAR MELON JUICE

MAKES 3 SERVINGS

¼ honeydew melon, rind
    removed

1 pear

½ cucumber

1. Assemble juicer for desired amount of pulp.

2. Juice honeydew, pear and cucumber; stir. Serve immediately.

KitchenAid®

RASPBERRY PEACH SMOOTHIE

MAKES 4 SERVINGS

1½ cups fresh or frozen peach slices

1 cup peach nectar

1 container (6 ounces) raspberry yogurt

¾ cup fresh or frozen raspberries

1 tablespoon honey

1 to 3 ice cubes

1. Combine peaches, nectar, yogurt, raspberries and honey in blender; blend until smooth. Add 3 ice cubes if using fresh fruit and 1 to 2 ice cubes if using frozen fruit; blend until smooth.

2. Pour into four glasses; serve immediately.

SPICY-SWEET GRAPEFRUIT JUICE

MAKES 3 SERVINGS

2 grapefruits, peeled

5 carrots

1 inch fresh ginger, peeled

1. Assemble juicer for desired amount of pulp.

2. Juice grapefruits, carrots and ginger; stir. Serve immediately.

KitchenAid®

CUBAN BATIDO

MAKES 2 SERVINGS

1½ cups cubed fresh pineapple

¾ cup milk

½ cup orange juice

3 tablespoons sugar

1 tablespoon fresh lime juice

1 cup ice

1. Combine pineapple, milk, orange juice, sugar, lime juice and ice in blender container. Process until smooth.

2. Pour into two glasses; serve immediately.

Tip: A batido is a popular Latin American drink made with water, milk, fruit and ice. It is similar in texture to a smoothie and literally means "beaten" in Portuguese.

CITRUS CARROT JUICE

MAKES 2 SERVINGS

1 orange, peeled

2 carrots

½ lemon, peeled

1. Assemble juicer for desired amount of pulp.

2. Juice orange, carrots and lemon; stir. Serve immediately.

KitchenAid®

TOFU, FRUIT AND VEGGIE SMOOTHIE

MAKES 2 SERVINGS

1 cup frozen pineapple chunks

½ cup (4 ounces) soft tofu

½ cup apple juice

½ cup orange juice

1 container (about 2½ ounces) baby food carrots

1. Combine pineapple, tofu, apple juice, orange juice and carrots in blender. Process 15 to 30 seconds or until smooth, pulsing to break up chunks.

2. Pour into two glasses; serve immediately.

ORANGE FENNEL SPROUT JUICE

MAKES 2 SERVINGS

2 oranges, peeled

2 stalks celery

1 bulb fennel

1 cup alfalfa sprouts

1. Assemble juicer for desired amount of pulp.

2. Juice oranges, celery, fennel and alfalfa sprouts; stir. Serve immediately.

KitchenAid®

LEMON MANGO SMOOTHIE

MAKES 1 SERVING

¾ cup mango nectar

1 cup frozen mango chunks

¼ cup lemon sorbet

2 tablespoons fresh lime juice

1 to 2 tablespoons honey*

¼ teaspoon grated lime peel

*Adjust honey as needed if fruit
is not as sweet as desired.*

1. Pour nectar into blender. Add mango, sorbet, lime juice, honey and lime peel. Process until smooth.

2. Pour into glass; serve immediately.

KitchenAid®

TANGERINE GINGER SIPPER

MAKES 2 SERVINGS

1 tangerine, peeled

1 pear

¼ lemon, peeled

½ inch fresh ginger, peeled

1. Assemble juicer for desired amount of pulp.

2. Juice tangerine, pear, lemon and ginger; stir. Serve immediately.

KitchenAid®

CITRUS PUNCH

MAKES 8 TO 10 SERVINGS (ABOUT 5 CUPS)

4 oranges, sectioned

1 pint strawberries, stemmed and halved

1 to 2 limes, cut into ⅛-inch slices

1 lemon, cut into ⅛-inch slices

1 cup fresh raspberries

2 cups orange juice

2 cups grapefruit juice

¾ cup lime juice

½ cup light corn syrup

1 bottle (750 mL) ginger ale, white grape juice, Asti Spumante or sparkling wine

1. Spread orange sections, strawberries, lime slices, lemon slices and raspberries on baking sheet. Freeze 4 hours or until firm.

2. Combine juices and corn syrup in 2-quart pitcher. Stir until corn syrup dissolves. Refrigerate 2 hours or until cold. Stir in ginger ale just before serving.

3. Divide frozen fruit among punch glasses or wine glasses. Fill with punch. Serve immediately.

GREEN ISLANDER SMOOTHIE

MAKES 1 SERVING

1 cup ice cubes

½ banana

¾ cup fresh pineapple chunks

½ cup packed torn spinach

½ cup packed kale, stemmed

1. Combine ice, banana, ¾ cup pineapple, spinach and kale in blender; blend until smooth.

2. Pour into glass; serve immediately.

KitchenAid®

Appetizers

GOAT CHEESE-STUFFED FIGS

MAKES 7 SERVINGS

7 fresh firm ripe figs

7 slices prosciutto

1 package (4 ounces) goat
cheese

Freshly ground black pepper

1. Preheat broiler. Line baking sheet or broiler pan with
foil. Cut figs in half vertically. Cut prosciutto slices in half
lengthwise to make 14 pieces (about 4 inches long and
1 inch wide).

2. Spread 1 teaspoon goat cheese onto cut side of
each fig half. Wrap prosciutto slice around fig and goat
cheese. Sprinkle with pepper.

3. Broil about 4 minutes or until cheese softens and figs
are heated through.

KitchenAid

APPETIZER CREAM PUFFS

MAKES 36 CREAM PUFFS

1 cup water

½ cup (1 stick) butter

¼ teaspoon salt

1 cup all-purpose flour

4 eggs

1 package (8 ounces) cream
cheese, softened

4 ounces tomato and basil-
flavored feta, crumbled

½ cup sour cream

⅓ cup finely chopped kalamata
or ripe olives

½ teaspoon lemon pepper

1. Preheat oven to 400°F. Grease two baking sheets.

2. Attach flat beater to stand mixer. Heat water, butter, and salt in medium saucepan over high heat to a full rolling boil. Reduce heat and quickly stir in flour, mixing vigorously until mixture leaves sides of pan in a ball. Place mixture in mixer bowl.

3. Add eggs, one at a time, beating on medium-low speed about 30 seconds after each addition. Stop and scrape bowl. Beat on medium speed 15 seconds. Drop dough onto prepared baking sheets in 36 mounds 2 inches apart.

4. Bake 10 minutes. *Reduce heat to 350°F.* Bake 25 minutes. Turn off oven. Remove baking sheets from oven. Cut small slit in side of each puff. Return to oven 10 minutes, leaving oven door ajar. Cool completely on wire racks.

5. For filling, combine cream cheese, feta cheese, sour cream, olives and lemon pepper in mixer bowl. Beat on medium-low speed 30 seconds or until blended.

6. Cut puffs in half and pipe or spoon about 1 tablespoon filling into each puff. Serve immediately.

COCONUT SHRIMP

MAKES 4 SERVINGS

Spicy Orange-Mustard Sauce
(recipe follows)

¾ cup all-purpose flour

¾ cup beer or water

1 egg

¾ teaspoon baking powder

½ teaspoon salt

¼ teaspoon ground red pepper

1 cup flaked coconut

1 cup panko bread crumbs
or 2 packages (3 ounces
each) ramen noodles,
crushed

20 jumbo raw shrimp, peeled
and deveined (with tails
on)

2 cups vegetable oil

1. Prepare Spicy Orange-Mustard Sauce. Line large plate with paper towels.

2. Whisk flour, beer, egg, baking powder, salt and red pepper in medium bowl. Combine coconut and bread crumbs in shallow bowl. Dip shrimp in beer batter; shake off excess. Coat with coconut mixture.

3. Heat oil in large skillet to 350°F. Cook shrimp in batches 3 minutes or just until golden, turning once halfway through cooking. Drain on prepared plate. Serve with Spicy Orange-Mustard Sauce.

Spicy Orange-Mustard Sauce: Combine ¼ cup coarse grain or Dijon mustard, 2 tablespoons honey, 2 tablespoons orange juice, 2 teaspoons grated orange peel, ½ teaspoon ground red pepper and ¼ teaspoon ground ginger in small bowl; stir until blended.

HONEY NUT BRIE

MAKES 16 TO 20 SERVINGS

¼ cup honey

¼ cup coarsely chopped pecans

1 tablespoon brandy (optional)

1 wheel (14 ounces) Brie cheese (about 5-inch diameter)

Crackers and apple slices

1. Preheat oven to 500°F. Combine honey, pecans and brandy, if desired, in small bowl. Place cheese on large round ovenproof platter or in 9-inch pie plate.

2. Bake 4 to 5 minutes or until cheese softens. Drizzle honey mixture over top of cheese. Bake 2 to 3 minutes longer or until topping is thoroughly heated. *Do not melt cheese.* Serve with crackers.

LOBSTER POT STICKERS

MAKES ABOUT 26 POT STICKERS

4 dried black Chinese mushrooms

¼ cup plus 2 teaspoons soy sauce, divided

3 teaspoons dark sesame oil, divided

1 tablespoon rice vinegar

8 ounces lobster flavored surimi, finely chopped

2 cups chopped napa or green cabbage

¼ cup chopped green onions

1 tablespoon minced fresh ginger

26 wonton wrappers

2 tablespoons vegetable oil, divided

1 cup chicken broth, divided

1. Place mushrooms in medium bowl; cover with warm water. Soak 20 to 40 minutes or until soft.

2. For sauce, whisk ¼ cup soy sauce, 1 teaspoon sesame oil and rice vinegar in small bowl until well blended; set aside.

3. Drain mushrooms; discard water. Cut off and discard stems. Chop caps; return to bowl. Add lobster, cabbage, green onions, ginger, remaining 2 teaspoons sesame oil and 2 teaspoons soy sauce; gently toss to combine.

4. Arrange wonton wrappers on clean work surface. Cut ½-inch triangle off all corners of wrappers to make rounded shapes. Working in batches, place about 2 teaspoons lobster mixture in center of each wrapper. Lightly moisten edges with water; fold in half. Pinch edges together to seal. Keep finished pot stickers covered with plastic wrap while filling remaining wrappers.

5. Heat 1 tablespoon vegetable oil in large nonstick skillet over medium heat. Add half of pot stickers; cook 5 to 6 minutes or until bottoms are golden brown, turning once.

6. Pour ½ cup broth into skillet; reduce heat to low. Cover and simmer 10 minutes or until liquid is absorbed. Repeat with remaining vegetable oil, pot stickers and broth. Serve immediately with sauce for dipping.

Tip: Pot stickers may be cooked immediately or covered tightly and stored in refrigerator up to 4 hours or frozen up to 3 months. To freeze, place pot stickers on baking sheet or shallow pan; freeze 30 minutes to firm slightly. Transfer to freezer food storage bag. (Do not thaw frozen pot stickers before cooking.)

KitchenAid®

PEARL-RICE BALLS

MAKES ABOUT 18 BALLS

½ cup sweet (glutinous) rice

2 to 3 drops yellow food
   coloring (optional)

3 dried black Chinese
   mushrooms

8 ounces ground pork or beef

1 egg white, lightly beaten

1 tablespoon minced green
   onion (white part only)

1½ teaspoons soy sauce

1½ teaspoons rice wine

½ teaspoon minced fresh
   ginger

½ teaspoon sugar

¼ teaspoon salt

   Pinch freshly ground black
   pepper

1½ teaspoons cornstarch

SAUCE

3 tablespoons soy sauce

1½ tablespoons white vinegar

¼ teaspoon minced garlic

⅛ teaspoon sugar

1. Place rice in medium bowl of cold water. Sort with fingers several times; drain. Repeat until water remains clear. Return rice to bowl; fill with warm water. Stir in food coloring, if desired. Soak rice 3 to 4 hours or cover and refrigerate overnight. Drain.

2. Place mushrooms in medium bowl; cover with warm water. Soak 20 to 40 minutes or until soft. Drain mushrooms; discard water. Cut off and discard stems. Chop caps; return to bowl. Add pork, egg white, green onion, 1½ teaspoons soy sauce, rice wine, ginger, ½ teaspoon sugar, salt and pepper; mix well. Stir in cornstarch.

3. Shape mixture into 1-inch balls (mixture will be fairly soft); roll each ball in prepared rice to coat, pressing lightly between hands to make rice adhere.

4. Place 12-inch bamboo steamer in wok. Add water to ½ inch below steamer. (Water should not touch steamer.) Remove steamer. Bring water to a boil over high heat.

5. Place pearl-rice balls in single layer in steamer lined with wet cloth, leaving about ½-inch space between balls; cover. Place steamer in wok. Cover and steam over high heat 40 minutes until rice is tender, adding boiling water as needed to maintain level.

6. Meanwhile for sauce, whisk 3 tablespoons soy sauce, vinegar, garlic and ⅛ teaspoon sugar in small bowl until well blended.

7. Remove pearl-rice balls to serving plate. Serve with sauce for dipping.

KitchenAid®

VIETNAMESE VEGETARIAN SPRING ROLLS

MAKES 14 ROLLS

12 dried Chinese black
   mushrooms (1 ounce)

1 large carrot, julienned

2 teaspoons sugar, divided

   Hoisin Peanut Dipping Sauce
   (page 79)

3 cups plus 2 tablespoons
   vegetable oil, divided

1 medium yellow onion, sliced

1 clove garlic, minced

1 tablespoon soy sauce

1 teaspoon sesame oil

1½ cups fresh bean sprouts
   (4 ounces), rinsed and
   drained

14 (7-inch) egg roll wrappers

1 egg, beaten

1. Place mushrooms in medium bowl; cover with hot water. Let stand 20 to 40 minutes.

2. Place carrot strips in small bowl. Add 1 teaspoon sugar; toss to coat. Let stand 15 minutes, tossing occasionally.

3. Prepare Hoisin Peanut Dipping Sauce; set aside.

4. Drain mushrooms, reserving ½ cup liquid. Squeeze out excess water. Cut stems off mushrooms; discard. Cut caps into thin slices; set aside.

5. Heat wok over medium-high heat 1 minute or until hot. Drizzle 2 tablespoons vegetable oil into wok and heat 30 seconds. Add onion; stir-fry 1 minute. Stir in mushrooms, garlic and reserved mushroom liquid. Reduce heat to medium. Cover and cook 3 minutes or until mushrooms are tender. Uncover; add soy sauce, sesame oil and remaining 1 teaspoon sugar. Stir-fry 3 to 5 minutes or until liquid has evaporated. Transfer to medium bowl; set aside to cool slightly.

6. Add carrot strips and bean sprouts to mushroom mixture; toss gently. Place one wrapper on work surface with corner facing you; keep remaining wrappers covered with plastic wrap. Drain mushroom mixture; place 3 tablespoons mixture on bottom third of wrapper. Brush edges of wrapper with some of beaten egg.

7. Fold bottom corner of wrapper up over filling. Fold in and overlap the opposite right and left corners to form 3½-inch-wide log; roll up tightly. Place on baking sheet; cover with plastic wrap. Repeat with remaining wrappers and filling.

8. Heat remaining 3 cups vegetable oil in wok over high heat to 375°F; adjust heat to maintain temperature. Fry rolls in batches 2 to 3 minutes or until golden brown, turning once. Drain on paper towels. Serve with sauce.

HOISIN PEANUT DIPPING SAUCE

MAKES ABOUT ½ CUP

2 tablespoons creamy peanut butter

2 tablespoons water

1 tablespoon soy sauce

⅓ cup hoisin sauce

½ teaspoon sesame oil

1 clove garlic, minced

Dash hot pepper sauce

1. Whisk peanut butter, water and soy sauce in small bowl until smooth.

2. Stir in hoisin sauce, sesame oil, garlic and hot pepper sauce. Pour into serving bowl.

LEEK STRUDELS

MAKES 9 SERVINGS

2 teaspoons vegetable oil

2 pounds leeks, cleaned and sliced (white parts only)

¼ teaspoon caraway seeds

¼ teaspoon salt

⅛ teaspoon freshly ground white pepper

¼ cup vegetable broth

3 sheets frozen phyllo dough, thawed

3 tablespoons butter, melted

1. Heat oil in large skillet over medium heat. Add leeks; sauté about 5 minutes or until tender. Stir in caraway seeds, salt and pepper. Add broth; bring to a boil over high heat. Reduce heat to low; cover and simmer about 5 minutes or until broth is absorbed. Let mixture cool to room temperature.

2. Preheat oven to 400°F. Cut each sheet of phyllo dough lengthwise into thirds. Brush one piece of phyllo dough with some of butter; spoon 2 tablespoons leek mixture near bottom of piece. Fold one corner over filling to make triangle. Continue folding as a flag, to make triangular packet.

3. Repeat with remaining phyllo dough, butter and leek mixture. Place on ungreased baking sheet; brush with butter. Bake about 20 minutes or until golden brown. Serve warm.

KitchenAid®

BAKED BRIE WITH NUT CRUST

MAKES 8 SERVINGS

⅓ cup pecans

⅓ cup almonds

⅓ cup walnuts

1 egg

1 tablespoon heavy cream

1 wheel (8 ounces) Brie cheese

2 tablespoons raspberry jam

1. Preheat oven to 350°F. Assemble Rotor Slicer/ Shredder with coarse shredding cone; attach to stand mixer. Shred nuts into shallow bowl or pie plate.

2. Whisk egg and cream in another shallow bowl until well blended.

3. Dip Brie into egg mixture, then into nut mixture, turning to coat all sides and pressing to adhere.

4. Place Brie on baking sheet; spread jam over top. Bake 15 minutes or until cheese is warm and soft.

KitchenAid®

SOFT PRETZEL BITES WITH CREAMY HONEY MUSTARD

MAKES 12 SERVINGS

¾ cup sour cream

¼ cup Dijon mustard

3 tablespoons honey

1⅔ cups warm water (110° to 115°F)

1 package (¼ ounce) active dry yeast

2 teaspoons sugar

½ teaspoon table salt

4½ cups all-purpose flour

2 tablespoons butter, softened

12 cups water

½ cup baking soda

Kosher salt

1. For creamy honey mustard, stir sour cream, mustard and honey in small bowl until smooth and well blended. Cover and refrigerate until ready to use.

2. Attach flat beater to stand mixer. Whisk 1⅔ cups warm water, yeast, sugar and table salt in mixer bowl. Let stand 5 minutes or until bubbly.

3. Add flour and butter to yeast mixture; mix on low speed until combined, scraping sides of bowl occasionally. Replace flat beater with dough hook; knead on low speed 5 to 7 minutes or until dough is smooth and elastic.

4. Place dough in large lightly greased bowl; turn once to grease surface. Cover and let rise in warm place 1 hour or until doubled.

5. Preheat oven to 450°F. Line baking sheets with foil; spray with nonstick cooking spray.

6. Punch down dough; turn out onto floured surface. Divide dough into 12 equal pieces. Roll each piece into 12-inch-long rope. Cut each rope into 8 equal pieces.

7. Bring 12 cups water to a boil in large saucepan. Stir in baking soda until dissolved. Working in batches, cook dough pieces 30 seconds. Remove to prepared baking sheets using slotted spoon.

8. Sprinkle dough evenly with kosher salt. Bake 12 minutes or until dark golden brown, rotating baking sheets halfway through baking time. Place pretzel bites in serving bowl. Serve warm with creamy honey mustard.

KitchenAid®

GOAT CHEESE CROSTINI WITH SWEET ONION JAM

MAKES 24 CROSTINI

1 tablespoon olive oil

2 medium yellow onions, thinly sliced

¾ cup dry red wine

¼ cup water

2 tablespoons packed brown sugar

1 tablespoon balsamic vinegar

1 teaspoon salt

¼ teaspoon freshly ground black pepper

2 ounces soft goat cheese

2 ounces cream cheese, softened

1 teaspoon chopped fresh thyme, plus additional for garnish

1 loaf (16 ounces) French bread, cut into 24 slices (about 1 inch thick), lightly toasted

1. Heat olive oil in large skillet over medium heat. Add onions; cook 10 minutes, stirring occasionally. Add wine, water, brown sugar, vinegar, salt and pepper; bring to a simmer. Reduce heat to low; cook 15 to 20 minutes or until all liquid is absorbed. (If mixture appears dry, stir in a few additional tablespoons water.) Cool 30 minutes or cover and refrigerate until ready to use.

2. Meanwhile, stir goat cheese, cream cheese and 1 teaspoon thyme in small bowl until well blended.

3. Spread goat cheese mixture evenly on each slice of bread. Top with onion jam. Garnish with additional thyme.

MOZZARELLA AND PROSCIUTTO BITES

MAKES 16 TO 20 PIECES

1 ball (8 ounces) fresh mozzarella cheese*

¼ cup chopped fresh basil

½ teaspoon freshly ground black pepper

6 to 8 thin slices prosciutto

Or substitute one 8-ounce container of small fresh mozzarella balls (ciliengini).

1. Soak 16 to 20 small bamboo skewers or toothpicks in water 20 minutes to prevent burning. Cut mozzarella into 1- to 1½-inch chunks. Place on paper towel-lined plate; sprinkle with basil and pepper, turning to coat all sides.

2. Cut prosciutto slices crosswise into thirds. Tightly wrap one slice around each piece of mozzarella, covering completely. Insert skewer into each piece. Freeze 15 minutes.

3. Preheat broiler. Line broiler pan or baking sheet with foil. Place skewers on prepared pan; broil about 3 minutes or until prosciutto begins to crisp, turning once. Serve immediately.

KitchenAid®

FRESH TOMATILLO SALSA

MAKES 3 CUPS

1 medium white onion, peeled and quartered

3 cloves garlic, peeled

1 jalapeño pepper, halved and seeded

9 fresh tomatillos, husked and hulled

2 avocados, peeled and pitted

½ cup packed fresh cilantro leaves

1 tablespoon fresh lime juice

1 teaspoon coarse salt

Tortilla chips

1. Combine onion, garlic and jalapeño in food processor; process on high about 30 seconds or until minced.

2. Add four tomatillos; process until pureed. Repeat with remaining tomatillos. Add avocado, cilantro, lime juice and salt; pulse 4 to 5 times or until almost smooth. Serve with tortilla chips.

Tip: Salsa may be made 2 to 3 days in advance. Store tightly covered in the refrigerator.

SUN-DRIED TOMATO CUCUMBER ROLLS

MAKES 15 TO 20 ROLLS

1 medium seedless cucumber, halved crosswise

1 package (8 ounces) cream cheese, softened

10 whole oil-packed sun-dried tomatoes, drained and rinsed

¼ cup crumbled feta cheese

¼ teaspoon dried oregano

¼ teaspoon salt

¼ teaspoon freshly ground black pepper

¼ teaspoon red pepper flakes

1 green onion, finely chopped

1. Assemble food processor with adjustable slicing disc; slide to third notch for medium slices. Place cucumber halves horizontally into large feed tube; slice on low speed. Transfer to bowl.

2. Replace slicing disc with multipurpose blade. Combine cream cheese, sun-dried tomatoes, feta cheese, oregano, salt, black pepper and red pepper flakes in food processor; pulse 15 times or until well blended. Stir in green onion.

3. Lay cucumbers flat on work surface. Spoon 2 teaspoons cheese mixture on bottom edge of each slice; roll up and secure with toothpicks. Serve immediately.

Tip: Make the filling up to 3 days in advance and store tightly wrapped in the refrigerator.

MANGO AND RED PEPPER SALSA

MAKES 3 CUPS SALSA

5 mangoes, pitted and peeled

2 red bell peppers, halved and seeded

¼ small red onion

¼ cup packed fresh cilantro leaves

1 jalapeño pepper, halved and seeded

1 clove garlic

1 tablespoon fresh lime juice

1½ teaspoons sugar

1 teaspoon kosher salt

Tortilla chips

1. Combine mangoes, bell peppers, onion, cilantro, jalapeño and garlic in food processor; pulse 10 to 15 times until coarsely chopped.

2. Stir in lime juice, sugar and salt with spatula. Serve with tortilla chips.

Tip: If your food processor has a dicing kit, use it to dice the bell pepper and onion.

KitchenAid®

Salads

ASPARAGUS ROLL-UPS

MAKES ABOUT 24 ROLL-UPS

- 1 pound asparagus
- 4 ounces cream cheese, softened
- ½ pound thinly sliced salami

1. Cut asparagus into lengths 1 inch longer than width of salami. Reserve bottoms for another use. Bring large skillet of salted water to a simmer over medium heat. Add asparagus; cook 4 to 5 minutes or until crisp-tender. Drain and immediately immerse in cold water to stop cooking. Drain; pat dry with paper towel.

2. Spread about 1 teaspoon cream cheese evenly over one side of each salami slice. Roll up 1 asparagus spear with each salami slice. Cover and refrigerate. Let stand at room temperature 10 minutes before serving.

KitchenAid®

FENNEL WHEAT BERRY SALAD

MAKES 4 TO 6 SERVINGS

3 cups water

½ cup wheat berries

¼ teaspoon salt

2 tablespoons balsamic vinegar

1 tablespoon olive oil

1 tablespoon honey

1¼ teaspoons whole fennel seeds, toasted

3 cups coleslaw mix

½ cup thinly sliced fennel bulb

1. Combine water, wheat berries and salt in medium saucepan. Bring to a boil. Reduce heat; cover and simmer about 1 hour or until wheat berries are tender. Drain off any water. Place wheat berries in large bowl; cover and refrigerate at least 1 hour.

2. For dressing, whisk vinegar, olive oil, honey and fennel seeds in small bowl.

3. Add coleslaw mix and sliced fennel to wheat berries. Drizzle with dressing; toss to coat. Serve immediately.

KitchenAid®

BULGUR, GREEN BEAN AND ORANGE SALAD

MAKES 4 TO 6 SERVINGS

⅔ cup bulgur

⅔ cup boiling water

1½ cups green beans (1-inch pieces)

2 tablespoons olive oil

2 tablespoons fresh lemon juice

½ teaspoon dried Greek seasonings

¼ teaspoon salt

Freshly ground black pepper

1 can (11 ounces) mandarin orange sections, drained

¼ cup slivered red onion

Spinach leaves (optional)

1. Place bulgur in medium bowl. Pour boiling water over bulgur; stir. Cover with plastic wrap; let stand 20 minutes or until bulgur is tender.

2. Bring small saucepan of salted water to a boil. Add green beans; cook 6 to 7 minutes or until tender; drain.

3. For dressing, whisk olive oil, lemon juice, Greek seasoning and salt in small bowl; season with pepper. Set aside.

4. Add beans, oranges and onion to bulgur. Drizzle dressing over salad; toss until well blended. Cover and refrigerate at least 30 minutes. Serve on spinach leaves, if desired.

KitchenAid

CALAMARI SALAD

MAKES 6 SERVINGS

¼ cup plus 1 tablespoon extra virgin olive oil, divided

1½ pounds cleaned squid (body tubes only)

Juice of 1 lemon

1 can (about 15 ounces) cannellini beans, rinsed and drained

1 cup thinly sliced celery

1 cup thinly sliced red bell pepper

½ cup thinly sliced white onion

3 tablespoons red wine vinegar

2 tablespoons chopped fresh parsley

1 tablespoon chopped fresh basil

1 tablespoon chopped fresh oregano

2 cloves garlic, minced

1 teaspoon salt

½ teaspoon red pepper flakes

1. Heat 1 tablespoon olive oil in large nonstick skillet over medium-high heat. Add squid; cook 2 minutes per side. Let cool slightly; cut into rings. Place in large bowl; drizzle with lemon juice. Add beans, celery, bell pepper and onion.

2. Whisk vinegar, parsley, basil, oregano, garlic, salt and red pepper flakes in small bowl. Slowly whisk in remaining ¼ cup olive oil until blended. Pour over squid mixture; toss to coat.

3. Refrigerate at least 1 hour. Serve chilled or at room temperature.

KitchenAid®

NECTARINE AND GOAT CHEESE SALAD

MAKES 4 TO 6 SERVINGS

1 package (5 ounces) mixed spring greens

2 nectarines, cut into thin slices

1 cup sliced celery

⅓ cup pine nuts, toasted (see Tip)

⅓ cup crumbled goat cheese

¼ cup creamy poppy seed dressing

1. Combine greens, nectarines, celery, pine nuts and goat cheese in large bowl; toss until well blended.

2. Drizzle dressing over salad; toss gently to coat.

Tip: To toast pine nuts, spread in single layer in heavy skillet. Cook over medium heat 1 to 2 minutes or until nuts are lightly browned, stirring frequently.

KitchenAid®

BEET AND ARUGULA SALAD

MAKES 4 TO 6 SERVINGS

3 medium beets, trimmed

6 cups baby arugula

2 tablespoons chopped shallot

1 tablespoon white wine
   vinegar

1 teaspoon Dijon mustard

¼ teaspoon salt

⅛ teaspoon freshly ground
   black pepper

3 tablespoons extra virgin
   olive oil

4 to 6 wedges (1 ounce each)
   aged Irish Cheddar cheese

1. Place beets in medium saucepan; add cold water to cover by 2 inches. Bring to a boil over medium-high heat; cook 35 to 40 minutes or until beets can easily be pierced with tip of knife. Drain; cool 15 minutes.

2. Peel beets; cut into ½-inch cubes. Transfer to medium bowl. Place arugula in separate medium bowl. Combine shallot, vinegar, mustard, salt and pepper in small bowl. Slowly whisk in olive oil until well blended. Toss beets with 1 tablespoon dressing. Toss arugula with remaining dressing.

3. Divide arugula among serving plates. Top with beets; garnish with cheese.

SPINACH SALAD WITH GOAT CHEESE-STUFFED MUSHROOMS AND SHALLOT VINAIGRETTE

MAKES 4 SERVINGS

¼ cup olive oil

3 tablespoons balsamic vinegar

2 teaspoons minced shallot

¼ teaspoon salt

8 cremini mushrooms

2 teaspoons honey

4 ounces herbed goat cheese

2 tablespoons cream cheese

1 package (5 ounces) baby spinach *or* 1 bunch spinach, washed and dried

4 tablespoons sliced or slivered toasted almonds

1. Combine olive oil, vinegar, shallot and salt in small bowl or jar with tight-fitting lid. Remove stems from mushrooms; place mushrooms cap side down on plate. Drizzle 2 tablespoons oil mixture over mushrooms; marinate 15 to 30 minutes. Add honey to remaining oil mixture; set aside.

2. Combine goat cheese and cream cheese in small bowl; set aside.

3. Preheat oven to 400°F. Place mushrooms cap side up in baking dish. Bake 10 minutes. Turn mushrooms over. Stuff each mushroom with about 1 tablespoon goat cheese mixture. Bake 5 to 10 minutes or until cheese is warm and soft.

4. Arrange spinach on large platter or individual serving plates.

5. Remove mushrooms from baking dish; whisk cooking liquid into dressing. Pour half of dressing over spinach; toss to coat. Arrange mushrooms on salad; drizzle remaining dressing over mushrooms. Sprinkle with almonds.

KitchenAid®

RUSTIC DRIED CHERRY SALAD

MAKES 4 SERVINGS

3 cups cubed French bread

¼ cup pecans, chopped

½ cup dried sweetened
   cherries, chopped

1 stalk celery, diced

3 tablespoons canola oil *or* 1½
   tablespoons canola oil and
   1½ tablespoons olive oil

3 tablespoons raspberry
   vinegar

2 tablespoons water

1 tablespoon honey

¼ teaspoon curry powder

1. Preheat oven to 350°F. Spread bread cubes on baking sheet. Bake 15 minutes or until toasted. Cool completely.

2. Toast pecans in medium skillet over medium heat 3 minutes or until lightly browned and fragrant, stirring frequently.

3. Combine bread, pecans, cherries and celery in large bowl.

4. Whisk oil, vinegar, water, honey and curry powder in small bowl. Pour over salad; toss until well blended.

KitchenAid®

GARLIC BREAD AND SALMON SALAD

MAKES 4 SERVINGS

4 slices Italian sourdough or whole wheat bread

1 clove garlic, cut in half

7½ ounces canned or cooked salmon, flaked

½ cup chopped green onions

1 cup cherry or grape tomatoes, halved

2 tablespoons white wine vinegar

1 tablespoon olive oil

1 tablespoon tomato juice

¼ teaspoon salt

¼ teaspoon freshly ground black pepper

2 tablespoons chopped fresh basil

1. Rub one side of each bread slice with garlic. Toast bread in toaster or under broiler until lightly browned. Cut into 1-inch cubes when cool enough to handle.

2. Combine salmon, green onions and tomatoes in serving bowl.

3. For dressing, whisk vinegar, olive oil, tomato juice, salt and pepper in small bowl. Pour over salmon mixture; toss to coat. Add bread cubes; toss until well blended. Sprinkle with basil.

Tip: Collect the juices left over from cutting the tomatoes to add to the dressing.

KitchenAid®

GRILLED BEET SALAD

MAKES 6 TO 8 SERVINGS

6 medium red beets (about 1½ pounds), peeled

1 medium yellow onion, cut into ½-inch wedges

½ pound carrots, halved lengthwise and cut into 1-inch pieces

¼ cup plus 2 tablespoons olive oil, divided

¼ cup balsamic vinegar

½ teaspoon dried rosemary

1 clove garlic, minced

½ teaspoon salt

¼ teaspoon freshly ground black pepper

6 cups chopped spring greens or 2 packages (5 ounces each) mixed spring greens

1 cup pecan pieces, toasted* or candied pecans

½ cup (2 ounces) crumbled Gorgonzola or goat cheese

*See page 12.

1. Prepare grill for direct cooking over medium-high heat.

2. Cut beets into 1-inch pieces; place in microwavable dish. Cover; microwave on HIGH 6 to 8 minutes or until slightly softened. Uncover; cool to room temperature. Pat beets dry with paper towels.

3. Divide beets, onion and carrots evenly between two 12×8-inch disposable foil pans. Drizzle 1 tablespoon olive oil over vegetables in each pan; stir to coat. Arrange vegetables in single layer. Cover loosely with foil. Place pans on grid over medium-high heat. Grill 22 to 25 minutes or until fork-tender, stirring frequently. Cool completely.

4. For dressing, whisk remaining ¼ cup olive oil, vinegar, rosemary, garlic, salt and pepper in small bowl.

5. Arrange greens in salad bowl or on platter. Add half of dressing; toss to coat. Top with grilled vegetables; drizzle with remaining dressing. Top with pecans and cheese. Serve immediately.

Note: To peel beets, trim ends, then peel with a vegetable peeler under running water to help minimize beet juice from staining your hands.

KitchenAid®

COBB SALAD

MAKES 4 SERVINGS

Blue Cheese Dressing (recipe follows)

1 package (10 ounces) torn mixed salad greens *or* 8 cups torn romaine lettuce

6 ounces cooked chicken,* cut into bite-size pieces

1 tomato, seeded and chopped

2 hard-cooked eggs, peeled and cut into bite-size pieces

4 slices bacon, crisp-cooked and crumbled

1 ripe avocado, diced

1 large carrot, julienned

2 ounces blue cheese, crumbled

See Poached Chicken on page 8.

1. Prepare Blue Cheese Dressing.

2. Place lettuce in serving bowl or spread on platter. Arrange chicken, tomato, eggs, bacon, avocado, carrot and cheese on top of lettuce. Serve with dressing.

Blue Cheese Dressing: Combine 1 cup mayonnaise, ⅔ cup crumbled blue cheese, 2 tablespoons fresh lemon juice and ¼ teaspoon freshly ground black pepper in small bowl; refrigerate until ready to serve.

KitchenAid®

SPRING GREENS WITH BLUEBERRIES, WALNUTS AND FETA CHEESE

MAKES 4 SERVINGS

1 tablespoon canola oil

1 tablespoon white wine vinegar or sherry vinegar

2 teaspoons Dijon mustard

½ teaspoon salt

½ teaspoon freshly ground black pepper

1 package (5 ounces) mixed spring greens

1 cup fresh blueberries

½ cup crumbled feta cheese

¼ cup chopped walnuts or pecans, toasted*

See page 12.

1. Whisk oil, vinegar, mustard, salt and pepper in large bowl.

2. Add greens and blueberries; toss gently to coat. Top with cheese and walnuts.

ITALIAN CROUTON SALAD

MAKES 6 SERVINGS

6 ounces French or Italian bread

¼ cup plain yogurt

¼ cup red wine vinegar

3 tablespoons olive oil

3 cloves garlic, minced

Salt and freshly ground black pepper

6 medium plum tomatoes, sliced (about 3¾ to 4 cups)

½ medium red onion, thinly sliced

3 tablespoons sliced fresh basil

2 tablespoons finely chopped fresh parsley

12 leaves red leaf lettuce *or* 4 cups prepared Italian salad mix

2 tablespoons freshly grated Parmesan cheese

1. Preheat broiler. Cut bread into ¾-inch cubes; place in single layer on baking sheet. Broil 4 inches from heat source 3 minutes or until bread is golden, stirring every 30 seconds to 1 minute. Place croutons in large bowl.

2. For dressing, whisk yogurt, vinegar, olive oil and garlic in small bowl until blended; season to taste with salt and pepper.

3. Add tomatoes, onion, basil and parsley to croutons; stir to combine. Pour dressing over salad; toss to coat. Cover and refrigerate 30 minutes or up to 1 day. (Croutons will be softer the following day.)

4. Place lettuce on serving plates. Evenly divide crouton mixture over lettuce. Sprinkle with cheese.

KitchenAid®

GREEN BEAN AND EGG SALAD

MAKES 4 TO 6 SERVINGS

1 pound green beans, trimmed and cut into 2-inch pieces

3 hard-cooked eggs, peeled and chopped

2 stalks celery, thinly sliced

½ cup Cheddar cheese cubes (¼-inch cubes)

¼ cup chopped red onion

⅓ cup mayonnaise

2 teaspoons cider vinegar

1½ teaspoons sugar

½ teaspoon salt

½ teaspoon celery seed

⅛ teaspoon freshly ground black pepper

1. Bring large saucepan of salted water to a boil. Add green beans; cook 6 to 7 minutes or until tender. Drain and rinse under cold running water to stop cooking.

2. Combine beans, eggs, celery, cheese and onion in large bowl.

3. For dressing, whisk mayonnaise, vinegar, sugar, salt, celery seed and pepper in small bowl. Add to salad; toss to coat.

4. Cover and refrigerate at least 1 hour before serving.

KitchenAid®

SPICY GRAPEFRUIT SALAD
WITH RASPBERRY DRESSING

MAKES 4 SERVINGS

2 cups washed watercress

2 cups mixed salad greens

3 medium grapefruit, peeled, sectioned and seeded

½ pound jicama, cut into thin strips

1 cup fresh raspberries

2 tablespoons chopped green onion

1 tablespoon honey

1 teaspoon balsamic vinegar

½ to ¾ teaspoon dry mustard

1. Combine watercress and salad greens in large bowl; divide evenly among four plates. Top evenly with grapefruit and jicama.

2. Reserve 12 raspberries for garnish. Combine remaining raspberries, green onion, honey, vinegar and mustard in food processor or blender; process until smooth and well blended.

3. Drizzle dressing over salads. Top salads with reserved raspberries.

FIESTA CORN SALAD

MAKES 4 TO 6 SERVINGS

5 large ears fresh corn

1 cup plain yogurt

3 tablespoons minced onion

1½ tablespoons fresh lime juice

1 clove garlic, minced

1 teaspoon ground cumin

1 teaspoon chili powder

¼ teaspoon salt

1½ cups shredded red cabbage

1 large tomato, chopped

1 medium green bell pepper,
   seeded and chopped

5 slices bacon, cooked and
   crumbled (optional)

1 cup coarsely crushed tortilla
   chips

1 cup (4 ounces) shredded
   Cheddar cheese

1. Remove husks and silk from corn. Bring large saucepan of water to a boil. Add corn; cover and cook 6 minutes or until tender. Drain and cool completely.

2. Meanwhile for dressing, whisk yogurt, onion, lime juice, garlic, cumin, chili powder and salt in small bowl.

3. Cut corn from cob using sharp knife. Combine corn, cabbage, tomato and bell pepper in large bowl. Pour dressing over vegetables; mix lightly.

4. Cover and refrigerate. Stir in bacon just before serving, if desired; sprinkle with chips and cheese.

KitchenAid®

ORANGE POPPY SEED SALAD

MAKES 4 SERVINGS

½ cup mayonnaise

¼ cup sour cream or plain yogurt

2 tablespoons honey

1 tablespoon lemon juice

1 teaspoon poppy seeds

1 package (5 ounces) mixed spring greens

2 oranges, peeled and sliced crosswise

1 small red onion, sliced and separated into rings

½ small jicama, cut into ½-inch strips

1. For dressing, whisk mayonnaise, sour cream, honey, lemon juice and poppy seeds in small bowl.

2. Arrange greens on serving plates; top with oranges, onion and jicama. Serve with dressing.

KitchenAid®

MARINATED TOMATO SALAD

MAKES 8 SERVINGS

1½ cups dry white wine or tarragon vinegar

½ teaspoon salt

¼ cup finely chopped shallots

2 tablespoons finely chopped chives

2 tablespoons fresh lemon juice

¼ teaspoon freshly ground white pepper

2 tablespoons extra virgin olive oil

6 plum tomatoes, quartered

2 large yellow tomatoes,* sliced into ½-inch thick slices

16 red cherry tomatoes, halved

16 small yellow pear tomatoes,* halved

Sunflower sprouts (optional)

Substitute 10 plum tomatoes, quartered, for yellow tomatoes and yellow pear tomatoes, if desired.

1. For dressing, combine vinegar and salt in large bowl; stir until salt is completely dissolved. Add shallots, chives, lemon juice and pepper; mix well. Slowly whisk in olive oil until well blended.

2. Add tomatoes to marinade; toss to coat. Cover; let stand at room temperature 30 minutes or up to 2 hours before serving.

3. To serve, divide salad among serving plates. Garnish with sunflower sprouts.

KitchenAid®

PASTA SALMON SALAD

MAKES 4 SERVINGS

8 ounces uncooked rotini
   pasta

1 can (7 ounces) salmon,
   drained, bones removed
   and flaked

1 cup sliced celery

½ cup chopped green onions

⅔ cup mayonnaise

1 tablespoon Dijon mustard

¼ teaspoon salt

⅛ teaspoon freshly ground
   black pepper

1. Cook pasta according to package directions until tender. Drain; rinse under cold running water to cool completely.

2. Combine pasta, salmon, celery and green onions in large bowl.

3. For dressing, whisk mayonnaise, mustard, salt and pepper. Add to salad; stir until well blended.

KitchenAid®

CARROT RAISIN SALAD WITH CITRUS DRESSING

MAKES 8 SERVINGS

¾ cup sour cream

¼ cup milk

1 tablespoon honey

1 tablespoon fresh lime juice

1 tablespoon orange juice

Grated peel of 1 medium orange

½ teaspoon salt

8 medium carrots, peeled and coarsely shredded

¼ cup raisins

⅓ cup chopped cashew nuts

1. For dressing, whisk sour cream, milk, honey, lime juice, orange juice, orange peel and salt in small bowl until smooth and well blended.

2. Combine carrots and raisins in large bowl. Add dressing; toss to coat. Cover and refrigerate 30 minutes. Gently toss before serving. Top with cashews.

KitchenAid®

EGGPLANT CAPRESE STACK

MAKES 6 SERVINGS

1 medium eggplant, sliced into ¼-inch rounds

¼ cup olive oil

½ teaspoon salt

1 cup panko bread crumbs

3 tablespoons freshly grated Parmesan cheese

1 teaspoon dried Italian seasoning

1 egg, beaten

2 tomatoes, sliced into ¼-inch slices

8 ounces fresh mozzarella cheese, sliced

Balsamic vinegar

Fresh basil leaves

1. Preheat oven to 350°F. Place eggplant slices on baking sheet. Drizzle with olive oil. Sprinkle with salt. Let stand 15 minutes.

2. Combine panko, Parmesan cheese and Italian seasoning in shallow bowl. Dip eggplant slices in egg, then in panko mixture, pressing to adhere. Place on same baking sheet. Bake 20 minutes. Remove from oven.

3. On serving platter, layer eggplant, tomato slices and mozzarella cheese twice making a stack. Drizzle with balsamic vinegar before serving. Garnish with basil.

KitchenAid®

LENTIL AND ORZO PASTA SALAD

MAKES 4 SERVINGS

8 cups water

½ cup dried lentils, rinsed and sorted

4 ounces uncooked orzo

1½ cups quartered grape or cherry tomatoes

¾ cup finely chopped celery

½ cup chopped red onion

2 ounces pitted olives (about 16), coarsely chopped

3 tablespoons cider vinegar

1 tablespoon olive oil

1 tablespoon dried basil

1 clove garlic, minced

⅛ teaspoon red pepper flakes

4 ounces feta cheese with sun-dried tomatoes and basil

1. Bring water to a boil in large saucepan over high heat. Add lentils; boil 12 minutes.

2. Add orzo; cook 10 minutes or just until tender. Drain and rinse under cold water to cool completely.

3. Meanwhile, combine tomatoes, celery, onion, olives, vinegar, olive oil, basil, garlic and red pepper flakes in large bowl. Add lentil mixture; toss until well blended. Fold in cheese. Let stand 15 minutes before serving.

KitchenAid®

THAI-STYLE WARM NOODLE SALAD

MAKES 4 SERVINGS

8 ounces uncooked vermicelli
or angel hair pasta

½ cup chunky peanut butter

¼ cup soy sauce

¼ to ½ teaspoon red pepper
flakes

2 green onions, thinly sliced

1 carrot, shredded

1. Cook pasta according to package directions.

2. Whisk peanut butter, soy sauce and red pepper flakes
in serving bowl until smooth.

3. Drain pasta, reserving 5 tablespoons water. Mix hot
pasta water with peanut butter mixture until smooth.
Add pasta; toss to coat. Stir in green onions and carrot.
Serve warm or at room temperature.

Note: Make this salad a heartier meal by mixing in
cubed tofu and/or cooked chicken or beef.

KitchenAid®

Soups and Stews

MINESTRONE SOUP

MAKES 4 TO 6 SERVINGS

¾ cup uncooked small shell pasta

2 cans (about 14 ounces each) vegetable broth

1 can (28 ounces) crushed tomatoes in tomato puree

1 can (about 15 ounces) cannellini beans, rinsed and drained

16 ounces cut-up fresh vegetables: green beans, broccoli, carrots and/or red bell pepper

2 tablespoons pesto sauce (page 8)

1. Cook pasta according to package directions. Drain and return to saucepan; keep warm.

2. Meanwhile, combine broth, tomatoes and beans in Dutch oven or large saucepan. Cover and bring to a boil over high heat. Reduce heat to low; simmer 3 to 5 minutes.

3. Add vegetables to broth mixture; bring to a boil. Reduce heat; cook 4 to 5 minutes or until vegetables are tender. Add pasta; cook until heated through. Ladle soup into bowls; top with pesto.

JAMBALAYA

MAKES 8 SERVINGS

1 tablespoon olive oil

28 ounces smoked sausage, cut into ¼-inch slices

1 onion, diced

2 stalks celery, diced

1 red bell pepper, diced

3 cloves garlic, chopped

1 tablespoon chopped fresh parsley

1 teaspoon dried oregano

1 teaspoon dried marjoram

1 teaspoon dried thyme

½ teaspoon paprika

Dash ground red pepper

½ cup dry white wine

3 cups water

1 can (about 14 ounces) diced tomatoes, undrained

½ cup tomato sauce

1 bay leaf

1½ cups uncooked long grain rice

1 pound uncooked medium shrimp, peeled and deveined

1. Heat olive oil in large skillet over medium-high heat. Add sausage, onion and celery; sauté 5 minutes. Add bell pepper and garlic; sauté 3 to 4 minutes. Add parsley, oregano, marjoram, thyme, paprika and ground red pepper; cook 1 minute, stirring constantly.

2. Add wine, stirring to scrape up browned bits from bottom of skillet. Add water, tomatoes, tomato sauce and bay leaf; stir in rice. Bring to a boil over high heat. Reduce heat; cover and simmer 20 to 25 minutes or until rice is tender.

3. Add shrimp; cook until shrimp are pink and opaque. Remove and discard bay leaf.

KitchenAid®

POZOLE

MAKES 6 SERVINGS

3 (6-inch) corn tortillas

1 tablespoon vegetable oil

1 large onion, chopped

1 tablespoon minced garlic

1 tablespoon dried oregano, crushed

1½ teaspoons ground cumin

2 cans (about 14 ounces each) chicken broth plus water to make 5 cups

1 pound boneless skinless chicken breasts

2 cans (15 ounces each) yellow hominy, drained

1 red or green bell pepper, chopped

1 can (4 ounces) diced mild green chiles

1 can (2¼ ounces) sliced black olives, drained

½ cup lightly packed fresh cilantro, coarsely chopped

1. Preheat oven to 450°F.

2. Cut tortillas into ¼-inch-wide strips. Place strips in single layer on baking sheet. Bake 3 to 4 minutes or until crisp. Do not let strips brown. Remove strips to plate to cool while preparing soup.

3. Heat oil in large saucepan over medium heat. Add onion, garlic, oregano and cumin; cover and cook about 6 minutes or until onion is golden, stirring occasionally. Add broth and water; cover and bring to a boil over high heat. Add chicken. Reduce heat to low; cover and simmer 8 minutes or until chicken is no longer pink in center. Remove chicken from broth and let cool slightly; cut into ½-inch cubes.

4. Meanwhile, add hominy, bell pepper, chiles and olives to broth. Cover and bring to a boil over medium-high heat. Reduce heat to medium-low; simmer 4 minutes or until bell pepper is crisp-tender. Return chicken to saucepan. Stir in cilantro. Top with toasted tortilla strips.

KitchenAid®

MOROCCAN LENTIL AND VEGETABLE SOUP

MAKES 6 SERVINGS

1 tablespoon olive oil

1 cup chopped onion

4 cloves garlic, minced

½ cup dried lentils, rinsed and sorted

1½ teaspoons ground coriander

1½ teaspoons ground cumin

½ teaspoon ground cinnamon

½ teaspoon freshly ground black pepper

1 container (32 ounces) vegetable broth

½ cup sliced celery

½ cup chopped sun-dried tomatoes (not packed in oil)

1 yellow squash, halved lengthwise and sliced crosswise

½ cup chopped green bell pepper

1 cup chopped plum tomatoes

½ cup chopped fresh Italian parsley

¼ cup chopped fresh cilantro or basil

1. Heat olive oil in medium saucepan over medium-high heat. Add onion and garlic; sauté 4 minutes or until onion is tender. Stir in lentils, coriander, cumin, cinnamon and black pepper; cook 2 minutes. Add broth, celery and sun-dried tomatoes; bring to a boil. Reduce heat to medium-low; cover and simmer 25 minutes.

2. Stir in squash and bell pepper; cover and cook 10 minutes or until lentils are tender.

3. Top with plum tomatoes, parsley and cilantro just before serving.

Tip: This soup tastes even better the next day after the flavors have had time to blend. Cover and refrigerate the soup overnight, reserving the plum tomatoes, parsley and cilantro until ready to serve.

KitchenAid®

CURRIED CREAMY SWEET POTATO SOUP

MAKES 4 SERVINGS

4 cups water

1 pound sweet potatoes, peeled and cut into 1-inch cubes

2 tablespoons butter, divided

2 cups finely chopped yellow onions

2 cups milk, divided

¾ teaspoon curry powder

½ teaspoon salt

Dash ground red pepper (optional)

1. Bring water to a boil in large saucepan over high heat. Add sweet potatoes; return to a boil. Reduce heat to medium-low; simmer, uncovered, 15 minutes or until potatoes are tender.

2. Meanwhile, melt 1 tablespoon butter in medium skillet over medium-high heat. Add onions; sauté 8 minutes or until tender and golden.

3. Drain potatoes; place in blender with onions, 1 cup milk, curry powder, salt and ground red pepper, if desired. Blend until completely smooth.

4. Return potato mixture to saucepan; stir in remaining 1 cup milk. Cook 5 minutes over medium-high heat or until heated through. Remove from heat; stir in remaining 1 tablespoon butter.

KitchenAid®

BUTTERNUT SQUASH AND MILLET SOUP

MAKES 6 SERVINGS

1 red bell pepper

1 tablespoon canola oil

2½ cups diced peeled butternut squash

1 medium red onion, chopped

1 teaspoon curry powder

½ teaspoon smoked paprika

½ teaspoon salt

⅛ teaspoon freshly ground black pepper

2 cups chicken broth

2 boneless skinless chicken breasts (about 4 ounces each), cooked and chopped*

1 cup cooked millet

See Poached Chicken on page 8.

1. Preheat broiler. Place bell pepper on broiler rack 3 to 5 inches from heat source, turning frequently with long handled tongs until blistered and charred on all sides. Transfer to food storage bag or paper bag; seal bag and let stand 15 to 20 minutes to loosen skin. Scrape off skin with paring knife. Cut off top and remove seeds.

2. Heat oil in large saucepan over high heat. Add squash, bell pepper and onion; sauté 5 minutes. Add curry powder, paprika, salt and black pepper; stir in broth. Bring to a boil; cover and cook 7 to 10 minutes or until vegetables are tender.

3. Puree soup in batches in blender or food processor (or use immersion blender). Return soup to saucepan. Stir in chicken and millet; cook until heated through.

KitchenAid®

CARIBBEAN CALLALOO SOUP

MAKES 6 SERVINGS

1 tablespoon olive oil

1 large onion, chopped

4 cloves garlic, minced

¾ pound boneless skinless chicken breasts, thinly sliced crosswise

1½ pounds butternut squash, cut into ½-inch cubes

3 cans (about 14 ounces each) chicken broth

2 jalapeño peppers, seeded and minced

2 teaspoons dried thyme

1 package (5 ounces) fresh spinach, torn

6 tablespoons toasted flaked coconut*

To toast coconut, spread in a single layer in heavy-bottomed skillet. Cook and stir 1 to 2 minutes or until lightly browned. Remove from skillet immediately.

1. Heat olive oil in large skillet over medium-low heat. Add onion and garlic; sauté 5 minutes or until onion is tender. Add chicken; cover and cook 5 to 7 minutes or until chicken is no longer pink in center.

2. Add squash, broth, jalapeño peppers and thyme; bring to a boil over medium-high heat. Reduce heat to low; cover and simmer 15 to 20 minutes or until squash is very tender.

3. Remove skillet from heat; stir in spinach until wilted. Ladle into bowls; sprinkle each serving with toasted coconut.

SHANTUNG TWIN MUSHROOM SOUP

MAKES 6 SERVINGS

1 package (1 ounce) dried
   shiitake mushrooms

2 teaspoons vegetable oil

1 large onion, coarsely chopped

2 cloves garlic, minced

2 cups sliced fresh white
   mushrooms

2 cans (about 14 ounces each)
   chicken broth

2 ounces cooked ham, cut into
   thin slivers

½ cup thinly sliced green onions

1 tablespoon dry sherry

1 tablespoon soy sauce

1 tablespoon cornstarch

1. Place shiitake mushrooms in small bowl; cover with boiling water. Let stand 20 minutes or until tender. Drain and rinse well; squeeze out excess water. Cut off and discard stems; slice caps.

2. Heat oil in large saucepan over medium heat. Add onion and garlic; sauté 1 minute. Stir in shiitake and white mushrooms; cook 4 minutes, stirring occasionally.

3. Add broth; bring to a boil over high heat. Reduce heat to medium; cover and simmer 15 minutes.

4. Stir in ham and green onions; cook until heated through. Whisk sherry and soy sauce into cornstarch in small bowl until smooth and well blended; stir into soup. Cook 2 minutes or until soup is thickened, stirring occasionally.

PASTA FAGIOLI

MAKES 4 TO 6 SERVINGS

6 slices (1-inch-thick) Italian or French bread

2 tablespoons butter, melted

Garlic powder

2 tablespoons olive oil

1 cup chopped onion

3 cloves garlic, minced

2 cans (about 14 ounces each) Italian-style stewed tomatoes, undrained

3 cups vegetable broth

2 zucchini, quartered lengthwise and sliced

1 can (about 15 ounces) cannellini beans, undrained

¼ cup chopped fresh Italian parsley

1 teaspoon dried basil

½ teaspoon salt

½ teaspoon dried oregano

¼ teaspoon freshly ground black pepper

4 ounces uncooked ditalini or small shell pasta

¼ cup shredded Parmesan or Asiago cheese

1. Preheat oven to 350°F. Place bread on baking sheet; brush with butter and sprinkle lightly with garlic powder. Bake 5 minutes or until lightly toasted. Cool completely. Cut into cubes.

2. Heat olive oil in Dutch oven or large saucepan over medium heat. Add onion and garlic; sauté 5 minutes or until onion is tender.

3. Add tomatoes, broth, zucchini, beans with liquid, parsley, basil, salt, oregano and pepper to Dutch oven; bring to a boil over high heat, stirring occasionally. Reduce heat to low; cover and simmer 10 minutes.

4. Add pasta; cover and simmer 10 minutes or just until pasta is tender. Ladle into bowls; top each serving with cheese and garlic bread cubes.

POTATO-CORN CHOWDER

MAKES 4 SERVINGS

1 tablespoon canola oil

1 cup chopped onion

½ cup chopped green bell pepper

2 cups cubed peeled potatoes

1 can (about 14 ounces) vegetable
   broth

1 cup corn

1 cup lima beans

1 tablespoon chopped fresh dill *or*
   1 teaspoon dried dill weed

½ teaspoon salt

¼ teaspoon freshly ground black
   pepper

2 cups milk, divided

3 tablespoons all-purpose flour

¼ cup chopped fresh parsley

1. Heat oil in large saucepan over medium heat. Add onion and bell pepper; sauté about 5 minutes or until tender.

2. Add potatoes, broth, corn, lima beans, dill, salt and black pepper. Bring to a boil over high heat. Reduce heat to medium-low; cover and simmer 10 to 12 minutes or until potatoes are tender.

3. Whisk ⅓ cup milk into flour in small bowl until smooth; stir into soup. Stir in remaining 1⅔ cups milk; cook over medium heat until mixture boils and thickens, stirring frequently. Cook 1 minute more. Ladle into four bowls; sprinkle each serving with parsley.

KitchenAid®

LAMB MEATBALL AND CHICKPEA SOUP

MAKES 4 TO 6 SERVINGS

1 pound ground lamb

¼ cup chopped onion

1 clove garlic, minced

1 teaspoon ground cumin

½ teaspoon salt

2 cups chicken broth

1½ cups fresh broccoli florets

1 tomato, peeled and chopped

1 can (about 15 ounces) chickpeas, rinsed and drained

½ teaspoon dried thyme

Salt and freshly ground black pepper

1. Combine lamb, onion, garlic, cumin and salt in medium bowl; mix lightly. Shape into 1-inch balls.* Brown meatballs in large skillet over medium-high heat, turning occasionally.

2. Meanwhile, bring broth to a boil in large saucepan over high heat. Add broccoli and tomato; return to a boil.

3. Reduce heat to medium-low. Add meatballs, chickpeas and thyme; cover and simmer 5 minutes. Season with salt and pepper.

To quickly shape uniform meatballs, place lamb mixture on cutting board; pat evenly into large square about 1 inch thick. Cut into 1-inch squares; shape each square into a ball.

ITALIAN WHITE BEAN SOUP

MAKES 8 TO 10 SERVINGS

1½ cups dried Great Northern or navy beans, rinsed and sorted

5 to 6 cups water

1 can (8 ounces) tomato sauce

1 tablespoon minced onion

2 teaspoons dried basil

2 cubes chicken bouillon

1 teaspoon dried parsley flakes

½ teaspoon minced fresh garlic

1½ cups uncooked medium pasta shells

8 ounces baby spinach leaves (optional)

Salt and freshly ground black pepper

¼ cup freshly grated Parmesan cheese

1. Place beans in large saucepan; cover with water. Bring to a boil over high heat; boil 2 minutes. Remove from heat; cover and let soak 1 hour.

2. Drain beans; discard water. Combine soaked beans, 5 cups water, pasta sauce, onion, basil, bouillon, parsley and garlic in Dutch oven. Bring to a boil over high heat. Reduce heat; cover and simmer 2 to 2½ hours.

3. Add pasta and spinach, if desired; cover and simmer 15 to 20 minutes or until pasta is tender. Season with salt and pepper. Top with cheese.

BARLEY STEW WITH
CORNMEAL-CHEESE DUMPLINGS

MAKES 4 SERVINGS

STEW

    1 tablespoon olive oil

    1 onion, chopped

    1 cup sliced zucchini

    1 cup sliced carrots

    ½ cup chopped parsnip

    2 cloves garlic, minced

    2 cans (11½ ounces each) spicy
        vegetable juice cocktail

    1 can (15 ounces) butter
        beans, drained

    1 can (about 14 ounces)
        stewed tomatoes,
        undrained

    1 cup water

    ⅓ cup quick pearl barley

    1 bay leaf

    2 tablespoons chopped fresh
        thyme

    1½ tablespoons chopped fresh
        rosemary

DUMPLINGS

    ⅓ cup all-purpose flour

    ⅓ cup cornmeal

    1 teaspoon baking powder

    ⅓ cup (1½ ounces) shredded
        Cheddar cheese

    ¼ cup milk

    1 tablespoon canola oil

1. Heat olive oil in large saucepan over medium-high heat. Add onion; sauté 5 minutes or until translucent. Add zucchini, carrots, parsnip and garlic; sauté until vegetables are slightly softened.

2. Add vegetable juice, beans, tomatoes, water, barley, bay leaf, thyme and rosemary; bring to a boil over high heat. Reduce heat to medium-low; cover and simmer 20 to 25 minutes or until barley is tender, stirring occasionally. Remove and discard bay leaf.

3. For dumplings, combine flour, cornmeal and baking powder in small bowl. Stir in cheese, milk and canola oil. Drop batter into four mounds onto boiling stew. Cover and simmer 10 to 12 minutes or until toothpick inserted near center of dumplings comes out clean.

KitchenAid®

CIOPPINO

MAKES 4 SERVINGS

4 cups Fish Stock (page 8) *or* 4 cups water plus 1 fish-flavored bouillon cube

1 tablespoon olive oil

1 large onion, chopped

1 cup sliced celery

1 clove garlic, minced

1 tablespoon dried Italian seasoning

¼ pound cod or other mild-flavored fish fillets, cut into ½-inch pieces

1 large tomato, chopped

1 can (10 ounces) baby clams, rinsed and drained (optional)

¼ pound small raw shrimp, peeled and deveined

¼ pound raw bay scallops

¼ cup flaked crabmeat

2 tablespoons fresh lemon juice

1. Prepare Fish Stock, if desired.

2. Heat olive oil in large saucepan over medium heat. Add onion, celery and garlic; sauté 5 minutes or until onion is soft. Add fish stock and Italian seasoning. Cover and bring to a boil over high heat.

3. Add fish and tomato to saucepan. Reduce heat to medium-low; simmer about 5 minutes or until fish is opaque.

4. Add clams, if desired, shrimp, scallops, crabmeat and lemon juice; simmer about 5 minutes or until shrimp and scallops are opaque.

KitchenAid®

Sandwiches, Burgers and Pizza

HAVARTI AND ONION SANDWICHES

MAKES 2 SANDWICHES

1½ teaspoons olive oil

⅓ cup thinly sliced red onion

4 slices pumpernickel bread

6 ounces dill Havarti cheese, cut into slices

½ cup prepared coleslaw

1. Heat olive oil in large skillet over medium heat. Add onion; sauté 5 minutes or until tender. Layer two bread slices with onion, cheese and coleslaw; top with remaining two bread slices.

2. Heat same skillet over medium heat. Add sandwiches; press down with spatula or weigh down with small plate. Cook 4 to 5 minutes per side or until cheese is melted and bread is toasted.

BARBECUED BEEF SANDWICHES

MAKES 12 SERVINGS

1 boneless beef chuck
  shoulder roast (about
  3 pounds)

2 cups ketchup

1 medium onion, chopped

¼ cup cider vinegar

¼ cup molasses

2 tablespoons Worcestershire
  sauce

2 cloves garlic, minced

½ teaspoon salt

½ teaspoon dry mustard

½ teaspoon freshly ground
  black pepper

¼ teaspoon garlic powder

¼ teaspoon red pepper flakes

  Sesame seed buns, split

1. Cut roast in half; place in 4-quart slow cooker. Combine ketchup, onion, vinegar, molasses, Worcestershire sauce, garlic, salt, mustard, black pepper and red pepper flakes in large bowl; pour over roast. Cover; cook on LOW 8 to 10 hours or on HIGH 4 to 5 hours.

2. Remove roast from sauce; cool slightly. Trim and discard excess fat from beef. Shred meat using two forks.

3. Let sauce stand 5 minutes to allow fat to rise. Skim off fat. Return shredded meat to slow cooker. Stir meat to evenly coat with sauce. Adjust seasonings. Cover; cook 15 to 30 minutes or until heated through.

4. Spoon filling into sandwich buns and top with additional sauce, if desired.

CUBAN PORK SANDWICHES

MAKES 8 SERVINGS

1 pork loin roast (about
   2 pounds)

½ cup orange juice

2 tablespoons fresh lime juice

1 tablespoon minced garlic

1½ teaspoons salt

½ teaspoon red pepper flakes

2 tablespoons yellow mustard

8 crusty bread rolls or bolillos,
   split in half (6 inches each)

8 slices Swiss cheese

8 thin ham slices

4 dill pickles, thinly sliced
   lengthwise

1. Preheat oven to 400°F. Grease 13×9-inch baking dish. Place pork in prepared dish.

2. Combine orange juice, lime juice, garlic, salt and red pepper flakes in small bowl. Pour over pork. Roast 50 to 55 minutes or until pork registers 145°F when tested with instant-read thermometer inserted into thickest part of roast. Transfer pork to cutting board; tent with foil and let stand 10 minutes. Remove foil; let pork stand until cool enough to handle. Cut into thin slices.

3. Spread mustard on cut sides of rolls. Divide pork slices among roll bottoms. Top each with Swiss cheese slice, ham slice and pickle slices; cover with top of roll.

4. Coat large skillet with cooking spray; heat over medium heat. Working in batches, arrange sandwiches in skillet. Cover with foil and top with plate to compress sandwiches; cook until bread is toasted and cheese is slightly melted. Serve immediately.

KitchenAid®

GRILLED PROSCIUTTO, BRIE AND FIG SANDWICHES

MAKES 2 SANDWICHES

¼ cup fig preserves

4 slices (½ to ¾ inch thick) Italian or country bread

Freshly ground black pepper

4 to 6 ounces Brie cheese, cut into ¼-inch-thick slices

2 slices prosciutto (about half of 3-ounce package)

¼ cup baby arugula

1½ tablespoons butter, divided

1. Spread preserves over two bread slices. Sprinkle pepper generously over preserves. Top with Brie, prosciutto, arugula and remaining bread slices.

2. Heat medium cast iron skillet over medium heat 5 minutes. Add 1 tablespoon butter; swirl to melt and coat bottom of skillet. Add sandwiches to skillet; cook over medium-low heat about 5 minutes or until bottoms of sandwiches are golden brown.

3. Turn sandwiches and add remaining ½ tablespoon butter to skillet. Tilt pan to melt butter and move sandwiches so butter flows underneath. Cover with foil; cook about 5 minutes or until cheese is melted and bread is golden brown.

KitchenAid®

HERBED MUSHROOM PIZZA

MAKES 4 SERVINGS

Crusty Pizza Dough (page 166) *or* 1 (12-inch) prepared pizza crust

2 tablespoons olive oil

8 ounces sliced cremini and/or shiitake mushrooms

1½ teaspoons minced garlic

½ teaspoon dried basil

½ teaspoon dried thyme

¼ teaspoon salt

¼ teaspoon freshly ground black pepper

⅓ cup pizza or marinara sauce

1½ cups (6 ounces) shredded mozzarella cheese

1. Prepare Crusty Pizza Dough, if desired. Preheat oven to 450°F.

2. Heat olive oil in large skillet over medium-high heat. Add mushrooms and garlic; cook 4 minutes, stirring occasionally. Stir in basil, thyme, salt and pepper.

3. Spread pizza sauce evenly over crust. Top with mushroom mixture; sprinkle with mozzarella cheese.

4. Bake directly on oven rack 8 minutes or until crust is golden brown and cheese is melted. Slide baking sheet under pizza to remove from oven. Cut into slices to serve.

HAM AND CHEESE QUESADILLAS WITH CHERRY JAM

MAKES 2 SERVINGS

1 tablespoon vegetable oil

1 cup thinly sliced red onion

1 small jalapeño pepper, seeded and minced

1 cup pitted fresh sweet cherries

1 tablespoon packed brown sugar

1 teaspoon balsamic vinegar

¼ teaspoon salt

3 ounces ham, thinly sliced

2 ounces Havarti cheese, thinly sliced

2 (9-inch) flour tortillas

2 teaspoons butter

1. Heat oil in large skillet over medium-high heat. Add onion and jalapeño; sauté 3 minutes or until onions are golden. Add cherries; sauté 1 minute. Stir in brown sugar, vinegar and salt. Cook over low heat 1 minute, stirring constantly. Remove from heat; cool slightly.

2. Arrange half of ham slices and half of cheese slices over one side of each tortilla. Top with one fourth of cherry jam. Fold tortillas in half. Set aside remaining jam.

3. Melt butter in skillet over medium heat. Add quesadillas; press down firmly with spatula. Cook 3 to 4 minutes per side or until golden and cheese is melted. Cut each quesadilla in half. Serve with reserved cherry jam.

KitchenAid®

PORK TENDERLOIN SLIDERS

MAKES 12 SANDWICHES

½ cup mayonnaise

1 canned chipotle pepper in adobo sauce, minced

2 teaspoons fresh lime juice

2 teaspoons chili powder

¾ teaspoon ground cumin

½ teaspoon salt

½ teaspoon freshly ground black pepper

2 tablespoons olive oil, divided

2 pork tenderloins (about 1 pound each)

12 green onions, ends trimmed

12 dinner rolls, sliced in half horizontally

12 slices Monterey Jack cheese

1. Combine mayonnaise, chipotle pepper and lime juice in small bowl. Cover and refrigerate.

2. Prepare grill for direct cooking over medium heat.

3. Combine chili powder, cumin, salt and black pepper in small bowl. Rub 1 tablespoon olive oil evenly over pork. Sprinkle spice mixture evenly over tenderloins, turning to coat all sides.

4. Grill pork, covered, 15 minutes or until 145°F, turning occasionally. Transfer to cutting board; tent with foil and let stand 10 minutes.

5. Meanwhile, coat green onions with remaining 1 tablespoon olive oil. Grill 3 minutes or until browned, turning frequently.

6. Coarsely chop green onions. Thinly slice pork. Evenly spread chipotle mayonnaise on bottom halves of rolls. Top with green onions, tenderloin slices, cheese and tops of rolls. Serve immediately.

TEMPEH MELT

MAKES 4 SERVINGS

3 teaspoons hamburger
    seasoning

1 teaspoon paprika

1 package (8 ounces)
    unseasoned soy tempeh

4 slices Swiss cheese

8 slices pumpernickel or
    marble rye bread

Thousand Island Sauce
    (recipe follows)

Dill pickle slices or
    sauerkraut

Red onion slices or
    caramelized red onion

1. Combine 1 cup water, hamburger seasoning and paprika in large skillet. Cut tempeh in half crosswise; add to skillet and bring to a boil over high heat. Reduce heat; simmer 20 minutes, turning tempeh occasionally. Remove tempeh from skillet; cut each piece in half.*

2. Prepare grill for direct cooking over medium-high heat. Grill tempeh, covered, 4 minutes per side. Top with cheese; grill 30 seconds or until cheese melts. Spread 1 tablespoon sauce over one piece of bread; top with tempeh, pickles, onions and another piece of bread.

Thousand Island Sauce: Combine ½ cup mayonnaise, ½ cup chili sauce, 1 tablespoon sweet pickle relish, 2 teaspoons Dijon mustard and dash ground red pepper in food processor. Process until smooth.

Tempeh can be poached in advance.

HOISIN BARBECUE CHICKEN SLIDERS

MAKES 16 SLIDERS

⅔ cup hoisin sauce

⅓ cup barbecue sauce

3 tablespoons quick-cooking tapioca

1 tablespoon sugar

1 tablespoon soy sauce

¼ teaspoon red pepper flakes

12 boneless skinless chicken thighs (3 to 3½ pounds)

16 dinner rolls or Hawaiian sweet rolls, split

½ medium red onion, finely chopped

Sliced pickles (optional)

1. Combine hoisin sauce, barbecue sauce, tapioca, sugar, soy sauce and red pepper flakes in slow cooker; mix well. Add chicken. Cover; cook on LOW 8 to 9 hours.

2. Remove chicken from sauce. Coarsely shred with two forks. Return shredded chicken to slow cooker; mix well.

3. Serve chicken and sauce on rolls with red onion and pickles, if desired.

KitchenAid®

GRILLED CHICKEN PARTY SANDWICH

MAKES 6 SERVINGS

¾ cup plus 1 to 2 tablespoons olive oil, divided

6 tablespoons fresh lime juice

4 cloves garlic, minced

2¼ teaspoons salt

¾ teaspoon freshly ground black pepper

2 boneless skinless chicken breasts (about ½ pound)

1 medium yellow onion

1 loaf ciabatta bread (16 ounces), cut in half lengthwise

¼ cup chopped fresh cilantro

6 ounces fresh mozzarella, sliced

1 medium tomato, thinly sliced

1. For marinade, combine ¾ cup olive oil, lime juice, garlic, salt and pepper in medium bowl.

2. Pour ¼ cup marinade into large resealable food storage bag. Add chicken. Seal bag; turn to coat. Marinate in refrigerator up to 2 hours; refrigerate remaining marinade.

3. Brush grid with 1 teaspoon olive oil. Prepare grill for direct cooking. Cut onion horizontally into ½-inch thick rings; thread onto skewers.

4. Remove chicken from marinade; discard marinade. Grill chicken, uncovered, 12 to 15 minutes or until internal temperature reaches 160°F, turning once. Brush onions with 1 tablespoon oil. Grill 8 to 12 minutes or until soft and browned, turning once. Grill bread, cut sides down, until lightly toasted.

5. Transfer chicken and onions to cutting board. Let chicken stand 10 minutes; thinly slice. Season onions with salt and pepper; separate rings.

6. Whisk reserved marinade; brush onto cut sides of bread. Sprinkle cilantro on bottom half of bread; top with cheese, tomato, chicken and onions. Top with remaining bread. Press down firmly. Wrap sandwich in foil. Place on grill over direct heat and top with large skillet to flatten. Grill 4 to 6 minutes or until cheese is melted. Slice sandwich into six pieces; serve immediately.

KitchenAid®

GRILLED PIZZA MARGHERITA

MAKES 4 SERVINGS

¾ cup pilsner or other light-colored beer

1 package (¼ ounce) active dry yeast

2 tablespoons plus 2 teaspoons extra virgin olive oil, divided

1¾ to 2½ cups all-purpose flour

1⅛ teaspoons salt, divided

1½ pints grape tomatoes, halved

1 clove garlic, minced

¼ teaspoon dried basil

⅛ teaspoon red pepper flakes

6 ounces fresh mozzarella, cut into 12 slices

10 fresh basil leaves, thinly sliced

1. Microwave beer in small microwavable bowl on HIGH 25 seconds. Stir in yeast and 2 teaspoons olive oil; let stand 5 minutes or until foamy.

2. Attach dough hook to stand mixer. Combine 1¾ cups flour and 1 teaspoon salt in mixer bowl; add beer mixture and stir until dough cleans side of bowl. Knead on low speed 5 minutes or until smooth and elastic, adding additional flour by tablespoons if dough is sticky. Divide dough in half and shape into balls. Dust with flour; place in separate medium bowls. Cover and let rise in warm place about 1½ hours or until doubled.

3. Heat 1 tablespoon olive oil in medium nonstick skillet over medium-high heat. Add tomatoes, garlic, dried basil, remaining ⅛ teaspoon salt and red pepper flakes; cook 3 to 4 minutes or until tomatoes are very soft, stirring occasionally. Remove from heat.

4. Oil grid; prepare grill for direct cooking.

5. Gently stretch each piece of dough into 9-inch circle on lightly floured surface. Transfer to floured baking sheets. Brush tops with remaining 1 tablespoon olive oil. Cover and let stand 10 minutes.

6. Reduce grill to medium heat. Carefully flip dough rounds onto grid, oiled side down. Grill, uncovered, 3 minutes or until bottom is golden and well marked. Turn crusts; spread each with half of tomato mixture, leaving ½-inch border. Top with cheese; cover and grill 3 minutes or until cheese is melted and crust is golden brown. Transfer to cutting board; sprinkle evenly with fresh basil. Serve immediately.

SAUSAGE, PEPPER AND ONION PIZZA

MAKES 4 SERVINGS

½ cup tomato sauce

1 clove garlic, minced

½ teaspoon dried basil

½ teaspoon dried oregano

⅛ teaspoon red pepper flakes

2 cooked Italian sausages

1 (12-inch) prepared pizza crust

1½ cups (6 ounces) shredded fontina cheese or pizza cheese blend

½ cup red onion pieces (1 inch)

1 cup bell pepper pieces (1 inch)

½ cup freshly grated Parmesan cheese

1. Preheat oven to 450°F. Combine tomato sauce, garlic, basil, oregano and red pepper flakes in small bowl. Cut sausages in half lengthwise, then cut crosswise into ½-inch slices.

2. Place pizza crust on pizza pan or baking sheet. Spread tomato sauce mixture over crust to within 1 inch of edge. Sprinkle fontina cheese over tomato sauce; top with sausage, onion and bell pepper. Sprinkle with Parmesan cheese.

3. Bake 12 minutes or until crust is crisp and cheeses are melted.

Tip: If you cook the sausage on the grill, grill a bell pepper and red onion rings with it until softened and lightly charred.

KitchenAid®

GOURMET BURGERS WITH PANCETTA AND GORGONZOLA

MAKES 4 SERVINGS

1½ pounds ground beef

4 ounces (about ½ cup) Gorgonzola or blue cheese crumbles

2 tablespoons mayonnaise

1 red bell pepper, quartered

4 thick slices red onion

4 egg or brioche rolls

Salt and freshly ground black pepper

Baby romaine lettuce

4 to 8 slices pancetta or bacon, crisp-cooked

1. Prepare grill for direct cooking. Shape beef into four patties about ¾ inch thick. Cover and refrigerate. Combine cheese and mayonnaise in small bowl; refrigerate until ready to serve.

2. Grill bell pepper and onion, covered, over medium-high heat 8 to 10 minutes or until browned, turning once. Transfer to plate; keep warm. Grill rolls, cut sides down, until lightly toasted, if desired.

3. Place patties on grid over medium heat. Grill, covered, 8 to 10 minutes (or uncovered 13 to 15 minutes) to medium (160°F) or to desired doneness, turning occasionally. Season with salt and black pepper.

4. Spread cheese mixture on cut surfaces of rolls. Top bottom half of each roll with lettuce, burger, pancetta, onion, bell pepper and top half of roll.

BRIE BURGERS WITH SUN-DRIED TOMATO AND ARTICHOKE SPREAD

MAKES 4 SERVINGS

1 cup canned quartered artichokes, drained and chopped

½ cup oil-packed sun-dried tomatoes, drained and chopped, divided

2 tablespoons mayonnaise

1 tablespoon plus 1 teaspoon minced garlic, divided

1 teaspoon freshly ground black pepper, divided

½ teaspoon salt, divided

1½ pounds ground beef

¼ cup chopped shallots

¼ pound Brie cheese, sliced

2 tablespoons butter, softened

4 egg or Kaiser rolls, split

Heirloom tomato slices

Arugula or lettuce leaves

1. Prepare grill for direct cooking.

2. Combine artichokes, ¼ cup sun-dried tomatoes, mayonnaise, 1 teaspoon garlic, ½ teaspoon pepper and ¼ teaspoon salt in small bowl; mix well.

3. Combine beef, shallots, remaining ¼ cup sun-dried tomatoes, 1 tablespoon garlic, ½ teaspoon pepper and ¼ teaspoon salt in large bowl; mix lightly. Shape into four patties.

4. Grill patties over medium heat, covered, 8 to 10 minutes (or uncovered 13 to 15 minutes) or until cooked through (160°F), turning occasionally. Top each burger with cheese during last 2 minutes of grilling.

5. Spread butter on cut sides of rolls; grill until lightly toasted. Spread artichoke mixture on bottom halves of rolls. Top with tomato slices, burger and arugula. Cover with top halves of rolls.

CRUSTY PIZZA DOUGH

MAKES DOUGH FOR 1 PIZZA CRUST

1 package (¼ ounce) active dry
   yeast

1 cup warm water (105° to 115°F)

2½ to 3½ cups all-purpose flour

2 teaspoons olive oil

½ teaspoon salt

1 tablespoon cornmeal

Toppings: pizza sauce, shredded
   cheese, cut-up vegetables,
   sliced tomatoes, cooked cubed
   chicken, pepperoni slices,
   shredded fresh basil, minced
   garlic

1. Attach dough hook to stand mixer. Dissolve
yeast in warm water in mixer bowl. Add 2½ cups
flour, olive oil and salt; mix on low speed 1 minute.
Knead on medium-low speed 4 to 5 minutes
or until dough is smooth and elastic, adding
remaining flour, ½ cup at a time. Shape dough
into a ball. Place in large lightly greased bowl; turn
once to grease surface. Cover and let rise in warm
place 1 hour or until doubled.

2. Preheat oven to 450°F. Grease 14-inch pizza
pan; sprinkle with cornmeal. Pat and stretch
dough to fit in pan, forming a rim around edge to
hold toppings. Top with pizza sauce and desired
toppings. Bake 15 to 20 minutes or until cheese is
melted and crust is lightly browned.

KitchenAid®

ROSEMARY PARMESAN CHICKEN FLATBREAD

MAKES 6 SERVINGS

Crusty Pizza Dough
(page 166)

2 tablespoons olive oil

1 tablespoon minced oil-
packed sun-dried
tomatoes

2 plum tomatoes, thinly sliced

1¼ cups shredded cooked
chicken breast (4 ounces)*

1½ to 2 cups baby spinach,
coarsely chopped

¼ cup freshly grated Parmesan
cheese

1 tablespoon minced fresh
rosemary

*See Poached Chicken on
page 8.

1. Prepare Crusty Pizza Dough through step 1.

2. Preheat oven to 400°F. Grease 15×10-inch jelly-roll pan. Punch down dough; pat and stretch dough to fit in prepared pan (if dough is difficult to stretch, cover and let rest 10 minutes). Bake 5 minutes.

3. Brush crust with olive oil; sprinkle evenly with sun-dried tomatoes. Layer with tomato slices, chicken, spinach, cheese and rosemary.

4. Bake 8 to 10 minutes or until crust is golden brown. Cut into slices to serve.

PANINI WITH FRESH MOZZARELLA AND BASIL

MAKES 4 SERVINGS

½ cup prepared vinaigrette

1 loaf (16 ounces) Italian bread, cut in half lengthwise

6 ounces fresh mozzarella cheese, cut into 12 slices

8 ounces thinly sliced oven-roasted deli turkey

12 to 16 whole fresh basil leaves

1 large tomato, thinly sliced

½ cup thinly sliced red onion

⅛ teaspoon red pepper flakes

1. Preheat indoor grill. Brush vinaigrette evenly over cut sides of bread.

2. Layer cheese, turkey, basil, tomato and onion evenly over bottom half of bread. Sprinkle with red pepper flakes. Cover with top half of bread; press down firmly. Cut into four sandwiches.

3. Place sandwiches on grill; close lid. Cook 5 to 7 minutes or until cheese is melted.

KitchenAid

SUPER MEATBALL SLIDERS

MAKES 24 SLIDERS

1 can (15 ounces) whole berry cranberry sauce

1 can (about 15 ounces) tomato sauce

⅛ teaspoon red pepper flakes (optional)

2 pounds ground beef or turkey

¾ cup plain dry bread crumbs

1 egg, lightly beaten

1 package (1 ounce) dry onion soup mix

Baby arugula leaves (optional)

24 small potato rolls or dinner rolls

6 slices (1 ounce each) provolone cheese, cut into quarters

1. Preheat oven to 350°F. Combine cranberry sauce, tomato sauce and red pepper flakes, if desired, in medium bowl.

2. Combine ground beef, bread crumbs, egg and soup mix in large bowl; mix well. Shape mixture into 24 meatballs (about 1¾ inches in diameter). Place in 13×9-inch baking pan or glass baking dish; pour sauce over meatballs, making sure all meatballs are covered in sauce.

3. Bake 40 to 45 minutes or until meatballs are cooked through (160°F), basting with sauce once or twice during cooking.

4. Place arugula leaves on rolls, if desired; top with meatballs, sauce and cheese.

SPANAKOPITA SANDWICHES

MAKES 4 SANDWICHES

1 tablespoon butter

¼ cup finely chopped onion

1 clove garlic, minced

2 packages (5 ounces each) fresh baby spinach, coarsely chopped

4 ounces crumbled feta cheese

¼ teaspoon dried oregano

Pinch of ground nutmeg

4 medium croissants, split

8 slices (1 ounce each) Monterey Jack cheese

1. Melt butter in large skillet over medium heat. Add onion and garlic; sauté 5 minutes or until onion is tender. Add spinach and 1 tablespoon water; cook 5 minutes or until spinach is wilted and dry. Remove from heat; stir in feta cheese, oregano and nutmeg.

2. Divide spinach mixture evenly among croissant bottoms; top with Monterey Jack cheese and croissant tops.

3. Wipe out skillet with paper towel; heat over medium heat. Add sandwiches; cover with large lid. Cook over low heat 5 to 6 minutes or until cheese is melted and bottoms of sandwiches are golden brown.

KitchenAid®

Pasta

SPICY ITALIAN SAUSAGE AND PENNE PASTA

MAKES 4 TO 6 SERVINGS

8 ounces uncooked penne pasta

1 pound bulk hot Italian sausage

1 cup chopped sweet onion

2 cloves garlic, minced

2 cans (about 14 ounces each) seasoned diced tomatoes

3 cups fresh broccoli florets

½ cup shredded Asiago or Romano cheese

1. Cook pasta according to package directions until al dente. Drain and return to saucepan; keep warm.

2. Meanwhile, crumble sausage into large skillet. Add onion; sauté over medium-high heat until sausage is cooked through. Drain fat. Add garlic; cook 1 minute. Stir in tomatoes and broccoli. Cover and cook 10 minutes or until broccoli is tender.

3. Add sausage mixture to pasta; toss to coat. Sprinkle with Asiago cheese.

BEEF AND SAUSAGE LASAGNA

MAKES 10 SERVINGS

2 tablespoons olive oil

1 large yellow onion, chopped

2 cloves garlic, minced

1 pound ground beef

1 pound Italian sweet sausage, casings removed

1 can (28 ounces) crushed tomatoes

1 can (8 ounce) tomato sauce

1 can (6 ounces) tomato paste

1 cup dry red wine

½ cup water

1 teaspoon dried basil

1 teaspoon dried oregano

1¼ teaspoons salt, divided

¼ teaspoon red pepper flakes

1 dried bay leaf

Olive oil

1 recipe Egg Pasta Dough or Semolina Pasta Dough (page 5)

1 container (32 ounces) ricotta cheese

1 cup freshly grated Parmesan cheese, divided

2 eggs, beaten

¼ teaspoon freshly ground black pepper

4 cups (16 ounces) shredded mozzarella cheese

1. For sauce, heat olive oil in Dutch oven or large saucepan over medium-high heat. Add onion; sauté about 3 minutes or until softened. Add garlic; cook 1 minute or until fragrant. Add beef and sausage; cook about 10 minutes or until no longer pink, stirring to break up meat. Add tomatoes, tomato sauce, tomato paste, wine, water, basil, oregano, ¾ teaspoon salt, red pepper flakes and bay leaf, stirring to scrape up browned bits from bottom of pan. Bring to a simmer. Reduce heat to medium-low; simmer 1 hour or until reduced by about one fourth, stirring frequently. Discard bay leaf.

2. Prepare pasta dough. Cut pasta into 5×4-inch noodles. Arrange in single layer on kitchen towel; let rest 10 minutes.

3. Meanwhile, preheat oven to 350°F. Lightly oil 15×10-inch baking dish. Bring large pot of salted water to boil. Cook lasagna noodles 2 minutes or until barely tender, stirring frequently. Drain and transfer to bowl of cold water to cool. Drain again and arrange in single layer on clean kitchen towels to remove excess water.

4. For filling, mix ricotta cheese, ½ cup Parmesan cheese, eggs, remaining ½ teaspoon salt and black pepper in large bowl. Spread 1 cup sauce in baking dish. Layer with four lasagna noodles, slightly overlapping. Spread with one third of sauce, half of filling and 2 cups mozzarella cheese. Repeat with four more noodles, half of remaining sauce, remaining filling and 2 cups mozzarella cheese. Finish with four noodles and sauce and sprinkle with remaining ½ cup Parmesan cheese. Cover with greased foil. (Lasagna can be cooled, covered and refrigerated for 1 day.)

5. Place dish on baking sheet. Bake 30 minutes. Uncover; bake 20 to 30 minutes (30 to 40 minutes for chilled lasagna) or until sauce is bubbly. Let stand 15 minutes before serving.

GINGER NOODLES WITH SESAME EGG STRIPS

MAKES 4 SERVINGS

6 ounces uncooked Chinese rice noodles or vermicelli

5 egg whites

6 teaspoons teriyaki sauce, divided

3 teaspoons sesame seeds, toasted,* divided

1 teaspoon dark sesame oil

½ cup vegetable broth

1 tablespoon minced fresh ginger

⅓ cup sliced green onions

*To toast sesame seeds, spread seeds in small skillet. Shake skillet over medium heat 2 minutes or until seeds begin to pop and turn golden.

1. Cook noodles according to package directions until tender. Drain and return to saucepan; keep warm.

2. Whisk egg whites, 2 teaspoons teriyaki sauce and 1 teaspoon sesame seeds in large bowl.

3. Heat sesame oil in large nonstick skillet over medium heat. Pour egg mixture into skillet; cook 1½ to 2 minutes or until bottom is set. Turn; cook 30 seconds to 1 minute or until cooked through. Gently slide onto cutting board; cut into ½-inch strips when cool enough to handle.

4. Add broth, ginger and remaining 4 teaspoons teriyaki sauce to skillet. Bring to a boil over high heat; reduce heat to medium. Add noodles; cook until heated through. Add egg strips and green onions; heat through. Sprinkle with remaining 2 teaspoons sesame seeds just before serving.

SPAGHETTI ALLA BOLOGNESE

MAKES 4 TO 6 SERVINGS

2 tablespoons olive oil

1 pound ground beef

1 medium onion, chopped

½ small carrot, finely chopped

½ stalk celery, finely chopped

1 cup dry white wine

½ cup milk

⅛ teaspoon ground nutmeg

1 can (about 14 ounces)
    whole tomatoes, coarsely
    chopped, juice reserved

1 cup beef broth

3 tablespoons tomato paste

1 teaspoon salt

1 teaspoon dried basil

½ teaspoon dried thyme

⅛ teaspoon freshly ground
    black pepper

1 bay leaf

1 package (16 ounces)
    uncooked spaghetti

1 cup freshly grated Parmesan
    cheese

1. Heat olive oil in large saucepan over medium heat. Add beef; cook 6 to 8 minutes, stirring to break up meat. Drain fat.

2. Add onion, carrot and celery; sauté 2 minutes. Stir in wine; cook 4 to 6 minutes or until wine has evaporated. Stir in milk and nutmeg; cook 3 to 4 minutes or until milk has almost evaporated. Remove from heat.

3. Press tomatoes with juice through sieve into meat mixture; discard seeds.

4. Stir in broth, tomato paste, salt, basil, thyme, pepper and bay leaf; bring to a boil over medium-high heat. Reduce heat; simmer 1 to 1½ hours or until most of liquid has evaporated and sauce thickens, stirring frequently. Remove and discard bay leaf.

5. Cook spaghetti according to package directions; drain and place in large bowl. Top with sauce; toss gently to coat. Sprinkle with cheese.

KitchenAid®

KALE, GORGONZOLA AND NOODLE CASSEROLE

MAKES 6 SERVINGS

6 ounces uncooked egg noodles or rotini pasta

1 large bunch kale, stems removed, coarsely chopped (about 8 cups chopped)

2 tablespoons butter

¼ cup chopped green onions

1 clove garlic, smashed

2 tablespoons all-purpose flour

2¼ cups half-and-half

4 ounces Gorgonzola cheese, crumbled

4 ounces fontina cheese, cut into small chunks

½ teaspoon salt

¼ teaspoon freshly ground black pepper

¼ teaspoon ground nutmeg

¼ cup panko bread crumbs

1. Preheat oven to 350°F. Grease 9-inch square baking dish.

2. Cook noodles according to package directions until al dente. Drain and return to saucepan; keep warm.

3. Place kale in large saucepan with 1 inch water; cover and bring to a simmer over medium heat. Cook kale 15 minutes or until tender. Drain well, pressing out excess liquid; set aside.

4. Melt butter in medium saucepan over medium-low heat. Add green onions and garlic; sauté 5 minutes. Discard garlic. Whisk in flour until smooth. Gradually whisk in half-and-half; cook until thickened, stirring frequently. Gradually add cheeses, stirring until melted. Stir in salt, pepper and nutmeg. Fold in noodles and kale; mix well.

5. Spoon into prepared baking dish. Sprinkle with bread crumbs. Bake 30 minutes or until bubbly. If desired, place dish until broiler for 30 seconds to brown.

KitchenAid®

PASTA AND POTATOES WITH PESTO

MAKES 6 SERVINGS

3 medium red potatoes, cut into chunks

8 ounces uncooked linguine

¾ cup peas

½ cup pesto sauce (page 8)

¼ cup plus 2 tablespoons freshly grated Parmesan cheese, divided

¼ teaspoon salt

¼ teaspoon freshly ground black pepper

1. Place potatoes in medium saucepan; cover with water. Bring to a boil over high heat. Reduce heat to medium; cook 10 minutes or until potatoes are tender. Drain and return to saucepan; keep warm.

2. Meanwhile, cook linguine according to package directions, adding peas during last 3 minutes of cooking; drain and return to saucepan. Add potatoes, pesto, ¼ cup cheese, salt and pepper; toss until blended. Sprinkle with remaining 2 tablespoons cheese just before serving.

KitchenAid®

PASTA WITH SPINACH AND RICOTTA

MAKES 4 SERVINGS

8 ounces uncooked tri-colored rotini pasta

1 tablespoon olive oil

1 package (10 ounces) frozen chopped spinach, thawed and squeezed dry

2 teaspoons minced garlic

1 cup ricotta cheese

½ cup water

4 tablespoons freshly grated Parmesan cheese, divided

Salt and freshly ground black pepper

1. Cook pasta according to package directions. Drain and return to saucepan; cover and keep warm.

2. Heat olive oil in large skillet over medium-low heat. Add spinach and garlic; sauté 5 minutes. Stir in ricotta cheese, water and 2 tablespoons Parmesan cheese. Season with salt and pepper.

3. Stir in pasta; sprinkle with remaining 2 tablespoons Parmesan cheese.

Tip: See Notes on Spinach on page 12 for instructions on substituting fresh spinach for frozen.

SPINACH AND MUSHROOM CANNELLONI

MAKES 6 TO 8 SERVINGS

1 recipe Egg Pasta Dough
(page 5)

18 ounces fresh spinach*

2 tablespoons olive oil

8 ounces cremini mushrooms,
chopped

1 small onion, finely chopped

1 clove garlic, minced

1 cup whole milk ricotta
cheese

½ cup plus ⅓ cup freshly
grated Parmesan cheese,
divided

1 egg

½ teaspoon salt

½ teaspoon freshly ground
black pepper

¼ teaspoon freshly grated
nutmeg, divided

3 cups whole milk

1 bay leaf

Additional salt and freshly
ground black pepper

7 tablespoons butter, divided,
plus more for baking dish

⅓ cup all-purpose flour

Shredded fresh basil

*Two 10-ounce packages frozen
chopped spinach, thawed and
squeezed dry, can be substituted
for the fresh spinach. Proceed to
step 2.

1. Prepare pasta dough. For filling, rinse spinach and shake dry; place in large saucepan with water clinging to leaves. Cover and cook over medium heat 7 minutes or until wilted and tender, stirring occasionally. Drain; rinse under cold running water until cool. Squeeze all excess liquid from spinach a handful at a time. Chop spinach and place in large bowl.

2. Heat olive oil in large skillet over medium-high heat. Add mushrooms; cook 6 minutes or until they give off their liquid, stirring occasionally. Add onion and garlic; cook about 5 minutes until mushroom liquid is evaporated, stirring occasionally. Transfer to bowl with spinach; let cool. Stir in ricotta cheese, ½ cup Parmesan cheese, egg, ½ teaspoon salt, ½ teaspoon pepper and ⅛ teaspoon nutmeg.

3. For cream sauce, bring milk and bay leaf to a simmer in medium saucepan over medium heat. Melt 5 tablespoons butter in separate medium saucepan over medium heat. Whisk in flour and reduce heat to medium-low. Let bubble without browning 1 minute. Gradually whisk in hot milk with bay leaf. Bring to simmer, whisking often; simmer 5 minutes or until slightly reduced. Remove and discard bay leaf. Add remaining ⅛ teaspoon nutmeg and season with additional salt and pepper. Dot top of sauce with 1 tablespoon butter to prevent skin from forming.

4. Roll pasta dough with Pasta Sheet Roller to thickness setting 5. Cut into 5-inch squares; place in single layer on floured surface. Let rest 10 minutes.

5. Preheat oven to 350°F. Bring large pot of salted water to a boil. Add pasta; cook 2 minutes or until barely tender, stirring frequently. Drain and transfer pasta to bowl of cold water to cool. Drain; place pasta squares on clean kitchen towels to remove excess water.

KitchenAid®

6. Spread about ½ cup cream sauce in large buttered baking dish. Place one pasta square on work surface; spoon 3 tablespoons filling along bottom edge and roll up from bottom. Place seam side down in baking dish. Repeat with remaining filling and pasta. Spread remaining sauce over pasta. Sprinkle with remaining ⅓ cup Parmesan cheese and

dot with remaining 1 tablespoon butter. (Cannelloni can be cooled, covered and refrigerated for up to 8 hours before baking.)

7. Bake about 25 minutes (35 minutes for chilled cannelloni) or until sauce is bubbly and top is golden brown. Let stand 5 minutes before serving. Garnish with shredded basil.

FETTUCCINE WITH PORK AND PORCINI RAGÙ

MAKES 4 TO 6 SERVINGS

1 ounce dried porcini mushrooms, rinsed

1 cup boiling water

3 tablespoons olive oil, divided

1½ pounds meaty pork neck

1 medium onion, chopped

2 cloves garlic, minced

2 tablespoons tomato paste

½ cup dry white wine

1 can (28 ounces) crushed tomatoes

1 tablespoon finely chopped fresh rosemary

½ teaspoon freshly ground black pepper

Salt

Semolina Pasta Dough (page 5), cut into fettuccine

Freshly grated Parmesan cheese

1. Combine dried mushrooms and boiling water in small bowl. Let stand 20 minutes or until mushrooms are softened. Remove mushrooms, reserving soaking liquid; coarsely chop mushrooms. Strain soaking liquid through fine-mesh sieve, leaving grit in bowl; set aside.

2. Heat 2 tablespoons olive oil in Dutch oven or large saucepan over medium-high heat. Add pork neck; cook about 6 minutes or until meaty parts are browned, turning occasionally. Transfer to plate.

3. Add remaining 1 tablespoon olive oil to Dutch oven; reduce heat to medium. Add onion; sauté about 5 minutes or until onion is translucent. Add garlic; cook 1 minute or until fragrant. Add tomato paste; cook 30 seconds, stirring constantly. Add wine, stirring to scrape up browned bits from bottom of pan. Stir in tomatoes, mushrooms, reserved soaking liquid, rosemary and pepper; bring to a boil over high heat.

4. Return pork to Dutch oven. Reduce heat to medium-low; cover and simmer about 1¾ hours or until meat is tender and falling off bones, stirring occasionally.

5. Remove pork from sauce; place on cutting board and let stand until cool enough to handle. Chop meat from bones, discarding bones. Return meat to sauce. Season with salt to taste.

6. Meanwhile, prepare pasta. Bring large pot of salted water to boil. Add pasta; cook 2 minutes or until barely tender, stirring occasionally. Drain and add to sauce; mix gently. Serve with Parmesan cheese.

SPAGHETTI WITH PESTO TOFU

MAKES 4 SERVINGS

1 package (14 ounces) extra firm tofu

¼ to ½ cup pesto sauce (page 8)

8 ounces uncooked spaghetti

3 cups marinara sauce

½ cup shredded Parmesan cheese

¼ cup pine nuts, toasted*

To toast pine nuts, spread in single layer in heavy skillet. Cook over medium heat 1 to 2 minutes or until nuts are lightly browned, stirring frequently.

1. Preheat oven to 350°F. Spray shallow baking dish with nonstick cooking spray.

2. Cut tofu into 1-inch cubes; place in medium bowl. Add pesto; toss to coat. Spread in prepared baking dish. Bake 15 minutes.

3. Meanwhile, cook spaghetti according to package directions. Drain and return to saucepan; stir in marinara sauce. Cook over low heat 5 minutes or until hot.

4. Divide spaghetti among four serving bowls. Top each serving with tofu cubes, Parmesan cheese and pine nuts.

KitchenAid®

CREAMY FETTUCCINE
WITH ASPARAGUS AND LIMA BEANS

MAKES 4 SERVINGS

8 ounces Egg Pasta Dough (page 5), cut into fettuccine or hot cooked dried fettuccine

2 tablespoons butter

2 cups (1-inch) fresh asparagus pieces

1 cup frozen lima beans

¼ teaspoon freshly ground black pepper

½ cup vegetable broth

1 cup half-and-half

1 cup freshly grated Parmesan cheese

1. Prepare pasta. Bring large saucepan of water to a boil. Add pasta; cook 2 minutes or until barely tender, stirring occasionally. Drain and return to saucepan; keep warm.

2. Meanwhile, melt butter in large skillet over medium-high heat. Add asparagus, lima beans and pepper; cook and stir 3 minutes. Add broth; simmer 3 minutes. Add half-and-half; simmer 3 to 4 minutes or until vegetables are tender.

3. Add vegetable mixture and cheese to fettuccine; toss until well blended. Serve immediately.

KitchenAid

MEDITERRANEAN MACARONI WITH CHICKEN AND ASPARAGUS

MAKES 4 TO 6 SERVINGS

8 ounces Eggless Dough for Pasta Press (page 7), cut into small macaroni *or* 2 cups uncooked elbow macaroni

1 tablespoon olive oil

1 red bell pepper, cut into slivers

¾ pound fresh asparagus, cut into 1-inch pieces

4 tablespoons butter, divided

¼ cup all-purpose flour

1¾ cups warm milk

1 teaspoon minced fresh thyme

Salt and freshly ground black pepper

1 cup (4 ounces) shredded mozzarella cheese

1 cup bite-size pieces cooked chicken*

4 ounces garlic and herb flavored goat cheese

¼ cup plain dry bread crumbs

See Poached Chicken on page 8

1. Prepare pasta.

2. Preheat oven to 350°F. Bring large saucepan of water to a oil. Add pasta; cook 2 minutes or until barely tender. Rinse under cold running water to stop cooking; set aside.

3. Meanwhile, heat olive oil in medium skillet over medium-high heat. Add bell pepper; sauté 3 minutes. Add asparagus; sauté 3 minutes or until crisp-tender. Remove from skillet.

4. Melt 3 tablespoons butter over medium-low heat in large saucepan until bubbly. Whisk in flour until smooth; cook 2 minutes without browning. Gradually whisk in milk. Cook 6 to 8 minutes over medium heat, whisking constantly until mixture begins to bubble and thickens slightly. Add thyme and season with salt and black pepper. Remove from heat. Stir in mozzarella cheese until melted.

5. Stir pasta, vegetables and chicken into cheese sauce. Crumble goat cheese into mixture; transfer to 2-quart baking dish. Top with bread crumbs and dot with remaining 1 tablespoon butter.

6. Bake 25 to 30 minutes or until sauce is bubbly and top is lightly browned.

KitchenAid®

CAULIFLOWER AND FARFALLE WITH GOUDA

MAKES 6 TO 8 SERVINGS

1 package (about 16 ounces) farfalle (bowtie) pasta

4 cups milk

2 cloves garlic, smashed

¼ cup (½ stick) plus 3 tablespoons butter, divided

5 tablespoons all-purpose flour

1 pound Gouda cheese, shredded

1 teaspoon dry mustard

⅛ teaspoon smoked paprika or regular paprika

Salt and freshly ground black pepper

1 head cauliflower, cut into florets

1 cup panko bread crumbs

1. Cook pasta according to package directions until almost tender. Remove pasta with slotted spoon; keep warm. Return water to a boil.

2. Meanwhile, bring milk and garlic to a boil in small saucepan. Reduce heat; keep warm.

3. Melt ¼ cup butter in large saucepan over medium heat; whisk in flour. Cook 1 minute, whisking constantly. Gradually whisk in milk. Bring to a boil. Reduce heat to medium low; cook 10 minutes or until thickened, stirring frequently. Remove from heat. Stir in cheese, mustard and paprika; whisk until melted. Season with salt and pepper. Keep warm.

4. Preheat broiler. Add cauliflower to boiling pasta water. Cook 3 to 5 minutes or just until tender; drain. Toss pasta and cauliflower with sauce mixture; transfer to 13×9-inch baking dish or individual baking dishes.

5. Melt remaining 3 tablespoons butter in small saucepan over medium heat. Add panko; stir just until moistened. Remove from heat. Sprinkle panko mixture over pasta mixture. Broil 2 minutes or until golden brown.

KitchenAid®

PEANUT-SAUCED LINGUINE

MAKES 6 SERVINGS

⅓ cup vegetable broth

3 tablespoons creamy peanut butter

2 tablespoons seasoned rice vinegar

2 tablespoons soy sauce

½ teaspoon red pepper flakes

12 ounces uncooked linguine

1½ pounds fresh asparagus, cut into 1-inch pieces (4 cups)

⅓ cup dry-roasted peanuts, chopped

1. Whisk broth, peanut butter, vinegar, soy sauce and red pepper flakes in small saucepan until smooth. Cook over low heat until heated through, stirring frequently. Keep warm.

2. Cook pasta according to package directions, adding asparagus during last 5 minutes of cooking. Drain and return to saucepan. Add peanut sauce; toss to coat. Sprinkle with peanuts just before serving.

KitchenAid®

PASTA WITH CARAMELIZED ONIONS AND GOAT CHEESE

MAKES 4 TO 6 SERVINGS

1 tablespoon olive oil

6 thinly sliced sweet onions

12 ounces uncooked campanelle or orecchiette pasta

2 cloves garlic, minced

¼ cup dry white wine

1 tablespoon chopped fresh sage *or* 1 teaspoon dried sage

1 teaspoon salt

¼ teaspoon freshly ground black pepper

½ cup milk

1 package (3 ounces) crumbled goat cheese

¼ cup chopped toasted walnuts

1. Heat olive oil in large skillet over medium heat. Add onions; cook 20 to 25 minutes or until golden and caramelized, stirring occasionally.

2. Meanwhile, cook pasta according to package directions. Drain and return to saucepan; keep warm.

3. Add garlic to onions in skillet; cook about 3 minutes or until softened. Add wine, sage, salt and pepper; cook until liquid has evaporated. Remove from heat. Add pasta, milk and goat cheese; stir until cheese is melted. Sprinkle with walnuts.

KitchenAid®

CAVATAPPI AND CHEDDAR AL FORNO

MAKES 4 TO 6 SERVINGS

8 ounces uncooked cavatappi
pasta (about 3 cups)

6 tablespoons butter, divided

3 shallots, thinly sliced

5 tablespoons all-purpose flour

1 cup milk

1 cup heavy cream

½ teaspoon salt

½ teaspoon dry mustard

2 drops hot pepper sauce
(optional)

3 cups (12 ounces) shredded
Cheddar cheese

1 cup peas

¼ cup dry bread crumbs

1. Preheat oven to 350°F. Cook pasta according to package directions until barely al dente. Rinse under cold running water to stop cooking; drain.

2. Meanwhile, melt 1 tablespoon butter in medium skillet over low heat. Add shallots; sauté 5 to 7 minutes or until well browned. Remove from heat.

3. Melt 4 tablespoons butter in large saucepan over medium heat until bubbly. Whisk in flour until smooth; cook 2 minutes without browning. Gradually whisk in milk and cream; cook 4 to 6 minutes until bubbly and thickened, whisking frequently. Stir in salt, mustard and hot pepper sauce.

4. Reduce heat to low; gradually stir in cheese until melted. Remove from heat. Stir in pasta, shallots and peas.

5. Transfer to 1½-quart baking dish; sprinkle with bread crumbs. Bake 20 to 25 minutes or until hot and bubbly.

FETTUCCINE ALLA CARBONARA

MAKES 4 SERVINGS

12 ounces uncooked
fettuccine

4 ounces pancetta or
bacon, cut crosswise
into ½-inch pieces

3 cloves garlic, cut into
halves

¼ cup dry white wine

⅓ cup heavy cream

1 egg

1 egg yolk

⅔ cup freshly grated
Parmesan cheese,
divided

Dash freshly ground
white pepper

1. Cook fettuccine according to package directions. Drain and return to saucepan; keep warm.

2. Sauté pancetta and garlic in large skillet over medium-low heat 4 minutes or until lightly browned. Drain and discard all but 2 tablespoons drippings from skillet.

3. Add wine to skillet; cook over medium heat 3 minutes or until almost evaporated. Add cream; cook 2 minutes, stirring frequently. Remove from heat; discard garlic.

4. Whisk egg and egg yolk in top of double boiler; place over simmering water, adjusting heat to maintain simmer. Whisk ⅓ cup cheese and pepper into egg mixture; whisk until thickened.

5. Pour pancetta mixture over fettuccine; toss to coat. Cook over medium-low heat until heated through. Add egg mixture; toss to coat. Serve with remaining ⅓ cup cheese.

KitchenAid®

Beef, Pork and Lamb

CHIPOTLE LAMB CHOPS WITH CRISPY POTATOES

MAKES 2 SERVINGS

4 lamb loin chops

2 teaspoons chipotle chili powder

Salt and freshly ground black pepper

8 ounces fingerling potatoes

3 tablespoons olive oil, divided

1. Rub lamb chops with chili powder. Season with salt and pepper.

2. Cut potatoes into ¼-inch-thick slices. Heat 2 tablespoons olive oil in large skillet over medium heat. Add potatoes, stirring to coat with oil; season with salt and pepper. Cook 15 to 20 minutes or until golden brown and crispy, stirring occasionally.

3. Meanwhile, heat remaining 1 tablespoon olive oil in medium skillet. Add lamb chops; cook 12 to 15 minutes or until medium-rare (145°F), turning once. Serve with potatoes.

HONEY-GLAZED SPARERIBS

MAKES ABOUT 4 SERVINGS

1 rack pork spareribs* (about 2 pounds)

¼ cup plus 1 tablespoon soy sauce, divided

3 tablespoons hoisin sauce

3 tablespoons dry sherry, divided

1 tablespoon sugar

1 teaspoon minced fresh ginger

2 cloves garlic, minced

¼ teaspoon Chinese five-spice powder

2 tablespoons honey

1 tablespoon cider vinegar

Sesame seeds (optional)

Ask your butcher to cut ribs down length of rack into two pieces so that each half is 2 to 3 inches wide.

1. Cut between bones of ribs to make 6-inch pieces. Trim excess fat. Place ribs in large resealable food storage bag.

2. For marinade, combine ¼ cup soy sauce, hoisin sauce, 2 tablespoons sherry, sugar, ginger, garlic and five-spice powder in small bowl; mix well. Pour over ribs. Seal bag tightly; place in large bowl. Refrigerate 8 hours or overnight, turning bag occasionally.

3. Preheat oven to 350°F. Line large baking pan with foil. Place ribs on rack in pan, reserving marinade. Bake 30 minutes; turn ribs. Brush with marinade; bake 40 minutes or until ribs are tender when pierced with fork.

4. Preheat broiler. For glaze, combine honey, vinegar, remaining 1 tablespoon soy sauce and 1 tablespoon sherry in small bowl; mix well. Brush half of mixture over ribs. Broil 4 to 6 inches from heat source 2 to 3 minutes or until ribs are glazed. Turn ribs; brush with remaining honey mixture. Broil until glazed. Cut into serving-size pieces. Sprinkle with sesame seeds, if desired.

KitchenAid®

ROSEMARY-LEMON PORK KABOBS

MAKES 4 SERVINGS

4 small red potatoes, quartered

1 pork tenderloin (about 1 pound), cut into 16 (1-inch) cubes

1 small red onion, quartered and layers separated

2 tablespoons olive oil, divided

½ teaspoon dried rosemary

Dash paprika

2 tablespoons fresh lemon juice

1 teaspoon grated lemon peel

½ clove garlic, minced

½ teaspoon salt

⅛ teaspoon freshly ground black pepper

1. Preheat broiler.

2. Place steamer basket in medium saucepan; fill saucepan with water to base of steamer. Bring to a boil over high heat. Add potatoes to steamer basket; steam 6 minutes or until crisp-tender. Rinse under cold water; pat dry with paper towels.

3. Thread potatoes onto four 10-inch metal skewers, alternating with pork and onion. Brush with 1 tablespoon olive oil; sprinkle with rosemary and paprika.

4. Place kabobs on baking sheet; broil 4 minutes. Turn; broil 4 minutes or until pork is barely pink in center.

5. Meanwhile, combine lemon juice, remaining 1 tablespoon olive oil, lemon peel, garlic, salt and pepper in small bowl. Spoon lemon mixture evenly over kabobs.

Tip: For an artful presentation, serve the pork, potatoes and onion on rosemary sprigs. Broil the skewers as directed, then remove the food and thread it onto short rosemary sprigs.

PEPPERED BEEF RIB-EYE ROAST

MAKES 6 TO 8 SERVINGS

1½ tablespoons whole black
    peppercorns

1 boneless beef rib-eye roast
    (2½ to 3 pounds), well
    trimmed

¼ cup Dijon mustard

2 cloves garlic, minced

¾ cup sour cream

2 tablespoons prepared
    horseradish

1 tablespoon balsamic vinegar

½ teaspoon sugar

1. Prepare grill for indirect cooking over medium heat with drip pan in center.

2. Place peppercorns in small resealable food storage bag. Squeeze out excess air; close bag securely. Pound peppercorns using flat side of meat mallet or rolling pin until cracked.

3. Pat roast dry with paper towels. Combine mustard and garlic in small bowl; spread over roast. Sprinkle with cracked pepper.

4. Place roast on grid directly over drip pan. Grill, covered, 1 hour or until internal temperature reaches 135°F for medium rare or 150°F for medium when tested with meat thermometer inserted into the thickest part of roast. (If using charcoal grill, add 4 to 9 briquets to both sides of the fire after 45 minutes to maintain medium heat.)

5. Meanwhile, combine sour cream, horseradish, vinegar and sugar in small bowl. Cover and refrigerate until ready to serve.

6. Transfer roast to cutting board; tent with foil. Let stand 10 to 15 minutes before carving. (Internal temperature will continue to rise 5° to 10°F during stand time.) Serve with sauce.

KitchenAid®

LAMB, FETA AND SUN-DRIED TOMATO SAUSAGES

MAKES ABOUT 3 POUNDS (16 TO 20 SAUSAGE LINKS)

2½ pounds boneless lamb shoulder (see Note), trimmed and cut into 2-inch strips

8 ounces sliced fresh (not salted or cured) pork fatback, cut into 1-inch pieces or coarsely chopped beef suet

⅓ cup chopped drained oil-packed sun-dried tomatoes

⅓ cup finely chopped yellow onion

2 cloves garlic, minced

2 teaspoons dried mint or basil

2½ teaspoons kosher salt *or* 2¼ teaspoons regular salt

¾ teaspoon red pepper flakes

3 ounces feta cheese, cut into ¼-inch cubes (about ¾ cup)

Sausage casings, soaked and drained

1. Spread lamb and fatback on baking sheet. Freeze about 1 hour or until semi-frozen and firm.

2. Assemble Food Grinder with coarse grinding plate; attach to stand mixer. Grind lamb and fatback into mixer bowl. Add sun-dried tomatoes, onion, garlic, mint, salt and red pepper flakes; mix well. Cover with plastic wrap; refrigerate until well chilled, at least 2 and up to 4 hours.

3. Meanwhile, freeze feta cheese 1 hour or until frozen. Just before stuffing, fold into lamb mixture.

4. Attach Sausage Stuffer to Food Grinder; stuff casings according to instruction booklet. Refrigerate sausages, uncovered, for at least 4 hours and up to 1 day.

5. Grill, broil or pan-fry sausages and serve hot.

Note: Lamb shoulder used to be a common cut for stews, but now most of it is cut into chops. Order it from your supermarket butcher or look for it at Halal butchers.

HONEY-MUSTARD AND BEER PULLED PORK SANDWICHES

MAKES 8 SERVINGS

1 tablespoon chili powder

2 teaspoons ground cumin

½ teaspoon salt

2 tablespoons yellow mustard

2 pounds bone-in pork shoulder roast

2 bottles (12 ounces each) beer, divided

¾ cup ketchup

3 tablespoons honey

2 tablespoons cider vinegar

8 soft sandwich rolls

24 bread and butter pickle chips

1. Prepare grill for indirect cooking over medium-low heat.

2. Combine chili powder, cumin and salt in small bowl. Spread mustard all over pork, then cover evenly with spice mixture. Transfer pork to rack in disposable foil pan. Reserve ¾ cup beer; pour enough remaining beer into foil pan to just cover rack beneath pork. Place tray on grid opposite heat source. Grill, covered, 4 to 6 hours or until internal temperature reaches 160°F. Transfer to cutting board. Tent with foil; let stand 15 minutes.

3. Combine reserved ¾ cup beer, ketchup, honey and vinegar in small saucepan. Bring to a boil over medium-high heat. Reduce heat to medium; cook and stir until thickened.

4. Shred pork with two forks, discarding any bone, fat or connective tissue. Combine pork and sauce in medium bowl; toss gently to combine. Serve on rolls with pickles.

PORK AND PARMESAN SAUSAGES

MAKES ABOUT 3½ POUNDS (10 TO 12 SAUSAGE LINKS)

3 pounds boneless and skinless pork shoulder, cut into 1½-inch strips

8 ounces sliced fresh (not salted or cured) pork fatback, cut into 1-inch pieces

¾ cup freshly grated Parmesan cheese

⅓ cup dry white wine

3 tablespoons finely chopped fresh parsley

4 cloves garlic, finely chopped

1 tablespoon kosher salt *or* 2½ teaspoons regular salt

2 teaspoons dried oregano

¾ teaspoon freshly ground black pepper

⅛ teaspoon ground allspice

Sausage casings, soaked and drained

1. Spread pork and fatback on baking sheet. Freeze about 1 hour or until semi-frozen and firm.

2. Assemble Food Grinder with coarse grinding plate; attach to stand mixer. Grind pork and fatback into mixer bowl. Add Parmesan, wine, parsley, garlic, salt, oregano, pepper and allspice; mix well. Cover with plastic wrap and refrigerate until well chilled, at least 2 and up to 4 hours.

3. Attach Sausage Stuffer to Food Grinder; stuff casings according to instruction booklet. Refrigerate sausages, uncovered, for at least 4 hours and up to 1 day.

4. Grill, broil or pan-fry sausages until cooked through and serve hot.

GREEK LAMB WITH TZATZIKI SAUCE

MAKES 6 TO 8 SERVINGS

2½ to 3 pounds boneless leg of lamb

8 cloves garlic, divided

¼ cup Dijon mustard

2 tablespoons minced fresh rosemary

2 teaspoons salt

2 teaspoons freshly ground black pepper

¼ cup plus 2 teaspoons olive oil, divided

1 small seedless cucumber

1 tablespoon chopped fresh mint

1 teaspoon fresh lemon juice

2 cups plain Greek yogurt

1. Untie and unroll lamb to lie flat; trim fat.

2. For marinade, mince 4 cloves garlic; place in small bowl. Add mustard, rosemary, salt and pepper; whisk in ¼ cup olive oil. Spread mixture evenly over lamb, coating both sides. Place lamb in large resealable food storage bag. Seal bag; refrigerate at least 2 hours or overnight, turning several times.

3. Meanwhile for tzatziki sauce, mince remaining 4 cloves garlic and mash to a paste; place in medium bowl. Peel and grate cucumber; squeeze to remove excess moisture. Add cucumber, mint, remaining 2 teaspoons olive oil and lemon juice to bowl with garlic. Add yogurt; mix well. Refrigerate until ready to serve.

4. Prepare grill for direct cooking. Grill lamb over medium-high heat 35 to 40 minutes until 140°F. Transfer to cutting board. Tent loosely with foil; let stand 5 to 10 minutes (temperature will rise 5°F).

5. Slice lamb and serve with tzatziki sauce.

KitchenAid®

PASTITSIO

MAKES 6 SERVINGS

1½ pounds ground beef

½ cup chopped onion

1 clove garlic, minced

1 can (about 14 ounces) diced
tomatoes

1 can (8 ounces) tomato sauce

2 tablespoons dried Greek
seasoning, divided

1 pound uncooked penne
pasta or elbow macaroni

¼ cup (½ stick) butter

¼ cup all-purpose flour

2 cups milk

2 eggs, lightly beaten

½ cup freshly grated Parmesan
cheese

1. Cook ground beef, onion and garlic in large skillet over medium heat 6 to 8 minutes or until beef is browned, stirring to break up meat. Drain fat. Add tomatoes, tomato sauce and 1½ tablespoons Greek seasoning. Reduce heat; simmer, uncovered, 25 to 30 minutes.

2. Meanwhile, cook pasta according to package directions. Drain and transfer to 2-quart baking dish. Preheat oven to 350°F.

3. Melt butter in medium saucepan over medium heat. Stir in flour; cook 2 minutes. Whisk in milk and remaining ½ tablespoon Greek seasoning; cook just until sauce thickens. Remove from heat. Stir about ¼ cup sauce into eggs in medium bowl. Whisk egg mixture back into saucepan. Cook over medium heat until mixture thickens. *Do not boil.* Stir in cheese.

4. Stir ½ cup cheese sauce into pasta. Top with meat sauce, then remaining cheese sauce. Bake, uncovered, 30 to 40 minutes or until top is golden. Let stand 15 minutes before serving.

SHEPHERD'S PIE

MAKES 4 TO 6 SERVINGS

3 medium russet potatoes
(1½ pounds), peeled and
cut into 1-inch pieces

½ cup milk

5 tablespoons butter, divided

1 teaspoon salt, divided

½ teaspoon freshly ground
black pepper, divided

2 medium onions, chopped

2 carrots, finely chopped

½ teaspoon dried thyme

1½ pounds ground lamb

3 tablespoons tomato paste

1 tablespoon Worcestershire
sauce

1½ cups reduced-sodium beef
broth

½ cup peas

1. Preheat oven to 350°F. Grease 1½-quart baking dish.

2. Place potatoes in large saucepan; add cold water to cover by 2 inches. Bring to a boil over medium-high heat; cook 16 to 18 minutes or until tender. Drain potatoes; return to saucepan.

3. Heat milk in small saucepan over medium-high heat until hot. Add 3 tablespoons butter, ½ teaspoon salt and ¼ teaspoon pepper; stir until butter is melted. Pour milk mixture into saucepan with potatoes; mash until smooth. Set aside.

4. Melt remaining 2 tablespoons butter in large skillet over medium heat. Add onions, carrots and thyme; cook 8 to 10 minutes or until vegetables are softened but not browned, stirring occasionally. Add lamb; cook over medium-high heat 4 minutes or until no longer pink. Drain excess fat. Return skillet to heat; cook 5 to 6 minutes or until lamb is lightly browned. Add tomato paste and Worcestershire sauce; cook 1 minute. Stir in broth; bring to a boil and cook 7 to 8 minutes or until nearly evaporated. Stir in peas, remaining ½ teaspoon salt and ¼ teaspoon pepper; cook 30 seconds. Pour mixture into prepared baking dish.

5. Spread mashed potatoes in even layer over lamb mixture; use spatula to swirl potatoes or fork to make crosshatch design on top.

6. Bake about 35 minutes or until filling is hot and bubbly and potatoes begin to brown.

KitchenAid®

PORK TENDERLOIN ROAST WITH FIG SAUCE

MAKES 4 SERVINGS

1 tablespoon olive oil

1 pork tenderloin roast
(about 1 pound)

2 teaspoons salt, divided

½ teaspoon freshly
ground black pepper

1 jar (about 8 ounces) fig
jam or preserves

¼ cup dry red wine

2 cloves garlic, minced

1 teaspoon dried
rosemary

¼ teaspoon red pepper
flakes

1. Preheat oven to 375°F. Heat olive oil in large skillet over medium heat. Add pork; brown on all sides. Sprinkle with 1 teaspoon salt and pepper; place in shallow roasting pan. Roast 15 minutes.

2. Meanwhile, combine fig jam and wine in same skillet; cook and stir over low heat 5 minutes or until melted and warm.

3. Brush small amount of fig sauce over tenderloin; roast 5 to 10 minutes or until 155°F. Transfer roast to cutting board. Tent with foil; let stand 10 minutes.

4. Combine garlic, remaining 1 teaspoon salt, rosemary and red pepper flakes in small bowl; sprinkle over pork. Cut pork into thin slices. Serve with remaining fig sauce.

KitchenAid®

ONION-WINE POT ROAST

MAKES 6 SERVINGS

2 tablespoons olive oil, divided

1 teaspoon salt, divided

½ teaspoon freshly ground black pepper

1 boneless beef chuck roast (about 3 pounds), trimmed

2 pounds yellow onions, cut in half and thinly sliced

2 tablespoons water

2 cups dry red wine

1. Heat 1 tablespoon olive oil in Dutch oven over medium-high heat. Sprinkle ½ teaspoon salt and pepper over beef; place in Dutch oven. Brown beef on both sides. Remove to plate.

2. Add remaining 1 tablespoon olive oil, onions and remaining ½ teaspoon salt to Dutch oven; cook over medium-high heat 10 minutes, stirring frequently. Stir in water, scraping up any browned bits from bottom of pan. Reduce heat to medium; partially cover and cook 15 minutes or until onions are deep golden brown, stirring occasionally.

3. Preheat oven to 300°F. Stir wine into onions; top with beef and any accumulated juices. Cover and bake 3 hours or until beef is fork-tender.

4. Remove beef from Dutch oven; skim fat from juices. Slice beef and serve with wine sauce.

KOFTAS (LAMB MEATBALLS IN SPICY GRAVY)

MAKES 6 SERVINGS

2 teaspoons Garam Masala (recipe follows)

2 pounds lamb shoulder, trimmed and cut into 2-inch strips

2 cloves garlic

2 eggs

1½ cups finely chopped onions, divided

½ cup chopped fresh cilantro

1½ teaspoons salt, divided

1 teaspoon minced fresh ginger

24 whole blanched almonds

1 to 3 tablespoons vegetable oil

1 teaspoon ground coriander

1 teaspoon ground cumin

1 teaspoon chili powder

½ teaspoon ground turmeric

2 tomatoes, seeded and chopped

½ cup water

1 cup plain yogurt

1. Prepare Garam Masala. Spread lamb on baking sheet. Refrigerate or freeze until slightly firm. Assemble Food Grinder with fine grinding plate; attach to stand mixer. Grind lamb and garlic into mixer bowl.

2. Add eggs, ½ cup onion, cilantro, Garam Masala, ½ teaspoon salt and ginger to lamb; mix well. Refrigerate at least 1 hour or overnight.

3. Shape mixture into 24 ovals or balls; insert 1 almond into each meatball. Heat 1 tablespoon oil in large skillet over medium-high heat. Add half of meatballs; cook 8 minutes or until browned, turning frequently. Remove meatballs from skillet. Repeat with remaining meatballs, adding additional oil as needed.

4. Reduce heat to medium. Add remaining 1 cup onion; sauté 6 to 8 minutes or until browned. Stir in remaining 1 teaspoon salt, coriander, cumin, chili powder and turmeric. Add tomatoes; cook 5 minutes or until tomatoes are tender.

5. Add water; bring mixture to a boil over high heat. Add meatballs; reduce heat to medium-low. Simmer 15 minutes or until cooked through. Remove meatballs from skillet to serving platter; keep warm.

6. Remove skillet from heat. Place yogurt in small bowl; stir in several spoonfuls of hot mixture. Stir yogurt mixture back into sauce in skillet. Cook over medium-low heat until sauce thickens. *Do not boil.* Pour sauce over meatballs.

KitchenAid®

BEEF AND BROCCOLI

MAKES 4 SERVINGS

1 pound beef tenderloin steaks

2 teaspoons minced fresh ginger

2 cloves garlic, minced

1 tablespoon vegetable oil

3 cups broccoli florets

¼ cup water

2 tablespoons teriyaki sauce

2 cups hot cooked rice

1. Cut beef crosswise into ⅛-inch-thick slices. Toss beef with ginger and garlic in medium bowl.

2. Heat oil in wok or large nonstick skillet over medium heat. Add half of beef mixture; stir-fry 2 to 3 minutes or until beef is barely pink in center. Remove to medium bowl. Repeat with remaining beef.

3. Add broccoli and water to wok; cover and steam 3 to 5 minutes or until broccoli is crisp-tender.

4. Return beef and any accumulated juices to wok. Add teriyaki sauce; cook until heated through. Serve over rice.

KitchenAid®

FRAGRANT BEEF WITH GARLIC SAUCE

MAKES 4 SERVINGS

1 boneless beef top sirloin
   steak (about 1¼ pounds)

⅓ cup teriyaki sauce

10 cloves garlic, peeled

½ cup beef broth

4 cups hot cooked rice

1. Place beef in large resealable food storage bag. Pour teriyaki sauce over beef. Seal bag; turn to coat. Marinate in refrigerator at least 30 minutes or up to 4 hours.

2. Combine garlic and broth in small saucepan. Bring to a boil over high heat. Reduce heat to medium; simmer, uncovered, 5 minutes. Cover and simmer 8 to 9 minutes or until garlic is softened. Transfer to blender or food processor; process until smooth.

3. Meanwhile, drain beef, reserving marinade. Place beef on rack of broiler pan. Brush with half of reserved marinade. Broil 5 to 6 inches from heat 6 minutes. Turn beef over; brush with remaining marinade. Broil 6 minutes.

4. Thinly slice beef; serve with garlic sauce and rice.

KitchenAid®

LAMB KEFTEDES WITH GREEK SALAD

MAKES 6 SERVINGS

LAMB KEFTEDES

3 slices multigrain bread, finely chopped

½ cup milk

1 cup finely diced onion

2 egg whites

1 tablespoon chopped fresh oregano

2 cloves garlic, minced

½ teaspoon salt

1 pound ground lamb

GREEK SALAD

1½ cups diced cucumber

1½ cups diced tomatoes

Juice of 1 lemon

1½ teaspoons olive oil

¼ teaspoon salt

⅛ teaspoon freshly ground black pepper

Lemon wedges (optional)

1. Combine bread and milk in large bowl; toss to coat. Let stand 20 to 30 minutes or until liquid is absorbed and bread is fully soaked.

2. Meanwhile, line baking sheet with parchment paper.

3. Add onion, egg whites, 1 tablespoon oregano, garlic and ½ teaspoon salt to bread cubes; gently toss. Add lamb; mix well. Shape mixture into 36 (½-inch) balls. Place on prepared baking sheet. Refrigerate 30 minutes.

4. Meanwhile for salad, combine cucumber, tomatoes, lemon juice, olive oil, ¼ teaspoon salt and pepper in medium bowl; mix gently. Set aside.

5. Preheat oven to 400°F. Place wire rack over rimmed baking sheet. Transfer meatballs to rack.

6. Bake 20 minutes or until cooked through, turning halfway through baking. If desired, reserve half of meatballs for Greek Lamb Pita Sandwiches (recipe follows). Serve meatballs with salad and lemon wedges, if desired.

GREEK LAMB PITA SANDWICHES

MAKES 6 SERVINGS

6 tablespoons hummus

3 pita bread rounds, cut in half and warmed

6 lettuce leaves

12 red onion slices

12 tomato slices

18 Lamb Keftedes

Spread 1 tablespoon hummus on inside of each pita bread half. Line with lettuce, onion and tomato. Fill each pita half with 3 meatballs. Serve immediately.

KitchenAid®

STEAK PARMESAN

MAKES 2 TO 3 SERVINGS

4 cloves garlic, minced

1 tablespoon olive oil

1 tablespoon coarse salt

1 teaspoon chopped fresh rosemary

1 teaspoon freshly ground black pepper

2 beef T-bone or Porterhouse steaks, cut 1 inch thick (about 2 pounds)

¼ cup freshly grated Parmesan cheese

1. Prepare grill for direct cooking. Combine garlic, olive oil, salt, rosemary and pepper in small bowl; press onto both sides of steaks. Let stand 15 minutes.

2. Place steaks on grid over medium-high heat. Cover; grill 14 to 19 minutes or until internal temperature reaches 145°F for medium rare, turning once.

3. Transfer steaks to cutting board; sprinkle with cheese. Tent with foil; let stand 5 minutes. Serve immediately.

Tip: For a smoky flavor, soak 2 cups hickory or oak wood chips in cold water to cover at least 30 minutes. Drain and scatter over hot coals before grilling.

KitchenAid®

Poultry

HONEY LEMON GARLIC CHICKEN

MAKES 4 SERVINGS

2 lemons, divided

2 tablespoons butter, melted

2 tablespoons honey

3 cloves garlic, chopped

2 sprigs fresh rosemary, leaves removed

1 teaspoon coarse salt

½ teaspoon freshly ground black pepper

3 pounds chicken (4 bone-in skin-on chicken thighs and 4 drumsticks)

1¼ pounds potatoes, cut into halves or quarters

1. Preheat oven to 375°F. Grate peel and squeeze juice from one lemon. Cut remaining lemon into slices.

2. Combine lemon peel, lemon juice, butter, honey, garlic, rosemary leaves, salt and pepper in small bowl; mix well. Combine chicken, potatoes and lemon slices in large bowl. Pour butter mixture over chicken and potatoes; toss to coat. Arrange in single layer on large rimmed baking sheet or in shallow roasting pan.

3. Bake about 1 hour or until potatoes are tender and chicken is cooked through (165°F). Cover loosely with foil if chicken skin is becoming too dark.

CHICKEN TIKKA MASALA MEATBALLS

MAKES 6 SERVINGS

MEATBALLS

1 pound ground chicken

½ cup plain dry bread crumbs

¼ cup finely chopped onion

1 egg

2 tablespoons chopped fresh
    cilantro

1 tablespoon minced fresh ginger

1 tablespoon tomato paste

2 cloves garlic, minced

½ teaspoon salt

TIKKA MASALA SAUCE

2 teaspoons sugar

2 teaspoons ground coriander

1 teaspoon ground cumin

½ teaspoon salt

½ teaspoon ground mustard seed

½ teaspoon ground red pepper

1 tablespoon vegetable oil

½ cup finely chopped onion

2 tablespoons minced fresh ginger

3 cloves garlic, minced

1 medium tomato, finely diced

½ cup water

½ cup coconut milk

1 tablespoon tomato paste

¼ cup chopped fresh cilantro

1. Preheat oven to 400°F. Line rimmed baking sheet with parchment paper.

2. For meatballs, combine chicken, bread crumbs, ¼ cup onion, egg, 2 tablespoons cilantro, 1 tablespoon ginger, 1 tablespoon tomato paste, 2 cloves garlic and ½ teaspoon salt in large bowl; mix well. Shape mixture by tablespoons into 30 meatballs. Place on prepared baking sheet. Bake 20 minutes. Keep warm.

3. For sauce, combine sugar, coriander, cumin, ½ teaspoon salt, mustard seed and ground red pepper in small bowl.

4. Heat oil in medium saucepan over medium heat. Add ½ cup onion; sauté 5 minutes or until just beginning to brown. Add 2 tablespoons ginger, spice mix and 3 cloves garlic; sauté 1 minute. Add tomato, water, coconut milk and 1 tablespoon tomato paste. Reduce heat to low; cook 10 minutes to allow flavors to develop. Add meatballs to saucepan; gently stir to coat evenly.

5. Spoon meatballs onto serving plates. Sprinkle with ¼ cup cilantro.

Serving Suggestion: Serve with naan and hot cooked brown rice.

KitchenAid®

DUCK BREAST WITH CHERRY SAUCE AND SWEET POTATO PANCAKES

MAKES 4 SERVINGS

CHERRY SAUCE

½ cup dried cherries

1 cup dry red wine

1 cup sour cherry preserves

¼ cup red wine vinegar

SWEET POTATO PANCAKES

2 sweet potatoes, peeled

1 russet potato, peeled

½ cup all-purpose flour

⅓ cup minced green onions

2 eggs, lightly beaten

½ teaspoon salt

½ teaspoon black pepper

¼ teaspoon ground nutmeg

Oil for frying

DUCK

4 boneless duck breasts
(about 2 pounds)

1. For cherry sauce, soak cherries in wine in small saucepan 15 minutes or until plump. Add cherry preserves and red wine vinegar. Simmer gently 10 minutes; keep warm until ready to serve.

2. For sweet potato pancakes, assemble Rotor Slicer/Shredder with coarse shredding cone; attach to stand mixer. Shred potatoes into mixer bowl. Squeeze as much moisture as possible out of shredded potatoes in colander or strainer.

3. Return potatoes to bowl. Add flour, green onions, eggs, salt, pepper and nutmeg; mix until combined. Heat ¼ inch of oil in large skillet over medium-high heat. Pat handfuls of potato mixture into cakes about 3 inches in diameter. Cook in batches without crowding pan 3 to 5 minutes per side until firm and browned. Keep warm.

4. Place duck breast, skin side up, on cutting board. Cut crisscross lines through skin and fat layer only. Cook, skin side down, in large skillet over medium heat 5 minutes or until fat is rendered and skin is browned, pouring off excess fat as needed. Turn and cook 5 minutes or until browned but still pink in center. Slice and keep warm.

5. Arrange duck and sweet potato pancakes on serving dishes. Top with Cherry Sauce.

KitchenAid®

SPICY BUTTERMILK OVEN-FRIED CHICKEN

MAKES 6 SERVINGS

1 whole chicken (about
    3 pounds), cut into
    serving pieces

2 cups buttermilk

1½ cups all-purpose flour

1 teaspoon salt

1 teaspoon ground red
    pepper

½ teaspoon garlic powder

¼ cup canola oil

1. Place chicken pieces in single layer in 13×9-inch baking dish. Pour buttermilk over chicken. Cover with plastic wrap; marinate in refrigerator at least 2 hours.

2. Preheat oven to 350°F. Combine flour, salt, red pepper and garlic powder in large bowl. Heat oil in large skillet over medium-high heat until hot.

3. Remove chicken pieces from buttermilk; coat with flour mixture and place in hot oil. Cook about 10 minutes or until brown and crisp on all sides. Place chicken in single layer in 13×9-inch baking dish.

4. Bake, uncovered, 30 to 45 minutes or until chicken is cooked through (165°F).

KitchenAid®

CORNISH HENS WITH WILD RICE AND PINE NUT PILAF

MAKES 4 SERVINGS

⅓ cup uncooked wild rice

4 Cornish hens (about 1¼ pounds each)

1 bunch green onions, cut into 2-inch pieces

3 tablespoons olive oil, divided

3 tablespoons soy sauce

⅓ cup pine nuts

1 cup chopped onion

1 teaspoon dried basil

2 cloves garlic, minced

2 jalapeño peppers, seeded and minced

½ teaspoon salt

Freshly ground black pepper

1. Preheat oven to 425°F. Cook rice according to package directions.

2. Stuff hens equally with green onions; place hens on rack in roasting pan. Roast 15 minutes.

3. Meanwhile, combine 1 tablespoon olive oil and soy sauce in small bowl. Baste hens with 1 tablespoon soy sauce mixture; roast 15 minutes or until cooked through (165°F). Baste with remaining soy sauce mixture. Let stand 15 minutes.

4. Heat large skillet over medium-high heat. Add pine nuts; cook 2 minutes or until golden, stirring constantly. Transfer to plate.

5. Add 1 tablespoon olive oil, onion and basil to same skillet; sauté 5 minutes or until browned. Add garlic; sauté 15 seconds. Remove from heat. Add rice, pine nuts, jalapeños, remaining 1 tablespoon olive oil and salt. Season with black pepper; toss gently to blend. Serve with hens.

CRISPY ROASTED CHICKEN

MAKES 8 TO 10 SERVINGS

1 roasting chicken or capon
(about 6½ pounds)

1 tablespoon peanut or
vegetable oil

2 cloves garlic, minced

1 tablespoon soy sauce

1. Preheat oven to 350°F. Line roasting pan with foil. Place chicken on rack in prepared pan.

2. Combine oil and garlic in small bowl; brush evenly over chicken. Roast 15 to 20 minutes per pound or until internal temperature reaches 170°F when tested with meat thermometer inserted into thickest part of thigh not touching bone.

3. *Increase oven temperature to 450°F.* Drain drippings from pan. Brush chicken evenly with soy sauce. Roast 5 to 10 minutes until skin is very crisp and deep golden brown. Transfer chicken to cutting board; let stand 10 to 15 minutes before carving. (Internal temperature will continue to rise 5° to 10°F during stand time.)

KitchenAid®

DUCK BREASTS WITH BALSAMIC HONEY SAUCE

MAKES 4 SERVINGS

- 3 tablespoons balsamic vinegar
- 3 tablespoons honey
- 2 tablespoons fresh lemon juice
- 4 boneless duck breasts (6 to 8 ounces each)
- Salt and freshly ground black pepper
- 1 shallot, minced

1. Whisk vinegar, honey and lemon juice in small bowl.

2. Score skin on duck breasts with tip of sharp knife in crosshatch pattern, being careful to cut only into the fat and not the meat. Season both sides of duck with salt and pepper. Cook duck breasts, skin side down, in large skillet over medium heat without turning 10 to 12 minutes or until skin is crisp and golden brown. Turn and cook about 8 minutes or until medium rare (130°F). Transfer duck to cutting board; let stand 10 minutes before slicing.

3. Meanwhile, drain all but 1 tablespoon fat from skillet. Add shallot to skillet; sauté over medium heat 2 to 3 minutes or until translucent. Add vinegar mixture; cook and stir about 5 minutes or until slightly thickened. Season with additional salt and pepper. Serve over duck.

HERBED CHICKEN AND APPLE SAUSAGES

MAKES ABOUT 3 POUNDS

3 pounds boneless chicken thighs with skin, excess fat trimmed, cut into 2-inch strips

1¼ cups (about 3 ounces) chopped dried apples

⅓ cup finely chopped shallots

3 tablespoons frozen apple juice concentrate, thawed

1 tablespoon kosher salt *or* 2¾ teaspoons regular salt

¾ teaspoon freshly ground white or black pepper

1 teaspoon dried sage

1 teaspoon crushed dried rosemary

½ teaspoon dried thyme

Sausage casings, soaked and drained

1. Spread chicken on baking sheet. Refrigerate or freeze until slightly firm.

2. Assemble Food Grinder with coarse grinding plate; attach to stand mixer. Grind chicken into mixer bowl. Add dried apples, shallots, apple juice concentrate, salt, pepper, sage, rosemary and thyme; mix well. Cover with plastic wrap and refrigerate 2 hours or until well chilled. Remove and wash grinder.

3. Attach Sausage Stuffer to Food Grinder; stuff casings according to instruction booklet. Refrigerate sausages, uncovered, at least 4 hours and up to 1 day to cure.

4. Grill, broil or pan-fry sausages until cooked through (165°F). Serve hot.

Tip: This breakfast sausage is equally delicious made into patties. After step 2, form mixture into 3-inch patties. Pan-fry until cooked through (165°F).

VENETIAN CHICKEN WITH CREAMY PESTO SAUCE

MAKES 6 TO 8 SERVINGS

2 tablespoons olive oil

2 red or yellow bell peppers, cut into chunks

2 pounds boneless skinless chicken breasts or thighs, cut into 1-inch chunks

1 teaspoon salt

½ teaspoon freshly ground black pepper

1 cup pesto sauce (page 8)

1 cup half-and-half

Hot cooked spaghetti

½ cup freshly grated Asiago or Parmesan cheese

1. Heat olive oil in large skillet over medium heat. Add bell peppers; sauté 3 minutes. Add chicken, salt and pepper; sauté 5 minutes.

2. Stir in pesto and half-and-half; cook, stirring occasionally, 3 minutes or until chicken is cooked through and bell peppers are tender (about 5 minutes for chicken thighs).

3. Serve over pasta; sprinkle with cheese.

KitchenAid®

COQ AU VIN

MAKES 4 SERVINGS

4 slices thick-cut bacon, cut into ½-inch pieces

1 pint pearl onions, blanched, stemmed and skins removed

1 cup sliced button mushrooms

1 tablespoon peanut oil

1 whole chicken (about 3 pounds), cut into serving pieces

3 tablespoons all-purpose flour

¼ cup tomato paste

1 can (about 14 ounces) chicken broth

1 cup dry red wine

1 clove garlic, minced

1 tablespoon fresh thyme *or* 1 teaspoon dried thyme

½ teaspoon salt

⅛ teaspoon freshly ground black pepper

1. Preheat oven to 350°F. Cook bacon in Dutch oven over medium heat until brown and crispy. Remove bacon with slotted spoon and drain on paper towels.

2. Add onions to bacon drippings; cook 7 minutes or until golden, stirring occasionally. Reduce heat to low; cover and cook 5 minutes. Transfer onions to bowl; set aside.

3. Return Dutch oven to medium-high heat. Add mushrooms; sauté 3 to 4 minutes or until tender. Add mushrooms to onions.

4. Add oil to bacon drippings in Dutch oven. Add chicken; cook 5 minutes per side or until browned. Transfer chicken to plate; set aside.

5. Drain all but 2 tablespoons drippings from Dutch oven. Add flour; sauté 1 minute. Stir in tomato paste; cook 1 minute. Add broth, wine, garlic, thyme, salt and pepper, stirring to scrape up browned bits from bottom of pan. Bring to a boil.

6. Add chicken, onions, mushrooms and bacon to Dutch oven. Cover and bake 45 minutes to 1 hour or until chicken is tender.

CHICKEN AND HERB STEW

MAKES 4 SERVINGS

½ cup all-purpose flour

½ teaspoon salt

¼ teaspoon freshly ground
   black pepper

¼ teaspoon paprika

4 chicken drumsticks

4 chicken thighs

2 tablespoons olive oil

12 ounces new potatoes,
   quartered

2 carrots, quartered
   lengthwise and cut into
   3-inch pieces

1 green bell pepper, cut into
   thin strips

¾ cup chopped onion

2 cloves garlic, minced

1¾ cups water

¼ cup dry white wine

2 cubes chicken bouillon

1 tablespoon chopped fresh
   oregano

1 teaspoon chopped fresh
   rosemary

2 tablespoons chopped fresh
   Italian parsley (optional)

1. Combine flour, salt, black pepper and paprika in shallow bowl. Coat chicken with flour mixture; shake off excess.

2. Heat olive oil in large skillet over medium-high heat. Add chicken; cook 8 minutes or until browned on both sides, turning once. Transfer to plate.

3. Add potatoes, carrots, bell pepper, onion and garlic to same skillet; cook and stir 5 minutes or until lightly browned. Add water, wine and bouillon; cook 1 minute, stirring to scrape up browned bits from bottom of skillet. Stir in oregano and rosemary.

4. Place chicken on top of vegetable mixture, turning several times to coat. Cover and simmer 45 to 50 minutes or until chicken is cooked through (165°F), turning occasionally. Garnish with parsley.

BASIL CHICKEN WITH RICE NOODLES

MAKES 4 SERVINGS

1 pound boneless skinless chicken breasts, cut into bite-size pieces

5 tablespoons soy sauce, divided

1 tablespoon dry white wine or rice wine (optional)

3 cloves garlic, minced

1 tablespoon grated fresh ginger

8 ounces uncooked rice noodles

1 red onion, sliced

1 yellow or red bell pepper, cut into strips

2 medium carrots, cut into matchstick-size pieces

2 jalapeño or serrano peppers, seeded and chopped

Juice of 2 limes

2 tablespoons packed brown sugar

1 tablespoon vegetable oil

1½ cups loosely packed basil leaves, shredded

1. Place chicken in shallow dish. Combine 3 tablespoons soy sauce, wine, if desired, garlic and ginger in small bowl. Pour over chicken and stir to coat. Marinate at room temperature 30 minutes or refrigerate up to 2 hours.

2. Place noodles in large bowl. Cover with hot water; let stand 15 minutes or until tender. Drain.

3. Combine onion, bell pepper, carrots and jalapeños in medium bowl. Whisk remaining 2 tablespoons soy sauce, lime juice and brown sugar in small bowl until sugar is dissolved.

4. Heat oil in large skillet or wok over medium-high heat. Add chicken with marinade; sauté 5 minutes or until cooked through. Add vegetables; cook and stir 4 to 6 minutes or until vegetables are crisp-tender.

5. Stir sauce and add to skillet; cook and stir 2 minutes. Add rice noodles and basil; toss to combine.

SPICY ALMOND CHICKEN WINGS

MAKES 6 TO 8 SERVINGS

3 pounds chicken drummettes

3 tablespoons vegetable oil

2 tablespoons jerk seasoning

½ teaspoon salt

1 cup slivered almonds, finely chopped

1. Place drummettes in large bowl. Add oil, jerk seasoning and salt; toss to coat. Cover and refrigerate 20 to 30 minutes.

2. Preheat oven to 400°F. Line large baking sheet with foil. Spray with nonstick cooking spray.

3. Place almonds in shallow bowl. Roll drummettes in almonds until coated. Place on prepared baking sheet.

4. Bake 30 to 35 minutes or until chicken is cooked through (165°F).

KitchenAid®

JALAPEÑO-LIME CHICKEN

MAKES 8 SERVINGS

8 chicken thighs

3 tablespoons jalapeño jelly

1 tablespoon olive oil

1 tablespoon fresh lime juice

1 clove garlic, minced

1 teaspoon chili powder

½ teaspoon freshly ground black pepper

⅛ teaspoon salt

1. Preheat oven to 400°F. Line 15×10-inch jelly-roll pan with foil; spray with nonstick cooking spray.

2. Arrange chicken in single layer in prepared pan. Bake 15 minutes; drain off juices.

3. Combine jelly, olive oil, lime juice, garlic, chili powder, pepper and salt in small bowl. Turn chicken; brush with half of jelly mixture.

4. Bake 20 minutes. Turn chicken; brush with remaining jelly mixture. Bake chicken 10 to 15 minutes or until cooked through (165°F).

KitchenAid®

SOFT TACOS WITH CHICKEN

MAKES 8 TACOS

8 (6- or 7-inch) corn tortillas

2 tablespoons butter

1 medium onion, chopped

1½ cups shredded cooked chicken

1 can (4 ounces) diced mild green chiles, drained

2 tablespoons chopped fresh cilantro

1 cup sour cream

Salt and freshly ground black pepper

1½ cups (6 ounces) shredded Monterey Jack cheese

1 avocado, diced

3 to 4 tablespoons green taco sauce

1. Preheat oven to 350°F. Stack and wrap tortillas in foil. Bake 15 minutes or until heated through.

2. Melt butter in large skillet over medium heat. Add onion; sauté 5 minutes or until tender. Add chicken, green chiles and cilantro; cook 3 minutes or until mixture is hot. Reduce heat to low. Stir in sour cream; season with salt and pepper. Heat gently; do not boil.

3. Spoon about 3 tablespoons chicken mixture into center of each tortilla; sprinkle with 2 tablespoons cheese. Top with avocado; drizzle with 1 to 2 teaspoons taco sauce. Sprinkle tacos with remaining cheese. Roll tortilla into cone shape or fold in half to eat.

KitchenAid®

GRILLED VIETNAMESE-STYLE CHICKEN WINGS

MAKES 2 DOZEN WINGS

3 pounds chicken wings

⅓ cup honey

¼ to ½ cup sliced lemongrass

¼ cup fish sauce

2 tablespoons chopped garlic

2 tablespoons chopped shallots

2 tablespoons chopped fresh ginger

2 tablespoons fresh lime juice

2 tablespoons canola oil

Sliced green onions (optional)

1. Remove and discard wing tips. Cut each wing in half at joint. Place wings in large resealable food storage bag.

2. Combine honey, lemongrass, fish sauce, garlic, shallots, ginger, lime juice and oil in food processor; process until smooth. Pour over wings. Seal bag; turn to coat. Marinate in refrigerator 4 hours or overnight.

3. Prepare grill for direct cooking over medium heat or preheat grill pan. Preheat oven to 350°F.

4. Remove wings from marinade; reserve marinade. Grill wings 10 minutes or until browned, turning and basting occasionally with marinade. Discard any remaining marinade.

5. Arrange wings in single layer on baking sheet. Bake 20 minutes or until cooked through. Sprinkle with green onions, if desired.

PINEAPPLE-HOISIN HENS

MAKES 4 SERVINGS

- 2 cloves garlic
- 1 can (8 ounces) crushed pineapple in juice, undrained
- 2 tablespoons rice vinegar
- 2 tablespoons soy sauce
- 2 tablespoons hoisin sauce
- 2 teaspoons minced fresh ginger
- 1 teaspoon Chinese five-spice powder
- 2 large Cornish hens (about 1½ pounds each), split in half

1. Mince garlic in blender or food processor. Add pineapple with juice; process until fairly smooth. Add vinegar, soy sauce, hoisin sauce, ginger and five-spice powder; process 5 seconds.

2. Place hens in large resealable food storage bag; pour pineapple mixture over hens. Seal bag; turn to coat. Marinate in refrigerator at least 2 hours or up to 1 day, turning bag once.

3. Preheat oven to 375°F. Drain hens; reserve marinade. Place hens, skin side up, on rack in shallow, foil-lined roasting pan. Roast 35 minutes.

4. Brush hens lightly with some reserved marinade; discard remaining marinade. Roast 10 minutes or until hens are browned and cooked through (165°F).

KitchenAid®

Fish and Seafood

BROILED TUNA AND RASPBERRY SALAD

MAKES 2 SERVINGS

½ cup ranch salad dressing

¼ cup raspberry vinegar

1½ teaspoons Cajun seasoning

1 thick-sliced tuna steak (about 6 to 8 ounces)

2 cups torn romaine lettuce leaves

1 cup torn mixed baby lettuce leaves

½ cup fresh raspberries

1. Combine salad dressing, vinegar and Cajun seasoning in small bowl. Pour ¼ cup mixture into resealable food storage bag; reserve remaining mixture. Add tuna to bag. Seal bag; turn to coat. Marinate in refrigerator 10 minutes, turning once.

2. Preheat broiler. Spray rack of broiler pan with nonstick cooking spray. Place tuna on rack. Broil tuna 4 inches from heat source 5 minutes. Turn tuna and brush with marinade; discard remaining marinade. Broil 5 minutes or until tuna flakes in center when tested with fork. Cool 5 minutes. Cut into ¼-inch-thick slices.

3. Toss lettuces in large bowl; divide evenly between two serving plates. Top with tuna and raspberries; drizzle with reserved dressing mixture.

ORANGE ALMOND SCALLOPS

MAKES 4 SERVINGS

3 tablespoons orange juice

1 tablespoon soy sauce

1 clove garlic, minced

1 pound bay scallops or halved sea scallops

1 tablespoon cornstarch

2 teaspoons vegetable oil, divided

1 green bell pepper, cut into slivers

1 can (8 ounces) sliced water chestnuts, drained and rinsed

3 tablespoons toasted blanched almonds

3 cups cooked rice

½ teaspoon finely grated orange peel

1. Combine orange juice, soy sauce and garlic in medium bowl. Add scallops; toss to coat. Marinate at room temperature 15 minutes or cover and refrigerate up to 1 hour.

2. Drain scallops; reserve marinade. Whisk cornstarch into marinade in small bowl until smooth and well blended.

3. Heat 1 teaspoon oil in wok or large nonstick skillet over medium heat. Add scallops; stir-fry 2 minutes or until scallops are opaque. Remove and reserve.

4. Add remaining 1 teaspoon oil to wok. Add bell pepper and water chestnuts; stir-fry 3 minutes.

5. Return scallops along with any accumulated juices to wok. Stir marinade mixture and add to wok; stir-fry 1 minute or until sauce boils and thickens. Stir in almonds. Serve over rice. Sprinkle with orange peel.

KitchenAid®

FRIED CALAMARI WITH TARTAR SAUCE

MAKES 2 TO 3 SERVINGS

Tartar Sauce (recipe follows)

1 pound cleaned squid (body tubes, tentacles or a combination), rinsed and patted dry

¾ cup plain dry bread crumbs

1 egg

1 tablespoon milk

Vegetable oil

Lemon wedges (optional)

1. Prepare Tartar Sauce; set aside. Line baking sheet with waxed paper. Cut squid into ¼-inch rings.

2. Place bread crumbs in medium bowl. Beat egg and milk in separate medium bowl. Add squid; stir to coat well. Transfer squid to bread crumbs; toss to coat. Place on prepared baking sheet. Refrigerate 15 minutes.

3. Heat 1½ inches oil in large heavy saucepan to 350°F; adjust heat to maintain temperature of oil. Fry squid in batches, 8 to 10 pieces at a time, 45 seconds or until golden brown. (Squid will pop and spatter during frying; do not stand too close to saucepan.) *Do not overcook squid or it will become tough.* Remove with slotted spoon; drain on paper towels.

4. Serve immediately with Tartar Sauce and lemon wedges, if desired.

TARTAR SAUCE

MAKES ABOUT 1⅓ CUPS

1⅓ cups mayonnaise

2 tablespoons chopped fresh Italian parsley

1 green onion, thinly sliced

1 tablespoon drained capers, minced

1 small sweet gherkin or pickle, minced

Combine all ingredients in small bowl; mix well. Cover and refrigerate until ready to serve.

KitchenAid®

SHRIMP PAD THAI

MAKES 2 TO 4 SERVINGS

½ cup plus 2 tablespoons chopped fresh cilantro, divided

1 jalapeño pepper, stemmed

2 tablespoons fresh lime juice

2 tablespoons rice vinegar or white vinegar

2 tablespoons water

2 tablespoons natural peanut butter

1½ tablespoons sugar

2 teaspoons soy sauce

¼ teaspoon red pepper flakes

4 ounces uncooked whole grain vermicelli or spaghetti, broken in half

8 ounces raw shrimp, peeled

3 ounces snow peas, cut in half diagonally

½ cup chopped green onions

2 ounces peanuts, toasted* and finely chopped

1 lime, quartered

To toast peanuts, spread in single layer in heavy skillet. Cook over medium heat 1 to 2 minutes or until nuts are lightly browned, stirring frequently.

1. For sauce, combine ½ cup cilantro, jalapeño, lime juice, vinegar, water, peanut butter, sugar, soy sauce and red pepper flakes in blender or food processor. Blend until smooth.

2. Cook pasta according to package directions, adding shrimp during last 3 minutes of cooking; cook until shrimp are opaque and pasta is tender. Add snow peas; drain immediately. Transfer to large bowl.

3. Stir in sauce until well blended. Sprinkle with green onions and peanuts; toss gently. Garnish with remaining 2 tablespoons cilantro and lime wedges.

KitchenAid®

MARINATED MUSSELS ON THE HALF SHELL

MAKES 3 DOZEN

½ cup Tomatillo Salsa (recipe follows)

36 mussels or small hard-shell clams

Boiling water

1 tablespoon olive oil

1 tablespoon fresh lime juice

Salt

1. Prepare Tomatillo Salsa.

2. Scrub mussels under cold water with stiff brush; discard any with open shells or with shells that don't close when tapped. If using mussels, pull out and discard brown, hairlike beards.

3. Arrange half of mussels in large skillet; pour in boiling water to depth of about ½ inch. Cover and simmer over medium heat 5 to 8 minutes or until shells open. As shells open, remove mussels with slotted spoon; set aside to cool. Discard any unopened mussels. Repeat with remaining mussels.

4. Remove mussels from shells with small knife. Separate shells; save half. Cover shells and refrigerate. Combine Tomatillo Salsa, olive oil and lime juice in large bowl. Add mussels; stir to coat. Season with salt to taste. Cover and refrigerate up to 24 hours.

5. Remove mussels from marinade; place one in each shell. Arrange on platter. Spoon any remaining marinade over mussels.

TOMATILLO SALSA

MAKES ABOUT 1½ CUPS

1 pound tomatillos (about 12 large)

½ cup finely chopped red onion

¼ cup coarsely chopped fresh cilantro

2 jalapeño or serrano peppers, stemmed, seeded and minced

1 tablespoon fresh lime juice

1 teaspoon olive oil

½ teaspoon salt

1. Remove papery husks from tomatillos; wash tomatillos and finely chop. Place in medium bowl.

2. Add onion, cilantro, jalapeño, lime juice, olive oil and salt; mix well. Cover and refrigerate 1 hour or up to 3 days for flavors to blend.

KitchenAid®

BROILED CAJUN FISH FILLETS

MAKES 4 SERVINGS

2 tablespoons all-purpose flour

½ cup seasoned dry bread crumbs

1 teaspoon dried thyme

½ teaspoon garlic salt

¼ teaspoon ground red pepper

¼ teaspoon black pepper

1 egg

1 tablespoon milk

4 scrod or orange roughy fillets, ½ inch thick (4 to 5 ounces each)

2 tablespoons butter, melted, divided

⅓ cup mayonnaise

2 tablespoons sweet pickle relish

1 tablespoon fresh lemon juice

1 teaspoon bottled horseradish

1. Preheat broiler. Line baking sheet with parchment paper.

2. Place flour in shallow bowl. Combine bread crumbs, thyme, garlic salt, red pepper and black pepper in another shallow bowl. Whisk egg and milk in third shallow bowl.

3. Coat each fillet with flour, then dip into egg mixture, letting excess drip back into bowl. Coat with bread crumb mixture. Place fillets on prepared baking sheet.

4. Brush 1 tablespoon butter evenly over fish. Broil 4 to 5 inches from heat source 3 minutes. Turn fish; brush with remaining 1 tablespoon butter. Broil 3 minutes or until fish begins to flake when tested with fork.

5. Meanwhile, combine mayonnaise, relish, lemon juice and horseradish in small bowl; mix well. Serve with fish.

KitchenAid®

OYSTER PO' BOYS

MAKES 4 SANDWICHES

Spicy Mayonnaise
(recipe follows)

¾ cup cornmeal

¼ cup all-purpose flour

½ teaspoon salt

⅛ teaspoon freshly ground
black pepper

2 pints shucked oysters,
drained

¾ cup vegetable oil

4 French bread rolls,* split

Lettuce leaves

Tomato slices

*Or substitute 1 loaf French
bread, split and cut into 4-inch
pieces.*

1. Prepare Spicy Mayonnaise.

2. Combine cornmeal, flour, salt and pepper in shallow bowl. Pat oysters dry with paper towels. Coat oysters with cornmeal mixture.

3. Heat oil in medium skillet over medium heat. Add oysters; fry in batches 5 minutes or until golden brown, turning once. Drain on paper towels.

4. Spread rolls with Spicy Mayonnaise; fill with lettuce, tomatoes and oysters.

SPICY MAYONNAISE

MAKES ABOUT ½ CUP

½ cup mayonnaise

2 tablespoons plain yogurt

1 clove garlic, minced

¼ teaspoon ground red pepper

Whisk mayonnaise, yogurt, garlic and red pepper in small bowl. Refrigerate until ready to use.

GRILLED FIVE-SPICE FISH WITH GARLIC SPINACH

MAKES 4 SERVINGS

1½ teaspoons grated lime peel

3 tablespoons fresh lime juice

4 teaspoons minced fresh ginger

½ to 1 teaspoon Chinese five-spice powder

½ teaspoon sugar

½ teaspoon salt

⅛ teaspoon freshly ground black pepper

2 teaspoons vegetable oil, divided

1 pound salmon steaks

½ pound fresh baby spinach leaves (about 8 cups lightly packed)

2 cloves garlic, minced

1. Combine lime peel, lime juice, ginger, five-spice powder, sugar, salt, pepper and 1 teaspoon oil in 2-quart baking dish. Add salmon; turn to coat. Cover and refrigerate 2 to 3 hours.

2. Combine spinach, garlic and remaining 1 teaspoon oil in large saucepan; sauté over medium heat 5 minutes or until spinach is wilted, adding water by teaspoons if spinach is too dry; keep warm.

3. Meanwhile, prepare grill for direct cooking over medium-high heat.

4. Remove salmon from marinade and place on oiled grid. Brush salmon with marinade. Grill salmon, covered, 4 minutes. Turn salmon; brush with marinade and grill 4 minutes or until fish just begins to flake when tested with fork. Discard remaining marinade.

5. Serve fish over bed of spinach.

KitchenAid®

MUSSELS IN BEER
WITH AIOLI AND CROUTONS

MAKES 4 SERVINGS

1 loaf (1 pound) French bread, cut into ¼-inch slices

4 pounds mussels

3 tablespoons olive oil, divided

1 shallot, chopped

1 bottle (12 ounces) lager

¾ cup water

½ cup mayonnaise

2 cloves garlic, minced

2 teaspoons fresh lemon juice

½ teaspoon Dijon mustard

⅛ teaspoon ground red pepper

1. Preheat oven to 450°F. Place bread on baking sheet. Bake 15 minutes or until golden, turning once.

2. Clean mussels under cold running water. Scrape off beard from shell. Discard open mussels that do not close when tapped.

3. Heat 1 tablespoon olive oil in large saucepan over medium heat. Add shallot; cook 1 minute or until translucent. Add lager and water. Increase heat to high; bring to a boil. Carefully add mussels. Cover and cook 3 to 5 minutes or until mussels open. Remove from heat and cool slightly. (Discard any mussels that do not open.)

4. Meanwhile for aioli, combine mayonnaise, remaining 2 tablespoons olive oil, garlic, lemon juice, mustard and red pepper in small bowl; mix well.

5. Spread each crouton with 1 teaspoon aioli. Serve mussels and broth in bowls with croutons.

HAZELNUT-COATED SALMON STEAKS

MAKES 4 SERVINGS

¼ cup hazelnuts

4 salmon steaks (about 5 ounces each)

1 tablespoon apple butter

1 tablespoon Dijon mustard

½ teaspoon salt

¼ teaspoon dried thyme

⅛ teaspoon freshly ground black pepper

1. Preheat oven to 375°F. Spread hazelnuts on ungreased baking sheet; bake 8 minutes or until lightly browned. Immediately transfer nuts to clean dry dish towel. Fold towel over nuts; rub vigorously to remove as much of skins as possible. Finely chop hazelnuts in food processor or with knife.

2. *Increase oven temperature to 450°F.* Place salmon in single layer in baking dish. Combine apple butter, mustard, salt, thyme and pepper in small bowl; brush over salmon. Top with hazelnuts, pressing to adhere.

3. Bake 14 to 16 minutes or until salmon begins to flake when tested with fork.

KitchenAid®

SALMON CAKES WITH RED PEPPER RELISH

MAKES 4 SERVINGS

¾ cup roasted red peppers, drained and finely chopped

2 tablespoons chopped fresh Italian parsley

1 tablespoon fresh lemon juice

2 teaspoons grated lemon peel, divided

3 teaspoons olive oil, divided

1 clove garlic, minced

3 cans (6 ounces each) skinless boneless salmon, drained and flaked

¼ cup plain dry bread crumbs

¼ cup finely chopped green onions

1 egg white

½ teaspoon salt

¼ teaspoon freshly ground black pepper

1. For relish, combine roasted peppers, parsley, lemon juice, 1 teaspoon lemon peel, 1 teaspoon olive oil and garlic in small bowl.

2. Combine salmon, bread crumbs, green onions, egg white, salt, black pepper and remaining 1 teaspoon lemon peel in medium bowl. Shape ⅓ cupfuls into eight 2½-inch diameter cakes.

3. Heat remaining 2 teaspoons olive oil in large skillet over medium-high heat. Cook salmon cakes 3 to 4 minutes per side or until browned. Serve with relish.

KitchenAid®

MAPLE SALMON AND SWEETS

MAKES 4 SERVINGS

½ **cup pure maple syrup**

2 **tablespoons butter, melted**

1½ **pounds skin-on salmon fillets**

2 **medium sweet potatoes,
    peeled and cut into ¼-inch
    slices**

1 **teaspoon salt**

¼ **teaspoon freshly ground
    black pepper**

1. Combine maple syrup and butter in small bowl. Place salmon in resealable food storage bag. Place sweet potatoes in another resealable food storage bag. Pour half of syrup mixture into each bag. Seal bags; turn to coat. Refrigerate at least 2 hours or overnight, turning bags occasionally.

2. Oil grid; prepare grill for direct cooking. Drain salmon and sweet potatoes; discard marinade. Season with salt and pepper.

3. Grill salmon, skin side down, on covered grill over medium heat 15 to 20 minutes or until fish begins to flake when tested with fork. (Do not turn.) Grill sweet potatoes, covered, in single layer on grill topper 15 minutes or until tender and slightly browned, turning once or twice or until tender and slightly browned.

KitchenAid®

TUNA TERIYAKI

MAKES 4 SERVINGS

4 tuna steaks (about
1½ pounds)

¼ cup soy sauce

2 tablespoons sake

1 tablespoon sugar

½ teaspoon minced fresh
ginger

¼ teaspoon minced garlic

1½ tablespoons vegetable oil

2 limes, cut into halves

Pickled ginger (optional)

*Salmon, halibut or swordfish can
be substituted for the tuna.*

1. Place tuna in single layer in baking dish. Whisk soy sauce, sake, sugar, ginger and garlic in small bowl until blended; pour over tuna. Cover and marinate in refrigerator 40 minutes, turning frequently.

2. Drain tuna, reserving marinade. Heat oil in large skillet over medium heat. Add tuna; cook 2 to 3 minutes per side or just until opaque and lightly browned.

3. Reduce heat to medium-low; pour reserved marinade over tuna. Add limes, cut side down, to skillet. Cook 1 minute or until tuna is coated and sauce is bubbly, turning once. Serve tuna with limes and pickled ginger, if desired.

ADRIATIC-STYLE HALIBUT

MAKES 4 SERVINGS

1 tomato, seeded and diced

⅓ cup coarsely chopped pitted kalamata olives

1 clove garlic, minced

4 skinless halibut or red snapper fillets (about 6 ounces each)

¾ teaspoon coarse salt

¼ teaspoon freshly ground black pepper

1 tablespoon olive oil

¼ cup dry white wine or vermouth

Additional salt and freshly ground black pepper

2 tablespoons chopped fresh basil

1. Preheat oven to 200°F. Combine tomato, olives and garlic in small bowl.

2. Season fish with salt and pepper. Heat olive oil in large nonstick skillet over medium heat. Add fish; cook 8 to 10 minutes or just until fish is opaque in center, turning once. Transfer to serving platter; keep warm in oven.

3. Add wine to skillet; cook over high heat until reduced to 2 tablespoons. Add tomato mixture; sauté 1 to 2 minutes or until heated through. Season with additional salt and pepper. Spoon tomato mixture over fish; sprinkle with basil.

KitchenAid®

Vegetarian Entrées

BROCCOLI, WHITE BEAN AND BULGUR GRATIN

MAKES 4 SERVINGS

⅔ cup uncooked bulgur

4 cups small broccoli florets

1 can (about 15 ounces) Great Northern beans, rinsed and drained

2 teaspoons olive oil

½ teaspoon dried thyme

½ teaspoon salt

⅛ teaspoon freshly ground black pepper

1 cup vegetable broth

¾ cup (3 ounces) shredded mozzarella cheese

1. Place bulgur in large bowl; add enough boiling water to cover by 1 inch. Let stand 25 minutes or until bulgur is tender and water is absorbed.

2. Preheat oven to 375°F. Grease 2-quart baking dish.

3. Steam broccoli in steamer basket over boiling water 4 minutes or until tender.

4. Combine bulgur, broccoli, beans, olive oil, thyme, salt and pepper in prepared baking dish; gently combine and spread into even layer. Pour broth over mixture; sprinkle evenly with cheese.

5. Bake 30 minutes or until golden brown and cheese is melted. Let stand 5 minutes before serving.

KitchenAid®

BUTTERNUT SQUASH GNOCCHI WITH SAVORY HERB BUTTER

MAKES 4 SERVINGS

1 butternut squash (about 2½ pounds), peeled, seeded, and cut into 1-inch pieces

1 to 2 cups all-purpose flour

3½ teaspoons salt, divided

¼ teaspoon freshly ground black pepper

4 quarts water

¼ cup (½ stick) butter

2 teaspoons minced garlic

1 teaspoon dried parsley flakes

1 teaspoon rubbed sage

½ teaspoon dried thyme

Juice of 1 lemon

¼ cup shredded Parmesan cheese

1. Place squash in large microwavable bowl. Cover with vented plastic wrap. Microwave on HIGH 6 to 7 minutes or until very tender. Let stand 10 minutes to cool slightly. Drain.

2. Mash squash or press through ricer into medium bowl. Add 1 cup flour, 2 teaspoons salt and pepper; mix well. Add additional flour if dough is too sticky.

3. Heavily dust cutting board or work surface with flour. Working in batches, scoop portions of dough onto board and roll into ½-inch-thick rope using floured hands. Cut each rope into ¾-inch pieces.

4. Bring water and 1 teaspoon salt to a boil in large saucepan over high heat. Drop 8 to 12 gnocchi into boiling water; cook about 2½ minutes or until gnocchi float to surface. Remove gnocchi with slotted spoon; drain on paper towels. Return water to a boil; repeat with remaining gnocchi.

5. Combine butter, garlic, parsley flakes, sage, thyme and remaining ½ teaspoon salt in large nonstick skillet. Heat over medium heat until butter is melted and just begins to brown. Add lemon juice; cook 30 seconds. Add gnocchi; gently toss to coat. Cook 2 minutes or until lightly browned and heated through. Serve gnocchi with cheese.

VEGETABLE ENCHILADAS

MAKES 6 SERVINGS

1 tablespoon vegetable oil

2 large poblano peppers or green bell peppers, cut into 2-inch strips

1 large zucchini, cut into 2-inch strips

1 large red onion, sliced

1 cup sliced mushrooms

1 teaspoon ground cumin

1 pound fresh tomatillos (about 8 large), peeled

½ to 1 jalapeño pepper, minced

1 clove garlic

½ teaspoon salt

1 cup loosely packed fresh cilantro

12 corn tortillas, warmed

2 cups (8 ounces) shredded Mexican cheese blend, divided

1. Preheat oven to 400°F.

2. Heat oil in large skillet over medium heat. Add poblano peppers, zucchini, onion, mushrooms and cumin; sauté 8 to 10 minutes or until vegetables are crisp-tender.

3. Meanwhile, place tomatillos in large microwavable bowl. Cover with vented plastic wrap. Microwave on HIGH 6 to 7 minutes or until very tender.

4. Combine tomatillos with juice, jalapeño, garlic and salt in food processor or blender; process until smooth. Add cilantro; pulse until combined and cilantro is coarsely chopped.

5. Divide vegetables evenly among tortillas. Spoon heaping tablespoon of cheese in center of each tortilla; roll up to enclose filling. Place in 13×9-inch baking dish. Pour tomatillo sauce evenly over enchiladas. Sprinkle with remaining 1 cup cheese.

6. Cover and bake 18 to 20 minutes or until cheese is melted and enchiladas are heated through.

SAVORY MUSHROOM AND BRIE TART

MAKES 4 SERVINGS

Single Crust Pie Pastry
(page 9)

2 tablespoons butter

1 package (4 ounces) sliced
exotic mushrooms (oyster,
shiitake, cremini)

⅓ cup chopped shallots or
sweet onion

1 tablespoon chopped fresh
thyme *or* 1 teaspoon dried
thyme

½ teaspoon salt

¼ teaspoon freshly ground
black pepper

3 eggs

½ cup half-and-half or whole
milk

4 ounces Brie cheese, rind
removed, cut into ¼-inch
cubes

1. Prepare Single Crust Pie Pastry.

2. Preheat oven to 350°F. Roll out pastry into 12-inch circle on lightly floured surface; fit into 10-inch tart pan with removable bottom and trim edge. Bake 10 minutes.

3. *Increase oven temperature to 375°F.* Melt butter in a large skillet over medium heat. Add mushrooms and shallots; cook 5 minutes, stirring occasionally. Stir in thyme, salt and pepper; cook 3 minutes or until mushroom liquid is absorbed. Remove from heat; let stand 5 minutes.

4. Beat eggs in large bowl. Stir in half-and-half and cheese. Add mushroom mixture; mix well. Pour into prepared pie crust.

5. Bake 25 to 30 minutes or until center is set and crust is golden brown. Cool on wire rack 10 minutes. Cut into wedges; serve warm or at room temperature.

KitchenAid®

POTATO GNOCCHI WITH TOMATO SAUCE

MAKES 4 SERVINGS

2 pounds baking potatoes (3 or 4 large)

Tomato Sauce (page 289)

⅔ to 1 cup all-purpose flour, divided

1 egg yolk

½ teaspoon salt

⅛ teaspoon ground nutmeg (optional)

Freshly grated Parmesan cheese

Slivered fresh basil

1. Preheat oven to 425°F. Pierce potatoes several times with fork. Bake 1 hour or until soft. Meanwhile, prepare Tomato Sauce.

2. Cut potatoes in half lengthwise; cool slightly. Scoop out potatoes from skins into medium bowl; discard skins. Mash potatoes until smooth. Add ⅓ cup flour, egg yolk, salt and nutmeg, if desired; mix well to form dough.

3. Turn out dough onto well-floured surface. Knead in enough remaining flour to form smooth dough. Divide dough into four pieces; roll each piece with hands on lightly floured surface into ¾- to 1-inch-wide rope. Cut each rope into 1-inch pieces; gently press thumb or tines of fork into center of each piece to make indentation. Transfer gnocchi to lightly floured kitchen towel in single layer to prevent sticking.

4. Bring 4 quarts salted water to a boil in large saucepan over high heat. To test cooking time, drop several gnocchi into water; cook 1 minute or until they float to surface. Remove from water with slotted spoon and taste for doneness. (If gnocchi start to dissolve, shorten cooking time by several seconds.) Cook remaining gnocchi in batches, removing with slotted spoon to warm serving dish.

5. Serve gnocchi with Tomato Sauce; sprinkle with cheese and basil.

KitchenAid®

SEITAN FAJITAS

MAKES 6 FAJITAS

1 package (1 ounce) fajita seasoning

2 packages (8 ounces each) seitan, sliced

1 tablespoon vegetable oil

1 red bell pepper, sliced

½ medium onion, sliced

1 package (8 ounces) sliced cremini mushrooms

6 (6- to 7-inch) tortillas, warmed

Toppings: salsa, sour cream, shredded cheese and guacamole

1. Dissolve seasoning according to package directions. Place seitan in large resealable food storage bag. Pour seasoning mixture over seitan. Seal bag; shake to coat.

2. Heat oil in large skillet over medium-high heat. Add bell pepper and onion; sauté 4 to 5 minutes or until crisp-tender. Add mushrooms; sauté 1 to 2 minutes or until mushrooms are softened. Add seitan and seasoning mixture; sauté 1 to 2 minutes or until seitan is heated through and vegetables are coated with seasoning.

3. Serve vegetables and seitan in tortillas with desired toppings.

KitchenAid®

VEGAN PESTO

MAKES 4 SERVINGS

1 pound uncooked fettuccine

1 cup packed fresh basil leaves

½ cup pine nuts, toasted*

2 cloves garlic

½ teaspoon salt

¼ teaspoon freshly ground
   black pepper

¼ cup plus 1 tablespoon olive
   oil, divided

*To toast pine nuts, in small
skillet. Heat over low heat
2 minutes or until light brown
and fragrant, stirring occasionally.*

1. Cook pasta according to package directions until tender. Drain and return to saucepan; keep warm.

2. Meanwhile, place basil, pine nuts, garlic, salt and pepper in food processor; drizzle with 1 tablespoon olive oil. Process about 10 seconds or until coarsely chopped. Stop and scrape side of bowl. With motor running, drizzle in remaining ¼ cup olive oil. Process about 30 seconds or until almost smooth. Toss with hot cooked pasta.

Note: Pesto can be made 1 week in advance. Transfer to jar with tight-fitting lid and store in refrigerator. Makes ½ cup pesto.

NUT ROAST

MAKES 6 TO 8 SERVINGS

1½ cups unsalted walnuts, pecans, almonds or cashews

2 tablespoons olive oil

1 onion, finely chopped

4 ounces cremini mushrooms (about 6 large), sliced

2 cloves garlic, minced

1 can (about 14 ounces) diced tomatoes

1 cup old-fashioned oats

2 eggs, lightly beaten

2 tablespoons all-purpose flour

1 tablespoon chopped fresh sage

1 tablespoon chopped fresh parsley

1 teaspoon chopped fresh thyme

Salt and freshly ground black pepper

1. Preheat oven to 350°F. Grease 8×4-inch loaf pan.

2. Place nuts in food processor. Pulse until finely chopped, allowing some larger pieces to remain. Transfer to large bowl.

3. Heat olive oil in medium skillet over medium heat. Add onion, mushrooms and garlic; sauté 3 minutes or until softened. Add to bowl with nuts.

4. Stir in tomatoes, oats, eggs, flour, sage, parsley and thyme until combined. Season with salt and pepper. Spoon mixture into prepared pan.

5. Bake 45 to 50 minutes or until firm and browned. Cool slightly; cut into slices to serve.

KitchenAid®

THAI VEGGIE CURRY

MAKES 4 TO 6 SERVINGS

2 tablespoons vegetable oil

1 onion, quartered and thinly sliced

1 to 3 tablespoons Thai red curry paste*

1 can (about 13 ounces) coconut milk

1 package (14 ounces) tofu, cubed

2 red or yellow bell peppers, cut into strips

1½ cups cauliflower and/or broccoli florets

1 cup snow peas

Salt and freshly ground black pepper

¼ cup slivered fresh basil

Hot cooked jasmine rice

*Thai red curry paste can vary in spiciness among brands. Start with 1 tablespoon and add additional, if desired.

1. Heat oil in large skillet or wok over medium-high heat. Add onion; sauté 2 minutes or until softened. Add 1 tablespoon curry paste, stirring to coat onion. Add coconut milk; bring to a boil, stirring to dissolve curry paste.

2. Add tofu, bell peppers and cauliflower; simmer over medium heat 4 to 5 minutes or until vegetables are crisp-tender. Stir in snow peas; simmer 2 to 5 minutes or until vegetables are tender and curry is heated through. Season with salt and pepper.

3. Sprinkle with basil; serve with rice.

ROASTED TOMATOES, BRIE AND NOODLES

MAKES 6 SERVINGS

1 pint grape tomatoes, halved lengthwise

2 teaspoons canola oil

¾ teaspoon salt, divided

6 ounces uncooked egg noodles

2 tablespoons butter

1 clove garlic, smashed

2 tablespoons all-purpose flour

2 cups half-and-half, heated

8 ounces ripe Brie, rind removed, cut into small pieces

2 tablespoons minced fresh chives

¼ cup finely chopped fresh basil

¼ teaspoon freshly ground pepper

¼ cup sliced almonds

1. Preheat oven to 425°F. Line baking sheet with foil and grease 9-inch square baking dish.

2. Spread tomatoes on prepared baking sheet. Sprinkle with canola oil and ¼ teaspoon salt. Roast 20 minutes or until tender and slightly shriveled. Set aside. *Reduce oven temperature to 350°F.*

3. Cook noodles according to package directions until al dente. Drain and return to saucepan; keep warm.

4. Melt butter in large saucepan over medium heat. Add garlic; cook 1 minute. Stir in flour until smooth. Gradually whisk in half-and-half; cook until thickened, stirring frequently. Discard garlic. Gradually stir in cheese until melted.

5. Add chives, basil, remaining ½ teaspoon salt and pepper. Stir in noodles. Drain off any liquid from tomatoes; fold into noodle mixture. Spread in prepared baking dish.

6. Bake 17 to 20 minutes or until sauce starts to bubble. Sprinkle with almonds; bake 8 to 10 minutes or until nuts turn light golden brown.

SPINACH RAVIOLI

MAKES 8 DOZEN RAVIOLI

2½ cups all-purpose flour

1 cup semolina flour

4 eggs, divided

½ cup water, divided

1 package (10 ounces) frozen chopped spinach, thawed and squeezed dry

2 cloves garlic

½ teaspoon salt

½ teaspoon freshly ground black pepper

¼ teaspoon ground nutmeg

1 cup ricotta cheese

½ cup shredded Asiago or Parmesan cheese, plus additional for serving

Grape tomatoes, halved

1. Attach flat beater to stand mixer. Combine all-purpose flour, semolina, 3 eggs and ¼ cup water in mixer bowl. Mix on low speed 30 seconds. Replace flat beater with dough hook. Knead on low speed 2 minutes, adding additional water by tablespoonfuls if needed until dough forms; knead 3 to 5 minutes or until dough is smooth and elastic. Shape dough into a ball; cover with dry towel and let rest 15 to 30 minutes.

2. Combine spinach, garlic, salt, pepper and nutmeg in food

processor; process until very finely chopped. Add ricotta cheese, ½ cup Asiago cheese and remaining 1 egg; process until smooth. Refrigerate until ready to use.

3. Attach Pasta Sheet Roller to stand mixer. Pull off a piece of dough and feed it through the pasta roller at thickness setting 1. Fold dough and run it through again. Continue folding and rolling dough at setting 1 until dough is smooth with no holes or frayed pieces. Rub all-purpose flour into dough if it feels sticky. Turn to thickness setting 2 and feed dough through rollers twice, making sure dough sheet extends the width of the roller. Repeat at settings 3 and 4; roll once at setting 5. Lay dough out on floured surface or clean tablecloth. Rub all-purpose flour over both sides of dough. Repeat with remaining dough.

4. Remove Pasta Sheet Roller; attach Ravioli Maker. Fold one dough sheet in half. Fit folded end of dough between rollers and rotate handle one quarter turn just until rollers just catch dough. Open dough and drape over sides of attachment. Fit hopper into ravioli attachment. Spread a spoonful of filling into hopper. Slowly turn rollers, adding more filling as needed. Lay finished sheet of ravioli on work surface. Repeat with remaining dough and filling.

5. Gently separate ravioli, removing selvage from middle and ends of ravioli sheet. (Do not stack uncooked ravioli as they will stick together.) Bring large saucepan of water to a boil. Add ravioli; cook 2 to 3 minutes or until al dente. Remove with slotted spoon and transfer to serving plates. Top with additional Asiago cheese and tomatoes.

Tip: Ravioli freeze well. Spread uncooked ravioli on a large baking sheet and freeze until firm. Transfer to freezer food storage bags or containers. Do not thaw before cooking.

KitchenAid®

VEGETARIAN CHILI WITH BROWN RICE

MAKES 6 SERVINGS

1 teaspoon canola oil

1 onion, chopped

1 green bell pepper, diced

1 red bell pepper, diced

1 stalk celery, diced

1 jalapeño pepper, minced

1 clove garlic, minced

2 cups vegetable broth

1 can (about 14 ounces) diced
   tomatoes

1 cup cooked brown rice

1 cup canned pinto beans,
   rinsed and drained

½ teaspoon dried oregano

½ teaspoon chipotle chili
   powder

½ teaspoon salt

¼ teaspoon freshly ground
   black pepper

¼ teaspoon ground cumin

6 tablespoons shredded
   Cheddar cheese

1. Heat oil in large saucepan over medium-high heat. Add onion, bell peppers, celery, jalapeño and garlic; sauté 7 minutes.

2. Add broth, tomatoes, rice, beans, oregano, chili powder, salt, black pepper and cumin. Bring to a boil over high heat. Reduce heat to medium; cover and cook 15 minutes or until vegetables are tender. Uncover; cook 10 minutes or until thickened.

3. Ladle chili into bowls; top with cheese.

VEGAN SLOPPY JOES

MAKES 4 TO 6 SERVINGS

1¾ cups boiling water

2 cups textured soy protein (TVP)

½ cup ketchup

½ cup barbecue sauce

2 tablespoons cider vinegar

1 tablespoon packed brown sugar

1 tablespoon soy sauce

1 teaspoon chili powder

1 tablespoon olive oil

½ cup chopped onion

½ cup chopped carrot

4 to 6 hamburger or hot dog buns

1. Pour boiling water over textured soy protein in large bowl; let stand 10 minutes.

2. For sauce, combine ketchup, barbecue sauce, vinegar, brown sugar, soy sauce and chili powder in medium bowl.

3. Heat olive oil in large saucepan over medium-high heat. Add onion and carrot; sauté 5 minutes or until vegetables are tender.

4. Stir in sauce; bring to a boil. Stir in reconstituted textured soy protein and ¾ cup water. Reduce heat to low; cover and cook 20 minutes. Serve sloppy joes in buns.

KitchenAid®

EXOTIC VEGGIE CHIPS

MAKES ABOUT 6 SERVINGS

3 tropical tubers (malanga, yautia, lila and/or taro roots)*

1 to 2 yellow (unripe) plantains

2 parsnips, peeled

1 medium sweet potato, peeled

1 lotus root,** peeled

Vegetable oil for deep frying

Coarse salt

These tropical tubers are all similar and their labels are frequently interchangeable or overlapping. They are available in the produce sections of Latin markets. Choose whichever tubers are available and fresh. Look for firm roots without signs of mildew or soft spots.

**Lotus root is available in the produce sections of Asian markets. The outside looks like a fat beige link sausage, but when sliced, the lacy, snowflake-like pattern inside is revealed.*

1. Line two baking sheets with paper towels. Peel thick shaggy skin from tubers, rinse and dry. Cut tubers into 3-inch lengths.

2. Assemble Rotor Slicer/Shredder with thin slicing cone; attach to stand mixer. Slice tubers and place in single layer on prepared baking sheets to absorb excess moisture. (Stack in multiple layers with paper towels between layers.) Peel thick skin from plantain. Slice and arrange on paper towels. Slice parsnips and sweet potato and transfer to paper towels. Trim lotus root and remove tough skin with paring knife; slice and transfer to paper towels.

3. Fill deep fryer or deep, heavy pot with oil and heat over medium-high heat to 350°F. Working in batches, deep fry each vegetable until crisp and slightly curled, stirring occasionally. Frying time will vary from 2 to 6 minutes depending on the vegetable. Remove vegetables with slotted spoon and drain on paper towels; immediately sprinkle with salt.

4. Once drained and cooled, combine chips. Serve at once or store in airtight containers at room temperature. To recrisp chips, bake in preheated 350°F oven 5 minutes.

SWISS ROSTI POTATOES

MAKES 4 SERVINGS

4 large russet potatoes (about 6 ounces each)*

¼ cup (½ stick) butter

Salt and freshly ground black pepper

1. Preheat oven to 400°F. Pierce each potato in several places with fork. Bake 1 hour or until fork-tender. Cool completely; refrigerate until cold.*

2. Peel potatoes with paring knife. Grate potatoes on large holes of metal grater or use large shredding disc of food processor.

3. Heat butter in large skillet over medium-high heat until melted and bubbly. Press grated potatoes evenly into skillet. (Do not stir or turn potatoes.) Season with salt and pepper. Cook 10 to 12 minutes until golden brown.

4. Turn off heat; invert serving plate over skillet. Turn potatoes out onto plate. Serve immediately.

Prepare potatoes several hours or up to 1 day in advance.

KitchenAid®

OVEN-ROASTED POTATOES AND ONIONS WITH HERBS

MAKES 6 SERVINGS

3 pounds unpeeled red potatoes, cut into 1½-inch cubes

1 sweet onion, coarsely chopped

3 tablespoons olive oil

2 tablespoons melted butter or bacon drippings

3 cloves garlic, minced

¾ teaspoon salt

¾ teaspoon freshly ground black pepper

⅓ cup packed chopped mixed fresh herbs, such as basil, chives, parsley, oregano, rosemary and/or thyme

1. Preheat oven to 450°F. Line large shallow roasting pan with foil. Arrange potatoes and onion in prepared pan.

2. Combine olive oil, butter, garlic, salt and pepper in small bowl. Drizzle over potatoes and onion; toss well to coat.

3. Bake 30 minutes. Stir; bake 10 minutes. Add herbs; toss well. Bake 10 minutes or until vegetables are tender and browned.

KitchenAid®

BUTTERNUT SQUASH OVEN FRIES

MAKES 4 SERVINGS

½ teaspoon garlic powder

½ teaspoon salt

¼ teaspoon ground red pepper

1 butternut squash (about 2½ pounds), peeled, seeded and cut into 2-inch sticks

1 tablespoon vegetable oil

1. Preheat oven to 425°F. Combine garlic powder, salt and red pepper in small bowl.

2. Place squash on baking sheet. Drizzle with oil and sprinkle with seasoning mix; gently toss to coat. Arrange in single layer.

3. Bake 20 to 25 minutes or until squash just begins to brown, stirring frequently.

4. Preheat broiler. Broil 3 to 5 minutes or until fries are browned and crisp. Spread on paper towels to cool slightly before serving.

KitchenAid®

CREAMED KALE

MAKES 4 TO 6 SERVINGS

2 large bunches kale (about 2 pounds)

2 tablespoons butter

2 tablespoons all-purpose flour

1½ cups milk

½ cup shredded Parmesan cheese, plus additional for garnish

2 cloves garlic, minced

¼ teaspoon salt

⅛ teaspoon ground nutmeg

1. Remove stems from kale; discard. Roughly chop leaves. Bring large saucepan of water to a boil. Add kale; cook 5 minutes. Drain.

2. Melt butter in large saucepan over medium heat. Whisk in flour until smooth; cook 1 minute without browning. Gradually whisk in milk. cook 4 to 5 minutes or until sauce boils and thickens, stirring frequently. Whisk in ½ cup cheese, garlic, salt and nutmeg.

3. Remove from heat; fold in kale until combined. Sprinkle with additional cheese.

KitchenAid®

CLASSIC BAKED MACARONI AND CHEESE

MAKES 8 SERVINGS

1 package (16 ounces) uncooked elbow macaroni

4 cups milk

4 cups (16 ounces) shredded sharp Cheddar cheese

4 cups (16 ounces) shredded American cheese

2 cups (8 ounces) shredded Muenster cheese

2 cups (8 ounces) shredded mozzarella cheese

½ cup plain dry bread crumbs (optional)

1. Preheat oven to 350°F. Cook macaroni according to package directions until al dente. Drain and place in 4-quart baking dish; keep warm.

2. Bring milk to a simmer in large saucepan over medium heat. Reduce heat to low. Gradually add cheeses, stirring constantly. Cook and stir 5 minutes or until smooth. Pour cheese sauce over macaroni; stir until well blended. Sprinkle with bread crumbs, if desired.

3. Bake 50 to 60 minutes or until bubbly and heated through.

Tip: Macaroni and cheese can also be baked in individual baking dishes or small cast iron skillets. Reduce baking time slightly.

CORN FRITTERS

MAKES 24 FRITTERS

1½ cups all-purpose flour

2 tablespoons sugar

2 teaspoons baking powder

½ teaspoon salt

1 can (8 ounces) cream-style corn

2 eggs

¼ cup milk

1 tablespoon butter, melted

Vegetable oil for deep frying

1. Attach flat beater to stand mixer. Combine flour, sugar, baking powder and salt in mixer bowl. Add corn, eggs, milk and butter; beat on low speed 1 minute or until well blended. Stop and scrape bowl; beat on medium-high speed 30 seconds.

2 Heat oil in large saucepan over medium-high heat to 375°F.

3. Drop tablespoonfuls of batter into oil; do not crowd pan. Cook until bubbles form on top; turn and cook until golden brown on all sides. Drain on paper towels. Repeat with remaining batter. Serve immediately.

KitchenAid®

PESTO RICE AND BEANS

MAKES 8 SERVINGS

1 can (about 14 ounces) vegetable broth

¾ cup uncooked long grain white rice

1½ cups fresh (1-inch) green bean pieces

1 can (about 15 ounces) Great Northern beans, rinsed and drained

½ cup pesto sauce (page 8)

Freshly grated Parmesan cheese (optional)

1. Combine broth and rice in medium saucepan. Bring to a boil over high heat. Reduce heat to low; cover and simmer 12 to 15 minutes or until rice is tender.

2. Meanwhile, bring another medium saucepan of water to a boil. Add green beans; cook 5 minutes or until crisp-tender. Drain and place in large bowl.

3. Add rice, Great Northern beans and pesto to green beans; mix well. Sprinkle with cheese, if desired.

ROASTED CAULIFLOWER WITH CHEDDAR BEER SAUCE

MAKES 4 TO 6 SERVINGS

1 large head cauliflower (about 2½ pounds), trimmed and cut into ½-inch florets

2 tablespoons vegetable oil, divided

½ teaspoon salt, divided

½ teaspoon freshly ground black pepper

2 medium shallots, finely chopped

2 teaspoons all-purpose flour

½ cup Irish ale

1 tablespoon spicy brown mustard

1 tablespoon Worcestershire sauce

1½ cups (6 ounces) shredded Cheddar cheese

1. Preheat oven to 450°F. Line large baking sheet with foil.

2. Combine cauliflower, 1 tablespoon oil, ¼ teaspoon salt and pepper in large bowl; toss to coat. Spread in single layer on prepared baking sheet.

3. Roast 25 minutes or until tender and lightly browned, stirring occasionally.

4. Meanwhile for sauce, heat remaining 1 tablespoon oil in medium saucepan over medium heat. Add shallots; sauté 3 to 4 minutes or until tender. Stir in flour and remaining ¼ teaspoon salt; cook 1 minute. Whisk in ale, mustard and Worcestershire sauce; bring to a simmer over medium-high heat. Reduce heat to medium-low; add cheese by ¼ cupfuls, stirring until cheese is melted before adding next addition. Cover and keep warm over low heat, stirring occasionally.

5. Transfer roasted cauliflower to large serving bowl; top with cheese sauce. Serve immediately.

KitchenAid®

CORN SOUFFLÉ

MAKES 6 SERVINGS

3 tablespoons all-purpose flour

1 tablespoon sugar

½ teaspoon freshly ground
    black pepper

3 eggs

2 cups corn

1 can (about 15 ounces)
    cream-style corn

1 cup (4 ounces) shredded
    Mexican cheese blend or
    Monterey Jack cheese

1 jar (2 ounces) chopped
    pimientos, drained

⅓ cup milk

1. Preheat oven to 350°F. Grease 8-inch round baking dish.

2. Attach flat beater to stand mixer. Combine flour, sugar and pepper in mixer bowl. Add eggs; beat on high speed until smooth. Stir in corn, cream-style corn, cheese, pimientos and milk. Pour into prepared baking dish.

3. Bake, uncovered, 55 minutes or until set. Let stand 15 minutes before serving.

COCONUT BUTTERNUT SQUASH

MAKES 4 TO 6 SERVINGS

1 tablespoon butter

½ cup chopped onion

1 pound butternut squash, peeled,
    seeded and cut into 1-inch pieces

1 pound sweet potatoes, peeled and cut
    into 1-inch pieces

1 can (13 ounces) coconut milk

3 tablespoons packed brown sugar,
    divided

½ teaspoon salt

½ teaspoon ground cinnamon

¼ teaspoon ground nutmeg

¼ teaspoon ground allspice

1 tablespoon grated fresh ginger

1. Melt butter in large skillet over medium-high heat. Add onion; sauté 5 minutes or until translucent. Add squash, sweet potatoes, coconut milk, 1 tablespoon brown sugar, salt, cinnamon, nutmeg and allspice; bring to a boil over medium-high heat. Reduce heat to low; cover and simmer 10 minutes. Uncover and cook 5 minutes or until vegetables are tender, stirring frequently. Remove from heat. Stir in ginger.

2. Transfer mixture to blender or food processor; blend until smooth. Spoon into serving bowls; sprinkle with remaining 2 tablespoons brown sugar.

FRESH CRANBERRY RELISH

MAKES 4 CUPS RELISH

2 cans (8 ounces each) pineapple chunks in juice

1 package (12 ounces) fresh or frozen cranberries

2 tablespoons powdered sugar

⅛ teaspoon ground cloves

1 teaspoon vanilla (optional)

1. Drain pineapple, reserving 2 tablespoons juice.

2. Combine half of pineapple and half of cranberries in food processor; process with on/off pulses until fruit is coarsely chopped. Transfer mixture to large bowl. Repeat with remaining pineapple and cranberries.

3. Stir sugar, reserved pineapple juice, cloves and vanilla, if desired, into fruit mixture; mix well. Serve immediately or cover and refrigerate up to 1 day before serving.

KitchenAid®

MASHED SWEET POTATOES WITH FRENCH MERINGUE

MAKES 6 SERVINGS

4 egg whites

Pinch cream of tartar

¾ cup sugar

Pinch salt

3 cups mashed, hot sweet potatoes (about 2 pounds uncooked)

2 tablespoons crystallized ginger, finely chopped

1 tablespoon butter, softened

1 to 2 tablespoons fresh orange juice

1. Preheat oven to 350°F.

2. Attach wire whip to stand mixer. Beat egg whites and cream of tartar in mixer bowl on high speed until soft peaks form. Combine sugar and salt in small bowl; gradually add to egg whites, beating on high speed until stiff peaks form.

3. Combine sweet potatoes, ginger, butter and orange juice in medium bowl; spread in 2-quart baking dish. Spread meringue over sweet potatoes.

4. Bake about 15 minutes or until meringue is golden. Serve immediately.

MUSHROOM GRATIN

MAKES 8 SERVINGS

4 tablespoons butter, divided

1 small onion, minced

8 ounces sliced cremini
mushrooms

2 cloves garlic, minced

4 cups cooked elbow
macaroni, rotini or other
pasta

2 tablespoons all-purpose flour

1 cup milk

½ teaspoon salt

½ teaspoon freshly ground
black pepper

½ teaspoon dry mustard

½ cup fresh bread crumbs

1 tablespoon olive oil

1. Preheat oven to 350°F. Grease shallow baking dish.

2. Melt 2 tablespoons butter in large skillet over
medium-high heat. Add onion; sauté 2 minutes. Add
mushrooms and garlic; sauté 6 to 8 minutes or until
vegetables soften. Remove from heat; stir in macaroni.

3. Melt remaining 2 tablespoons butter in medium
saucepan over low heat. Whisk in flour until smooth;
cook 2 minutes without browning. Gradually whisk in
milk. Bring to a boil over medium-high heat, whisking
constantly. Reduce heat to a simmer. Add salt, pepper
and mustard; cook 5 to 7 minutes or until sauce thickens,
whisking frequently.

4. Pour sauce over mushroom mixture; stir to coat.
Spoon into prepared baking dish. Top with bread
crumbs; drizzle with olive oil.

5. Cover and bake 15 minutes. Uncover and bake
10 minutes or until filling is bubbly and topping is
browned.

CABBAGE COLCANNON

MAKES 6 SERVINGS

1 pound new red potatoes, halved

1 tablespoon vegetable oil

1 small onion, thinly sliced

½ small head green cabbage, thinly sliced

Salt and freshly ground black pepper

3 tablespoons butter

1. Place potatoes in medium saucepan; add water to cover. Bring to a boil over medium heat; cook 20 minutes or until tender. Drain well.

2. Heat oil in large skillet over medium-high heat. Add onion; sauté 8 minutes or until onion is lightly browned. Add cabbage; cook and stir 5 minutes or until softened.

3. Add potatoes to skillet; cook until heated through. Slightly mash potatoes. Season to taste with salt and pepper. Top each serving with ½ tablespoon butter.

KitchenAid®

KOHLRABI AND CARROT SLAW

MAKES 8 SERVINGS

2 pounds kohlrabi bulbs, peeled

4 carrots

1 red bell pepper, chopped

1 pint grape tomatoes, halved

2 green onions, thinly sliced

⅓ cup mayonnaise

⅓ cup plain yogurt

2 tablespoons cider vinegar

2 tablespoons finely chopped
   fresh parsley

1 teaspoon dried dill weed

¼ teaspoon salt

¼ teaspoon ground cumin

⅛ teaspoon freshly ground black
   pepper

1. Assemble Rotor Slicer/Shredder with coarse shredding cone; attach to stand mixer. Shred kohlrabi and carrots into mixer bowl. Add bell pepper, tomatoes and green onions.

2. Whisk mayonnaise, yogurt, vinegar, parsley, dill, salt, cumin and black pepper in small bowl until smooth. Add to vegetables; toss to coat. Cover and refrigerate until ready to serve.

KitchenAid®

CARAMELIZED BRUSSELS SPROUTS

MAKES 4 SERVINGS

1 tablespoon vegetable oil

1 pound brussels sprouts, ends trimmed and discarded, thinly sliced

¼ cup dried cranberries

2 teaspoons packed brown sugar

½ teaspoon salt

1. Heat oil in large skillet over medium-high heat. Add brussels sprouts; sauté 10 minutes or until crisp-tender and beginning to brown.

2. Add cranberries, brown sugar and salt; sauté 5 minutes or until browned.

KitchenAid®

BREADS

Breads

BOSTON BLACK COFFEE BREAD

MAKES 1 LOAF

½ cup rye flour

½ cup cornmeal

½ cup whole wheat flour

1 teaspoon baking soda

½ teaspoon salt

¾ cup strong brewed coffee,
    room temperature or cold

⅓ cup molasses

¼ cup canola oil

¾ cup raisins

1. Preheat oven to 325°F. Grease and flour 9×5-inch loaf pan.

2. Combine rye flour, cornmeal, whole wheat flour, baking soda and salt in large bowl. Stir in coffee, molasses and oil until mixture forms thick batter. Fold in raisins. Pour batter into prepared pan.

3. Bake 50 minutes or until toothpick inserted into center comes out clean. Cool completely in pan on wire rack.

PRETZEL ROLLS

MAKES 12 ROLLS

1¼ cups lager or pale ale, at room temperature

3 tablespoons packed brown sugar

2 tablespoons milk

2 tablespoons butter, melted

1 package (¼ ounce) active dry yeast

3 to 4 cups bread flour, divided

2 teaspoons salt

4 quarts water

½ cup baking soda

Kosher salt

1. Attach flat beater to stand mixer. Combine lager, brown sugar, milk, butter and yeast in mixer bowl. Stir in 1 cup flour and 2 teaspoons salt on low speed, adding enough additional flour to make stiff dough that cleans the bowl.

2. Replace flat beater with dough hook. Knead on low speed 5 to 7 minutes or until smooth and slightly tacky, adding additional flour as needed. Shape dough into ball. Place in large lightly greased bowl; turn once to grease surface. Cover and let rise in warm place 1 hour or until doubled.

3. Turn out dough onto lightly floured work surface; knead briefly. Shape into 12 equal pieces. Shape each into smooth ball by gently pulling top surface to underside; pinch bottom to seal. Place on ungreased baking sheet. Cover with plastic wrap; let rise in warm place 30 minutes or until doubled.

4. Preheat oven to 425°F. Grease second baking sheet.

5. Bring water and baking soda to a boil in large saucepan. Add rolls to water, a few at a time; cook until puffed, turning once. Drain on clean kitchen towel. Place rolls 2 inches apart on prepared baking sheet. Cut 1½-inch-wide X in top of each roll using kitchen shears. Sprinkle with kosher salt.

6. Bake 15 to 18 minutes or until crisp and brown. Remove from baking sheet; cool on wire rack.

SWEDISH LIMPA BREAD

MAKES 12 SERVINGS

¾ cup plus 4 teaspoons water, divided

4 tablespoons molasses, divided

2 tablespoons butter

1 teaspoon instant coffee granules

½ teaspoon caraway seeds, crushed

½ teaspoon whole fennel seeds, crushed

1¾ to 2 cups all-purpose flour, divided

½ cup rye flour

1 package (¼ ounce) active dry yeast

1 tablespoon sugar

1½ teaspoons grated orange peel

1 teaspoon salt

¼ teaspoon whole fennel seeds

¼ teaspoon whole caraway seeds

1. Heat ¾ cup water, 3 tablespoons molasses and butter in small saucepan over low heat until temperature reaches 120° to 130°F. Stir in coffee granules.

2. Attach flat beater to stand mixer. Combine 1½ cups all-purpose flour, rye flour, yeast, sugar, orange peel, salt and crushed caraway and fennel seeds in mixer bowl. Stir in water mixture on low speed to form soft but sticky dough. Gradually add additional all-purpose flour to form rough dough.

3. Replace flat beater with dough hook. Knead on low speed 2 minutes or until soft dough forms, gradually adding remaining all-purpose flour to prevent sticking, if necessary. Cover with towel; let rest 5 minutes. Knead on low speed 5 to 8 minutes or until dough is smooth and elastic. Shape dough into a ball. Place in large lightly greased bowl; turn once to grease surface. Cover with lightly greased plastic wrap. Let rise in warm place about 1 hour or until almost doubled.

4. Grease 8×4-inch loaf pan. Punch down dough; roll into 12×7-inch rectangle. Starting with one short end, roll up tightly. Pinch seams and ends to seal. Place seam side down in prepared pan. Cover loosely with plastic wrap. Let rise in warm place 1 hour or until doubled.

5. Preheat oven to 350°F. Stir remaining 1 tablespoon molasses and 4 teaspoons water in small bowl; set aside. Uncover loaf; make 3 diagonal slashes on top of dough using sharp knife.

6. Bake 40 to 45 minutes or until loaf sounds hollow when tapped. Brush top with molasses mixture and sprinkle with whole fennel and caraway seeds halfway through baking time. Brush again with molasses mixture about 10 minutes before removing loaf from oven. Cool in pan on wire rack 5 minutes. Remove from pan; cool completely on wire rack.

KitchenAid®

TRIPLE CHOCOLATE STICKY BUNS

MAKES 12 ROLLS

2¾ cups bread flour

⅓ cup plus 1 tablespoon unsweetened cocoa powder, divided

¼ cup granulated sugar

1 package (¼ ounce) active dry yeast

1 teaspoon salt

½ cup sour cream

1 egg

¼ cup warm water (130°F)

10 tablespoons butter, divided

⅔ cup packed brown sugar, divided

2 tablespoons light corn syrup

½ teaspoon ground cinnamon

½ cup coarsely chopped walnuts, toasted*

½ cup semisweet chocolate chips

To toast walnuts, spread in single layer on baking sheet. Bake in preheated 350°F oven 8 to 10 minutes or until golden brown, stirring frequently.

1. Attach flat beater to stand mixer. Whisk flour, ⅓ cup cocoa, granulated sugar, yeast and salt in mixer bowl. Whisk sour cream and egg in small bowl until well blended. Add water, 3 tablespoons butter and sour cream mixture to flour mixture; beat on medium speed 3 minutes.

2. Replace flat beater with dough hook. Knead on medium-low speed about 6 minutes. Place dough in large lightly greased bowl; turn once to grease surface. Cover and let rise in warm place about 40 minutes. (Dough will not double in size.)

3. Meanwhile, prepare topping and filling. Grease 9-inch round cake pan. Combine ⅓ cup brown sugar, 4 tablespoons butter, corn syrup and remaining 1 tablespoon cocoa in small saucepan. Heat over medium heat until brown sugar dissolves and mixture bubbles around edge, stirring frequently. Pour into prepared pan.

4. Combine remaining ⅓ cup brown sugar and cinnamon in small bowl. Melt remaining 3 tablespoons butter.

5. Roll out dough into 12×8-inch rectangle on very lightly floured surface. Brush with melted butter and sprinkle with brown sugar-cinnamon mixture. Sprinkle with walnuts and chocolate chips; gently press filling into dough. Starting with long side, roll up tightly; pinch seam to seal. Using serrated knife, cut crosswise into 12 slices; arrange over topping in pan. Cover and let rise in warm place about 35 minutes or until doubled. Preheat oven to 375°F.

6. Bake about 25 minutes or just until buns in center of pan are firm to the touch. Immediately invert onto serving plate. Serve warm or at room temperature.

KitchenAid®

HERB GARLIC BAGUETTES

MAKES 2 LOAVES

1 package (¼ ounce) active dry yeast

1 teaspoon sugar

¼ cup warm water (105° to 115°F)

3¼ to 3½ cups all-purpose flour

1 tablespoon chopped fresh basil *or* 1 teaspoon dried basil

2 teaspoons chopped fresh oregano *or* ½ teaspoon dried oregano

2 teaspoons chopped fresh thyme *or* ½ teaspoon dried thyme

1 teaspoon minced garlic

1 teaspoon salt

¾ cup cold water

1 egg

1 teaspoon water

1. Dissolve yeast and sugar in warm water in small bowl.

2. Attach flat beater to stand mixer. Combine 3¼ cups flour, basil, oregano, thyme, garlic and salt in mixer bowl. With mixer running on medium-low speed, gradually add yeast mixture and cold water until blended. If dough is sticky, add remaining ¼ cup flour.

3. Replace flat beater with dough hook. Knead on medium-low speed 5 to 7 minutes or until dough is smooth and elastic. Shape dough into a ball. Place in large lightly greased bowl, turning once to grease surface. Cover and let rise in warm place 1½ to 2 hours or until doubled.

4. Grease two baking sheets. Turn out dough onto lightly floured surface. Knead several times to remove air. Divide dough in half; shape each half into 12-inch long loaf. Place each loaf on prepared baking sheet. Make 3 to 4 shallow diagonal slices in top of each loaf with sharp knife. Whisk egg and 1 teaspoon water in small bowl; brush over loaves. Reserve remaining egg mixture. Cover loaves with greased plastic wrap. Let rise in warm place 1 to 1½ hours or until doubled.

5. Preheat oven to 450°F. Brush top of each loaf again with egg mixture. Bake 15 to 18 minutes or until deep golden brown. Immediately remove to wire rack; cool completely.

CINNAMON ROLLS

MAKES 18 ROLLS

1 package (¼ ounce) active dry yeast

¼ cup warm water (100° to 110°F)

½ cup plus 1 tablespoon milk, divided

¼ cup granulated sugar

5 tablespoons butter, melted, divided

1 egg

1 teaspoon vanilla

½ teaspoon salt

2½ to 2¾ cups all-purpose flour, divided

½ cup packed brown sugar

1 tablespoon ground cinnamon

⅓ cup raisins (optional)

½ cup powdered sugar, sifted

1. Attach flat beater to stand mixer. Dissolve yeast in warm water in mixer bowl; let stand 5 minutes or until bubbly.

2. Add ½ cup milk, granulated sugar, 2 tablespoons butter, egg, vanilla and salt; beat on medium speed until blended. Add 2½ cups flour; beat until soft dough forms.

3. Replace flat beater with dough hook. Add enough remaining flour, 1 tablespoon at a time, if necessary to prevent sticking. Knead on low speed 5 minutes or until dough is smooth and elastic.

4. Shape dough into a ball. Place dough in large lightly greased bowl; turn once to grease surface. Cover and let rise in warm place about 1 hour or until doubled.

5. Grease two 8-inch round cake pans. Combine brown sugar, 1 tablespoon butter and cinnamon in small bowl.

6. Punch down dough. Roll out dough into 18×8-inch rectangle on lightly floured surface. Brush with remaining 2 tablespoons butter; spread with brown sugar mixture. Sprinkle with raisins, if desired. Starting with long side, roll up dough jelly-roll style; pinch seam to seal. Cut crosswise into 1-inch slices; arrange slices cut sides up in prepared pans. Cover loosely and let rise in warm place 30 to 40 minutes or until almost doubled. Preheat oven to 350°F.

7. Bake 18 minutes or until golden brown. Remove to wire racks to cool slightly.

8. For glaze, whisk powdered sugar and remaining 1 tablespoon milk in small bowl until smooth. Drizzle glaze over warm rolls.

DRESDEN STOLLEN

MAKES 1 LOAF

¼ cup golden raisins

¼ cup chopped candied cherries

¼ cup slivered almonds

¼ cup candied orange peel

2 tablespoons brandy or rum

¼ cup warm water (105° to 115°F)

4 tablespoons sugar, divided

2 packages (¼ ounce each) active dry yeast

4 strips lemon peel (each about 2½ inches)

2¾ cups all-purpose flour, divided

⅓ cup cold butter, cut into 5 pieces

½ teaspoon salt

1 egg

½ teaspoon almond extract

2 to 5 tablespoons milk

2 tablespoons butter, melted, divided

1 egg white, lightly beaten

3 tablespoons powdered sugar

1. Combine raisins, cherries, almonds, orange peel and brandy in small bowl; set aside.

2. Combine water, 1 tablespoon sugar and yeast in small bowl. Let stand 5 minutes or until bubbly.

3. Place remaining 3 tablespoons sugar and lemon peel in food processor. Process until peel is minced. Add 2¾ cups flour, ⅓ cup cold butter and salt. Process about 15 seconds or until mixed. Add yeast mixture, egg and almond extract; process 10 seconds or until blended.

4. With motor running, slowly drizzle in just enough milk through feed tube until dough forms a ball that cleans side of bowl. Process until ball turns around bowl about 25 times. Turn off processor and let dough stand 1 to 2 minutes.

5. Turn on processor and gradually drizzle in enough remaining milk to make dough that is soft, smooth and satiny, but not sticky. Process until dough turns around bowl about 15 times.

6. Turn dough onto lightly floured surface. Shape into a ball, cover with inverted bowl or plastic wrap and let stand 20 minutes.

7. Knead reserved fruit mixture into dough on well-floured surface. Sprinkle with additional flour, if necessary, to keep dough from becoming sticky. Shape dough into a ball and place in large lightly greased bowl, turning once to grease surface. Cover loosely with plastic wrap and let rise in warm place about 1 hour or until doubled.

8. Punch down dough. Roll or pat dough into 9×7-inch oval on large greased baking sheet. Brush with 1 tablespoon melted butter. Make a crease lengthwise in dough with handle of wooden spoon just off center. Fold smaller section over larger one. Brush top with egg

white. Cover and let stand in warm place 45 minutes or until almost doubled.

9. Preheat oven to 350°F. Bake 25 to 30 minutes or until evenly browned.

Immediately remove to wire rack. Brush with remaining 1 tablespoon melted butter; sprinkle with powdered sugar. Cool completely.

KitchenAid®

GANNAT (FRENCH CHEESE BREAD)

MAKES 1 LOAF

3 to 6 tablespoons warm
water (105° to 115°F)

1 package (¼ ounce) active
dry yeast

1 teaspoon sugar

2½ cups all-purpose flour

¼ cup (½ stick) butter,
softened

1 teaspoon salt

2 eggs

1 cup (4 ounces) shredded
Emmentaler Swiss,
Gruyère, sharp Cheddar
or Swiss cheese

1 teaspoon vegetable oil

1. Combine 3 tablespoons water, yeast and sugar in small bowl. Stir to dissolve yeast; let stand 5 minutes or until bubbly.

2. Place flour, butter and salt in food processor. Process 15 seconds or until mixed. Add yeast mixture and eggs; process 15 seconds or until blended.

3. With processor running, very slowly drizzle just enough remaining water through feed tube until dough forms a ball that cleans side of bowl. Process until ball turns around bowl about 25 times. Turn off processor and let dough stand 1 to 2 minutes.

4. Turn on processor and gradually drizzle in enough remaining water to make dough that is soft, smooth and satiny but not sticky. Process until dough turns around bowl about 15 times.

5. Turn out dough onto lightly floured surface. Shape into a ball and place in large lightly greased bowl, turning once to grease surface. Cover and let stand in warm place 1 hour or until doubled.

6. Punch down dough. Place dough on lightly greased surface; knead cheese into dough. Roll or pat into 8-inch circle. Place in well greased 9-inch round cake or pie pan. Brush with oil. Let stand in warm place about 45 minutes or until doubled.

7. Preheat oven to 375°F. Bake 30 to 35 minutes or until browned and bread sounds hollow when tapped. Immediately remove from pan; cool on wire rack.

KitchenAid®

TREACLE BREAD (BROWN SODA BREAD)

MAKES 6 TO 8 SERVINGS

2 cups all-purpose flour

1 cup whole wheat flour

1 teaspoon baking soda

½ teaspoon salt

½ teaspoon ground ginger

1¼ cups buttermilk, plus additional as needed

3 tablespoons dark molasses (preferably blackstrap)

1. Preheat oven to 375°F. Line baking sheet with parchment paper.

2. Combine all-purpose flour, whole wheat flour, baking soda, salt and ginger in large bowl; mix well. Combine 1¼ cups buttermilk and molasses in small bowl; mix well.

3. Stir buttermilk mixture into flour mixture. Add additional buttermilk by tablespoonfuls if needed to make dry, rough dough. Turn out dough onto floured surface; knead 8 to 10 times or just until smooth; do not overknead. Shape dough into round loaf about 1½ inches thick. Place on prepared baking sheet.

4. Use floured knife to cut halfway through dough, scoring into quarters (called farls in Ireland). Sprinkle top of dough with additional flour, if desired.

5. Bake about 35 minutes or until bread sounds hollow when tapped. Remove to wire rack to cool slightly. Serve warm.

Note: Treacle Bread can be sliced or pulled apart into farls.

CINNAMON-NUT BUBBLE RING

MAKES 12 SERVINGS

¾ cup plus 1½ tablespoons milk, divided

5 tablespoons butter, divided

3 cups bread flour, divided

¾ cup granulated sugar, divided

1 package (¼ ounce) active dry yeast

1 teaspoon salt

4½ teaspoons ground cinnamon, divided

1 egg

½ cup finely chopped walnuts

1 cup powdered sugar

1. Combine ¾ cup milk and 2 tablespoons butter in small saucepan; heat to 120°F.

2. Attach flat beater to stand mixer. Whisk 1 cup flour, ¼ cup granulated sugar, yeast, salt and ½ teaspoon cinnamon in mixer bowl. Add milk mixture and egg; beat on medium speed 3 minutes.

3. Replace flat beater with dough hook; knead in walnuts and enough remaining flour to form soft dough on low speed. Knead on medium-low speed 5 minutes. Place dough in large lightly greased bowl; turn once to grease surface. Cover and let rise in warm place about 30 minutes or until doubled.

4. Spray 10-inch tube pan with nonstick cooking spray. Melt remaining 3 tablespoons butter; place in shallow bowl. Combine remaining ½ cup granulated sugar and 4 teaspoons cinnamon in another shallow bowl.

5. Punch down dough. Roll pieces of dough into 2-inch balls. Roll balls in melted butter; coat with cinnamon-sugar. Arrange in prepared pan. Cover and let rise about 30 minutes or until doubled. Preheat oven to 350°F.

6. Bake 30 minutes or until golden brown. Cool in pan on wire rack 10 minutes; remove from pan. Combine powdered sugar and remaining 1½ tablespoons milk in small bowl; whisk until smooth. Drizzle glaze over bread.

KitchenAid®

OATMEAL RAISIN NUT BREAD

MAKES 1 LOAF

3 cups bread flour, divided

1 cup old-fashioned oats

1 package (¼ ounce) active dry yeast

1½ teaspoons salt

1½ teaspoons ground cinnamon

1 cup plus 2 tablespoons warm water (130°F)

¼ cup maple syrup

2 tablespoons canola oil

1 cup raisins

¾ cup chopped pecans

1. Attach flat beater to stand mixer. Whisk 1 cup flour, oats, yeast, salt and cinnamon in mixer bowl. Combine water, maple syrup and oil in medium bowl. Add to flour mixture; beat 3 minutes on medium speed.

2. Replace flat beater with dough hook; beat in enough remaining flour until soft dough forms. Knead on medium-low speed 6 to 8 minutes or until dough is smooth and elastic. Add raisins and pecans; knead until well incorporated. Shape dough into a ball. Place in large lightly greased bowl; turn once to grease surface. Cover and let rise in warm place about 40 minutes or until doubled.

3. Grease 9×5-inch loaf pan. Punch down dough. Roll out dough into 14×8-inch rectangle on lightly floured surface. Starting with short side, roll up tightly; pinch seam to seal. Place seam side down in prepared pan. Cover and let rise about 30 minutes or until doubled. Preheat oven to 375°F.

4. Bake 30 to 40 minutes or until top is browned and loaf sounds hollow when tapped (200°F).

KitchenAid®

LOADED BANANA BREAD

MAKES 1 LOAF

1½ cups all-purpose flour

2½ teaspoons baking powder

¼ teaspoon salt

6 tablespoons (¾ stick) butter, softened

⅓ cup granulated sugar

⅓ cup packed brown sugar

2 eggs

3 ripe bananas, mashed

½ teaspoon vanilla

1 can (8 ounces) crushed pineapple, drained

⅓ cup flaked coconut

¼ cup mini chocolate chips

⅓ cup chopped walnuts (optional)

1. Preheat oven to 350°F. Grease 9×5-inch loaf pan. Whisk flour, baking powder and salt in small bowl.

2. Attach flat beater to stand mixer. Beat butter, granulated sugar and brown sugar in mixer bowl on medium speed until light and fluffy. Beat in eggs, one at a time, scraping down bowl after each addition. Add bananas and vanilla. Beat just until combined.

3. Gradually beat flour mixture into banana mixture on low speed just until combined. Fold in pineapple, coconut and chocolate chips. Spoon batter into prepared pan. Top with walnuts, if desired.

4. Bake 50 minutes or until toothpick inserted into center comes out almost clean. Cool in pan 1 hour; remove to wire rack.

SOFT PRETZELS

MAKES 12 PRETZELS

1 package (¼ ounce) active dry
    yeast

¼ cup warm water (105° to
    115°F)

1 cup brown ale, at room
    temperature

1 tablespoon sugar

1 tablespoon olive oil

2 teaspoons kosher salt,
    divided

3¾ to 4 cups all-purpose flour

2 cups hot water

1 teaspoon baking soda

1 egg, well beaten

2 tablespoons butter, melted

1. Attach flat beater to stand mixer. Sprinkle yeast over warm water in mixer bowl; let stand 5 minutes. Add ale, sugar, olive oil, ¾ teaspoon salt and enough flour to make soft dough on low speed.

2. Replace flat beater with dough hook. Knead on medium-low speed 5 to 7 minutes or until dough is smooth and elastic. Shape dough into a ball. Place in large lightly greased bowl; turn once to grease surface. Cover and let rise in warm place 45 minutes or until doubled.

3. Punch down dough. Divide into 12 pieces. Roll each piece into rope about 20 inches long. If dough becomes too difficult to roll, let stand 10 minutes. Shape ropes into pretzels.

4. Combine hot water and baking soda in pie plate. Dip pretzels into mixture; place on lightly greased baking sheet. Cover loosely and let stand in warm place 15 to 20 minutes. Brush pretzels with egg; sprinkle with remaining 1¼ teaspoons salt.

5. Preheat oven to 425°F. Bake 10 minutes or until golden brown. Brush pretzels with melted butter.

Variation: Sprinkle a small amount of finely shredded cheese over pretzels before baking—Parmesan, Asiago or Cheddar are good choices. Or add ½ cup (2 ounces) shredded Cheddar cheese to the dough during the last minute of kneading.

CINNAMON RAISIN BREAD

MAKES 2 LOAVES

¼ cup (½ stick) butter

1 cup plus 2 tablespoons milk

2 tablespoons honey

2 eggs

4 cups all-purpose flour

2½ teaspoons salt

2½ teaspoons active dry yeast

1 cup raisins

2 tablespoons melted butter, divided

8 teaspoons sugar

4 teaspoons ground cinnamon

1. Melt ¼ cup butter in small saucepan over low heat; stir in milk and honey until mixture is warm but not hot. Whisk in eggs; remove from heat.

2. Attach flat beater to stand mixer. Combine flour, salt and yeast in mixer bowl. Add egg mixture and raisins; mix on low speed until dough forms.

3. Replace flat beater with dough hook. Knead on low speed 5 to 7 minutes or until dough is smooth and elastic. Shape dough into a ball. Place in large lightly greased bowl; turn once to grease surface. Cover and let rise in warm place 1 to 1½ hours or until dough is doubled.

4. Grease and flour two 8×4-inch loaf pans. Punch down dough. Divide in half; shape each half into 8×10-inch rectangle. Brush with 1 tablespoon melted butter. Combine sugar and cinnamon in small bowl. Reserve 2 teaspoons cinnamon-sugar; sprinkle remaining cinnamon-sugar evenly over dough.

5. Roll up dough, starting with short sides; place in prepared loaf pans. Cover and let rise in warm place 1 to 1½ hours or until almost doubled. Preheat oven to 375°F.

6. Bake 35 minutes or until golden brown (180°F), rotating pans once. Brush tops with remaining 1 tablespoon melted butter; sprinkle with reserved cinnamon-sugar. Cool in pans 10 minutes. Remove to wire rack; cool completely.

KitchenAid®

MALTY MAPLE CORNBREAD

MAKES 8 SERVINGS

1 cup coarse ground yellow cornmeal

1 cup porter or dark ale

¼ cup maple syrup

1 cup all-purpose flour

1 tablespoon baking powder

½ teaspoon salt

2 eggs

¼ cup (½ stick) butter, melted

1. Preheat oven to 400°F. Grease 9-inch square baking pan. Combine cornmeal, porter and maple syrup in small bowl.

2. Sift flour, baking powder and salt into large bowl. Stir in cornmeal mixture, eggs and butter until well blended. Pour batter into prepared pan.

3. Bake 20 minutes or until toothpick inserted into center comes out clean. Cool in pan 10 minutes. Serve warm.

Note: For an extra-flavorful crust, place the greased pan in the oven for several minutes to preheat. When batter is ready, pour into hot pan and bake as directed. The cornbread will develop a thick, brown crust with a deep, rich flavor.

KitchenAid®

IRISH SODA BREAD

MAKES 12 SERVINGS

2½ cups all-purpose flour

1¼ cups whole wheat flour

1 cup currants

¼ cup sugar

1 tablespoon baking powder

2 teaspoons caraway seeds

1 teaspoon salt

½ teaspoon baking soda

½ cup (1 stick) butter, cut into small pieces

1½ cups buttermilk

1 egg

1. Preheat oven to 350°F. Grease large baking sheet.

2. Attach flat beater to stand mixer. Combine all-purpose flour, whole wheat flour, currants, sugar, baking powder, caraway seeds, salt and baking soda in mixer bowl. Add butter; mix on low speed until mixture resembles coarse crumbs.

3. Whisk buttermilk and egg in medium bowl. Add to flour mixture; mix on low speed until slightly sticky dough forms. Transfer dough to prepared baking sheet; shape into 8-inch round.

4. Bake 50 to 60 minutes or until bread is golden and crust is firm. Cool on baking sheet 10 minutes. Remove to wire rack; cool completely.

BLUEBERRY HILL BREAD

MAKES 1 LOAF

2 cups all-purpose flour

¾ cup packed brown sugar

2 teaspoons baking powder

1 teaspoon baking soda

1 teaspoon salt

½ teaspoon ground nutmeg

¾ cup buttermilk

1 egg

3 tablespoons oil or melted butter

1 cup fresh or thawed frozen blueberries

1. Preheat oven to 350°F. Grease 8½×4½-inch loaf pan.

2. Combine flour, brown sugar, baking powder, baking soda, salt and nutmeg in bowl of food processor; process 5 seconds to mix. Whisk buttermilk, egg and oil in medium bowl; pour over flour mixture. Process 5 to 10 seconds or just until flour is moistened. Do not overprocess; batter should be lumpy.

3. Sprinkle blueberries over batter. Pulse just to mix blueberries into batter. (Batter will be stiff.) Spread in prepared pan.

4. Bake 50 to 60 minutes or until toothpick inserted into center comes out clean. Cool in pan 15 minutes. Remove to wire rack; cool completely.

KitchenAid®

Muffins, Scones and Biscuits

HAM AND SWISS CHEESE BISCUITS

MAKES ABOUT 18 BISCUITS

2 cups all-purpose flour

2 teaspoons baking powder

½ teaspoon baking soda

½ cup (1 stick) cold butter, cut into small pieces

⅔ cup buttermilk

½ cup (2 ounces) shredded Swiss cheese

2 ounces ham, minced

1. Preheat oven to 450°F. Grease baking sheet.

2. Combine flour, baking powder and baking soda in medium bowl. Cut in butter with pastry blender until mixture resembles coarse crumbs. Add buttermilk; stir until soft dough forms. Stir in cheese and ham.

3. Turn out dough onto floured surface. Gently knead 10 to 12 times. Roll or pat dough to ½-inch thickness. Cut dough with 2-inch round biscuit cutter. Place on prepared baking sheet.

4. Bake 10 minutes or until golden brown. Serve warm.

COCONUT SCONES WITH ORANGE BUTTER

MAKES 8 SCONES

Orange Butter (recipe follows)

1¾ cups all-purpose flour

1 tablespoon baking powder

2 tablespoons sugar

½ teaspoon salt

5 tablespoons cold butter

1 egg

1 cup heavy cream, divided

2 tablespoons milk

2 teaspoons grated orange peel

½ cup plus ⅓ cup flaked coconut, divided

1. Preheat oven to 400°F. Line baking sheet with parchment paper. Prepare Orange Butter.

2. Combine flour, baking powder, sugar and salt in large bowl. Cut in butter with pastry blender until mixture resembles coarse crumbs.

3. Whisk egg, ¾ cup cream, milk and orange peel in medium bowl; stir in ½ cup coconut. Add to flour mixture; stir just until dough forms.

4. Turn out dough onto floured surface. Pat into 8-inch circle, about ¾-inch thick. Cut into eight triangles. Brush tops of scones with remaining ¼ cup cream; sprinkle with remaining ⅓ cup coconut. Place 2 inches apart onto prepared baking sheet.

5. Bake 12 to 15 minutes or until scones are golden brown and coconut is toasted. Cool on wire rack 15 minutes. Serve warm with Orange Butter.

ORANGE BUTTER

MAKES ABOUT ½ CUP

½ cup (1 stick) butter, softened

2 tablespoons fresh orange juice

1 tablespoon grated orange peel

2 teaspoons sugar

Attach flat beater to stand mixer. Place butter, orange juice, orange peel and sugar in mixer bowl. Mix on low speed until creamy and well blended.

MAPLE WALNUT MUFFINS

MAKES 12 MUFFINS

½ cup plus 3 tablespoons maple syrup, divided

¼ cup chopped walnuts

2 tablespoons butter, melted

2 cups all-purpose flour

¾ cup sugar

2 teaspoons baking powder

½ teaspoon baking soda

½ teaspoon salt

¼ teaspoon ground cinnamon

¾ cup plus 1 tablespoon milk

½ cup vegetable oil

1 egg

½ teaspoon vanilla

1. Preheat oven to 400°F. Grease 12 standard (2½-inch) muffin cups. Place 2 teaspoons maple syrup, 1 teaspoon walnuts and ½ teaspoon butter in each muffin cup.

2. Combine flour, sugar, baking powder, baking soda, salt and cinnamon in large bowl; mix well.

3. Whisk milk, oil, egg, remaining 3 tablespoons maple syrup and vanilla in medium bowl until well blended. Add to flour mixture; stir just until blended. Spoon batter evenly into prepared muffin cups. Place muffin pan on baking sheet to catch any drips (maple syrup may overflow slightly).

4. Bake 20 to 25 minutes or until toothpick inserted into centers comes out clean. Invert pan onto wire rack covered with waxed paper. Cool muffins slightly; serve warm.

HONEY SCONES WITH CHERRY COMPOTE

MAKES 8 SCONES

Cherry Compote (recipe follows)

2 cups all-purpose flour

½ cup old-fashioned oats

2 tablespoons packed brown sugar

1 tablespoon granulated sugar

1 tablespoon baking powder

½ teaspoon salt

6 tablespoons butter, melted

1 egg

¼ cup heavy cream

¼ cup milk

3 tablespoons honey

1. Prepare Cherry Compote. Preheat oven to 425°F. Line baking sheet with parchment paper.

2. Combine flour, oats, brown sugar, granulated sugar, baking powder and salt in large bowl. Whisk butter, egg, cream, milk and honey in medium bowl until well blended. Add to flour mixture; stir just until dough forms.

3. Turn out dough onto lightly floured surface. Pat into 8-inch round about ¾ inch thick. Cut into eight triangles; place 1 to 2 inches apart on prepared baking sheet.

4. Bake 12 to 15 minutes until golden brown. Cool on wire rack 15 minutes. Serve with compote.

CHERRY COMPOTE

MAKES ABOUT 2 CUPS

1 pound fresh Bing cherries, pitted and halved

¼ cup sugar

¼ cup water

2 tablespoons fresh lemon juice

1. Combine cherries, sugar, water and lemon juice in medium heavy saucepan. Bring to a boil over medium heat, stirring to dissolve sugar. Boil 2 minutes; remove cherries with slotted spoon and set aside.

2. Reduce heat to medium-low; simmer 2 to 4 minutes or until thickened.

3. Return cherries to saucepan; remove from heat. Cool 1 hour before serving.

KitchenAid®

CLASSIC SCONES

MAKES 16 SCONES

2 cups all-purpose flour

2 tablespoons sugar

2 teaspoons baking powder

½ teaspoon salt

⅓ cup butter, softened

½ cup heavy cream

2 eggs, divided

1 teaspoon water

1. Preheat oven to 425°F. Grease large baking sheet. Attach flat beater to stand mixer. Combine flour, sugar, baking powder and salt in mixer bowl. Add butter; mix on medium-low speed 30 seconds or until well blended.

2. Add cream and 1 egg; mix on medium-low speed 30 seconds or until soft dough forms. Turn out dough onto lightly floured surface; knead three times. Divide dough in half. Pat each half into circle about ½-inch thick. Cut each circle into eight wedges.

3. Bake 10 to 12 minutes or until golden brown. Cool slightly on wire rack. Serve warm.

KitchenAid®

CHOCOLATE POPOVERS

MAKES 6 POPOVERS

¾ cup plus 2 tablespoons all-purpose flour

¼ cup granulated sugar

2 tablespoons unsweetened cocoa powder

¼ teaspoon salt

4 eggs

1 cup milk

2 tablespoons butter, melted

½ teaspoon vanilla

Powdered sugar

1. Position rack in lower third of oven. Preheat oven to 375°F. Grease 6-cup popover pan or six 6-ounce custard cups; set custard cups in jelly-roll pan.

2. Sift flour, granulated sugar, cocoa and salt into medium bowl. Attach flat beater to stand mixer. Beat eggs at low speed of electric mixer 1 minute. Beat in milk, butter and vanilla. Beat in flour mixture until smooth. Pour batter into prepared pan.

3. Bake 50 minutes. Dust with powdered sugar; serve immediately.

CARAMELIZED ONION, BACON AND PARMESAN MUFFINS

MAKES 12 SERVINGS

6 slices bacon, chopped

2 cups chopped onions

3 teaspoons sugar, divided

¼ teaspoon dried thyme

1½ cups all-purpose flour

¾ cup freshly grated Parmesan cheese

2 teaspoons baking powder

½ teaspoon salt

¾ cup lager or other light-colored beer

2 eggs

¼ cup extra virgin olive oil

1. Preheat oven to 375°F. Grease 12 standard (2½-inch) muffin cups or line with paper baking cups.

2. Cook bacon in large skillet over medium heat until crisp, stirring occasionally. Remove with slotted spoon to paper towel-lined plate. Add onions, 1 teaspoon sugar and thyme to skillet; cook 12 minutes or until onions are golden brown, stirring occasionally. Cool 5 minutes; stir in bacon.

3. Combine flour, cheese, baking powder, salt and remaining 2 teaspoons sugar in large bowl. Whisk lager, eggs and olive oil in medium bowl. Add to flour mixture; stir just until moistened. Gently stir in onion mixture. Spoon batter evenly into prepared muffin cups.

4. Bake 15 minutes or until toothpick inserted into centers comes out clean. Cool in pan 5 minutes; remove to wire rack. Serve warm.

KitchenAid®

PUMPKIN-GINGER SCONES

MAKES 12 SCONES

½ cup sugar, divided

2 cups all-purpose flour

2 teaspoons baking powder

1 teaspoon ground cinnamon

½ teaspoon baking soda

½ teaspoon salt

¼ cup (½ stick) cold butter, cut into small pieces

1 egg

½ cup solid-pack pumpkin

¼ cup sour cream

½ teaspoon grated fresh ginger *or* 2 tablespoons finely chopped crystallized ginger

1 tablespoon butter, melted

1. Preheat oven to 425°F.

2. Reserve 1 tablespoon sugar. Combine remaining sugar, flour, baking powder, cinnamon, baking soda and salt in large bowl. Cut in ¼ cup butter with pastry blender until mixture resembles coarse crumbs. Beat egg in medium bowl; beat in pumpkin, sour cream and ginger until well blended. Stir into flour mixture until soft dough forms that pulls away from side of bowl.

3. Turn out dough onto well-floured surface. Knead 10 to 12 times. Roll dough using floured rolling pin into 9×6-inch rectangle. Cut dough into six 3-inch squares with floured knife. Cut each square diagonally in half, making 12 triangles; place 2 inches apart on ungreased baking sheets. Brush tops of scones with melted butter; sprinkle with reserved sugar.

4. Bake 10 to 12 minutes or until golden brown. Cool 10 minutes on wire racks. Serve warm.

LEMON-GLAZED ZUCCHINI MUFFINS

MAKES 12 MUFFINS

2 cups all-purpose flour

⅔ cup granulated sugar

1 tablespoon baking powder

2 teaspoons grated lemon peel

1 teaspoon salt

½ teaspoon ground nutmeg

½ cup chopped walnuts, pecans or hazelnuts

½ cup dried fruit bits or golden raisins

½ cup milk

⅓ cup vegetable oil

2 eggs

1 cup packed shredded zucchini, undrained

¼ cup powdered sugar

1 to 1½ teaspoons fresh lemon juice

1. Preheat oven to 400°F. Line 12 standard (2½-inch) muffin cups with paper baking cups.

2. Combine flour, granulated sugar, baking powder, lemon peel, salt and nutmeg in large bowl; stir in nuts and fruit. Whisk milk, oil and eggs in medium bowl until blended. Stir into flour mixture; add zucchini, stirring just until moistened. Spoon evenly into prepared muffin cups.

3. Bake 20 to 25 minutes or until toothpick inserted into centers comes out clean. Remove from pan to wire rack; cool slightly. Meanwhile, whisk powdered sugar and lemon juice in small bowl until smooth. Drizzle over warm muffins.

ORANGE SCONES WITH BERRIES

MAKES 6 SCONES

1¼ cups all-purpose flour

4 tablespoons sugar, divided

1½ teaspoons baking powder

¼ teaspoon salt

1 ounce cold cream cheese, cut into small pieces

1 tablespoon cold butter, cut into small pieces

1 egg

¼ cup milk

1 tablespoon plus 1 teaspoon finely grated orange peel

1½ cups fresh strawberries, sliced, divided

1⅓ cups fresh blueberries, divided

1 tablespoon orange liqueur (optional)

1½ cups vanilla ice cream (optional)

1. Preheat oven to 425°F. Grease baking sheet or line with parchment paper.

2. Combine flour, 2 tablespoons sugar, baking powder and salt in medium bowl. Cut in cream cheese and butter with pastry blender until mixture resembles coarse crumbs. Whisk egg, milk and orange peel in small bowl. Add to flour mixture; stir just until moistened.

3. Turn out dough onto floured surface; gather dough into a ball. If dough is sticky, sprinkle with a little additional flour; knead 10 to 12 times. Press dough into 9×3-inch rectangle, about ½ inch thick. Cut into three squares; cut squares in half. Place 1 inch apart on prepared baking sheet.

4. Bake 12 to 14 minutes or until lightly browned. Remove to wire rack.

5. Meanwhile, combine ½ cup strawberries, ⅓ cup blueberries and remaining 2 tablespoons sugar in food processor; process until smooth. Transfer to medium bowl; stir in remaining berries and liqueur, if desired. Let stand 15 minutes.

6. Slice scones and serve with berry sauce and ice cream, if desired.

SWEET CHERRY BISCUITS

MAKES ABOUT 10 BISCUITS

2 cups all-purpose flour

2 tablespoons sugar

4 teaspoons baking powder

½ teaspoon salt

½ teaspoon crushed dried
   rosemary

½ cup (1 stick) cold butter, cut
   into small pieces

¾ cup milk

½ cup dried sweetened
   cherries, chopped

1. Preheat oven to 425°F.

2. Combine flour, sugar, baking powder, salt and rosemary in large bowl. Cut in butter with pastry blender until mixture resembles coarse crumbs. Add milk; stir until soft dough forms. Stir in cherries.

3. Pat dough to 1-inch thickness on floured surface. Cut dough with 3-inch biscuit cutter. Place biscuits 1 inch apart on ungreased baking sheet.

4. Bake about 15 minutes or until golden brown. Cool on wire rack 5 minutes before serving.

KitchenAid®

CLASSIC BLUEBERRY MUFFINS

MAKES 15 MUFFINS

2 cups all-purpose flour

¾ cup sugar

2 teaspoons baking powder

½ teaspoon baking soda

½ teaspoon salt

½ teaspoon ground cinnamon

1½ cups fresh or frozen
blueberries (do not thaw)

¾ cup plus 2 tablespoons milk

½ cup (1 stick) butter, melted

1 egg

1 teaspoon vanilla

1. Preheat oven to 400°F. Grease 15 standard (2½-inch) muffin cups or line with paper baking cups.

2. Combine flour, sugar, baking powder, baking soda, salt and cinnamon in large bowl; mix well. Place ¼ cup flour mixture in medium bowl; add blueberries and toss to coat.

3. Whisk milk, butter, egg and vanilla in medium bowl until well blended. Add to flour mixture; stir just until blended. Fold in blueberries. Spoon batter evenly into prepared muffin cups.

4. Bake 20 to 25 minutes or until toothpick inserted into centers comes out clean. Cool in pan 2 minutes; remove to wire rack. Serve warm or at room temperature.

COUNTRY BUTTERMILK BISCUITS

MAKES ABOUT 9 BISCUITS

2 cups all-purpose flour

1 tablespoon baking powder

2 teaspoons sugar

½ teaspoon salt

½ teaspoon baking soda

⅓ cup shortening

⅔ cup buttermilk*

Or substitute soured fresh milk. To sour milk, combine 2½ teaspoons lemon juice plus enough milk to equal ⅔ cup. Stir; let stand 5 minutes before using.

1. Preheat oven to 450°F.

2. Combine flour, baking powder, sugar, salt and baking soda in medium bowl. Cut in shortening with pastry blender until mixture resembles coarse crumbs. Add buttermilk; stir until soft dough forms that clings together and forms a ball.

3. Turn out dough onto well-floured surface. Gently knead dough 10 to 12 times. Roll or pat dough to ½-inch thickness. Cut dough with floured 2½-inch biscuit cutter. Place 2 inches apart on ungreased baking sheet.

4. Bake 8 to 10 minutes or until golden brown. Serve warm.

Drop Biscuits: Prepare Country Buttermilk Biscuits as directed through step 2, increasing buttermilk to 1 cup. Stir batter with wooden spoon about 15 strokes. *Do not knead.* Drop dough by heaping tablespoonfuls 1 inch apart onto greased baking sheets. Bake as directed in step 4. Makes about 18 biscuits.

Sour Cream Dill Biscuits: Prepare Country Buttermilk Biscuits as directed through step 2, omitting buttermilk. Combine ½ cup sour cream, ⅓ cup milk and 1 tablespoon chopped fresh dill in small bowl until well blended. Stir into dry ingredients and continue as directed in step 3. Makes about 9 biscuits.

Bacon and Onion Biscuits: Prepare Country Buttermilk Biscuits as directed through step 2, adding 4 slices crumbled crisp-cooked bacon and ⅓ cup chopped green onions to flour-shortening mixture before adding buttermilk. Continue as directed in step 3. Makes about 9 biscuits.

CINNAMON SUGARED PUMPKIN-PECAN MUFFINS

MAKES 12 SERVINGS

8 tablespoons sugar, divided

2½ teaspoons ground cinnamon, divided

1 cup 100% bran cereal

1 cup milk

1 cup all-purpose flour

1 tablespoon baking powder

½ teaspoon baking soda

½ teaspoon salt

1 cup solid-pack pumpkin

1 egg

1 tablespoon vanilla

1 package (2 ounces) pecan chips (½ cup)

1. Preheat oven to 400°F. Grease 12 standard (2½-inch) muffin cups or line with paper baking cups. Combine 2 tablespoons sugar and ½ teaspoon cinnamon in small bowl for topping; set aside.

2. Combine cereal and milk in large bowl; let stand 5 minutes to soften. Meanwhile, combine flour, remaining 6 tablespoons sugar, remaining 2 teaspoons cinnamon, baking powder, baking soda and salt in large bowl; mix well.

3. Whisk pumpkin, egg and vanilla into cereal mixture. Gently fold in flour mixture just until blended. *Do not overmix.* Spoon batter evenly into prepared muffin cups; sprinkle with pecan chips and cinnamon-sugar topping.

4. Bake 20 to 25 minutes or until toothpick inserted into centers comes out clean. Cool in pan 3 minutes; remove to wire rack. Serve warm or at room temperature.

KitchenAid®

BACON-CHEDDAR MUFFINS

MAKES 12 MUFFINS

2 cups all-purpose flour

¾ cup sugar

2 teaspoons baking powder

½ teaspoon baking soda

½ teaspoon salt

¾ cup plus 2 tablespoons milk

⅓ cup butter, melted

1 egg, beaten

1 cup (4 ounces) shredded
   Cheddar cheese

½ cup crumbled crisp-cooked
   bacon (about 6 slices)

1. Preheat oven to 350°F. Grease 12 standard (2½-inch) muffins cups or line with paper baking cups.

2. Combine flour, sugar, baking powder, baking soda and salt in large bowl; mix well.

3. Whisk milk, butter and egg in small bowl. Add to flour mixture; stir just until blended. Fold in cheese and bacon. Spoon batter evenly into prepared muffin cups.

4. Bake 15 to 20 minutes or until toothpick inserted into centers comes out clean. Cool in pan 2 minutes; remove to wire rack. Serve warm or at room temperature.

KitchenAid®

Cookies

CLASSIC MACAROONS

MAKES ABOUT 3 DOZEN COOKIES

1 package (14 ounces) flaked coconut

¾ cup sugar

6 tablespoons all-purpose flour

¼ teaspoon salt

4 egg whites

1 teaspoon vanilla

1 cup semisweet or bittersweet chocolate chips, melted

1. Preheat oven to 325°F. Line cookie sheets with parchment paper or grease and dust with flour.

2. Combine coconut, sugar, flour and salt in large bowl; mix well. Beat in egg whites and vanilla. Drop batter by tablespoonfuls 2 inches apart onto prepared cookie sheets.

3. Bake 20 minutes or until set and light golden brown. Immediately remove to wire racks; cool completely.

4. Dip cooled cookies in melted chocolate; place on waxed paper-lined tray. Let stand at room temperature until chocolate is set.

FROSTED SUGAR COOKIES

MAKES ABOUT 6 DOZEN COOKIES

2 cups all-purpose flour

1 teaspoon baking powder

½ teaspoon salt

1 cup granulated sugar

¾ cup (1½ sticks) butter, softened

2 egg whites

1 teaspoon vanilla

Vanilla Frosting (recipe follows)

Assorted decors

1. Preheat oven to 375°F. Line cookie sheets with parchment paper. Combine flour, baking powder and salt in medium bowl.

2. Attach flat beater to stand mixer. Beat sugar and butter in mixer bowl on medium speed until fluffy. Beat in egg whites and vanilla. Add flour mixture on low speed until well blended. Wrap dough in plastic wrap; refrigerate 3 to 4 hours.

3. Roll dough on well-floured surface to ¼-inch thickness. Cut out dough with 2-inch cookie cutters; place on prepared cookie sheets.

4. Bake 8 to 10 minutes or until lightly browned. Remove to wire racks; cool completely.

5. Meanwhile, prepare Vanilla Frosting. Frost cookies; sprinkle with decors.

VANILLA FROSTING

MAKES ABOUT ½ CUP FROSTING

2 cups powdered sugar

2 to 3 tablespoons milk, divided

1 teaspoon vanilla

1. Whisk powdered sugar, 2 tablespoons milk and vanilla in medium bowl.

2. Add additional 1 tablespoon milk, if necessary, until desired spreading consistency is reached.

KitchenAid®

CHOCOLATE CHIP SKILLET COOKIE

MAKES 8 SERVINGS

1¾ cups all-purpose flour

1 teaspoon baking soda

1 teaspoon salt

¾ cup (1½ sticks) butter, softened

¾ cup packed brown sugar

½ cup granulated sugar

2 eggs

1 teaspoon vanilla

1 package (12 ounces) semisweet chocolate chips

Sea salt (optional)

Ice cream (optional)

1. Preheat oven to 350°F. Combine flour, baking soda and salt in medium bowl.

2. Attach flat beater to stand mixer. Beat ¾ cup butter, brown sugar and granulated sugar in mixer bowl on medium speed until creamy. Beat in eggs and vanilla until well blended. Gradually beat in flour mixture at low speed just until blended. Stir in chocolate chips. Press batter evenly into well-seasoned large (10-inch) cast iron skillet. Sprinkle lightly with sea salt, if desired.

3. Bake about 35 minutes or until top and edges are golden brown but cookie is still soft in center. Cool on wire rack 10 minutes; cut into wedges. Serve warm with ice cream, if desired.

KitchenAid®

BANANA SANDIES

MAKES ABOUT 2 DOZEN SANDWICH COOKIES

2⅓ cups all-purpose flour

1 cup (2 sticks) butter, softened

¾ cup granulated sugar

¼ cup packed brown sugar

1 medium banana, cut into ¼-inch slices (about ½ cup)

1 teaspoon vanilla

¼ teaspoon salt

⅔ cup chopped pecans

Cream Cheese Frosting (recipe follows)

Yellow food coloring (optional)

1. Preheat oven to 350°F. Line cookie sheets with parchment paper.

2. Attach flat beater to stand mixer. Combine flour, butter, granulated sugar, brown sugar, banana, vanilla and salt in mixer bowl. Beat on medium speed 2 to 3 minutes, scraping bowl often, until well blended. Stir in pecans. Shape dough into 1-inch balls. Place 2 inches apart on prepared cookie sheets; flatten to ¼-inch thickness with bottom of glass dipped in sugar.

3. Bake 12 to 15 minutes or until edges are lightly browned. Remove to wire racks; cool completely.

4. Prepare Cream Cheese Frosting; tint with food coloring, if desired. Spread 1 tablespoon frosting over bottom halves of cookies; top with remaining cookies.

Cream Cheese Frosting: Beat 8 ounces softened cream cheese and ½ cup (1 stick) butter in mixer bowl on medium speed until fluffy. Gradually add 1 package (16 ounces) powdered sugar and 1 teaspoon vanilla. Beat until well blended.

KitchenAid®

EXTRA-CHOCOLATEY BROWNIE COOKIES

MAKES ABOUT 4 DOZEN COOKIES

2 cups all-purpose flour

½ cup unsweetened Dutch process cocoa powder

1 teaspoon baking soda

¾ teaspoon salt

1 cup (2 sticks) butter, softened

1 cup packed brown sugar

½ cup granulated sugar

2 eggs

2 teaspoons vanilla

1 package (11½ ounces) semisweet chocolate chunks

2 cups coarsely chopped walnuts or pecans

1. Preheat oven to 350°F. Whisk flour, cocoa, baking soda and salt in medium bowl until well blended.

2. Attach flat beater to stand mixer. Beat butter in mixer bowl on medium speed 1 minute or until light and fluffy. Add brown sugar and granulated sugar; beat 2 minutes or until fluffy. Add eggs and vanilla; beat until well blended. Add flour mixture; beat on low speed until blended. Stir in chocolate chunks and walnuts.

3. Drop dough by heaping tablespoonfuls 2 inches apart onto ungreased cookie sheets; flatten slightly.

4. Bake 8 to 10 minutes or until set. Cool on cookie sheets 2 minutes. Remove to wire racks; cool completely.

KitchenAid®

OAT, CHOCOLATE AND HAZELNUT BISCOTTI

MAKES ABOUT 4 DOZEN BISCOTTI

1½ cups whole wheat flour

1 cup all-purpose flour

1 cup old-fashioned oats

2 teaspoons baking powder

½ teaspoon salt

½ teaspoon ground cinnamon

1½ cups sugar

½ cup (1 stick) butter, softened

3 eggs

1 teaspoon vanilla

2 cups toasted hazelnuts
   (see Tip)

¾ cup semisweet chocolate
   chunks

1. Preheat oven to 325°F. Line cookie sheet with parchment paper. Combine whole wheat flour, all-purpose flour, oats, baking powder, salt and cinnamon in large bowl.

2. Attach flat beater to stand mixer. Beat sugar and butter in mixer bowl on high speed until light and fluffy. Beat in eggs and vanilla. Gradually beat in flour mixture on low speed. Stir in hazelnuts and chocolate.

3. Divide dough into two equal portions. Shape into 10- to 12-inch-long logs; flatten slightly to 3-inch width. Place on prepared cookie sheet.

4. Bake 30 minutes. Cool completely on baking sheet. *Reduce oven temperature to 300°F.* Transfer logs to cutting board; cut diagonally into ½-inch slices with serrated knife. Arrange slices, cut side up, on cookie sheet. Bake 10 to 15 minutes or until golden brown. Turn slices; bake 5 to 10 minutes or until golden brown. Remove to wire racks; cool completely.

Tip: To toast hazelnuts, preheat oven to 325°F. Spread hazelnuts on a baking sheet; bake 5 to 7 minutes. Place nuts in a clean kitchen towel and rub to remove skins.

KitchenAid®

MINI LEMON SANDWICH COOKIES

MAKES 4½ DOZEN SANDWICH COOKIES

2 cups all-purpose flour

1¼ cups (2½ sticks) butter, softened, divided

½ cup granulated sugar, divided

⅓ cup heavy cream

1 teaspoon grated lemon peel

⅛ teaspoon lemon extract

¾ cup powdered sugar

2 to 3 teaspoons lemon juice

1 teaspoon vanilla

Yellow food coloring (optional)

1. For cookies, attach flat beater to stand mixer. Combine flour, 1 cup butter, ¼ cup granulated sugar, cream, lemon peel and lemon extract in mixer bowl. Beat on medium speed 2 to 3 minutes or until well blended. Divide dough into thirds. Wrap each piece in plastic wrap; refrigerate until firm.

2. Preheat oven to 375°F. Place remaining ¼ cup granulated sugar in shallow bowl. Roll out each piece of dough to ⅛-inch thickness on well-floured surface. Cut out dough with 1½-inch round cookie cutter. Dip both sides of each cookie in granulated sugar. Place 1 inch apart on ungreased cookie sheets; pierce several times with fork.

3. Bake 6 to 9 minutes or until cookies are slightly puffed but not browned. Cool on cookie sheets 1 minute. Remove to wire racks; cool completely.

4. For filling, combine powdered sugar, remaining ¼ cup butter, lemon juice and vanilla in mixer bowl. Beat on medium speed 1 to 2 minutes or until smooth. Tint with food coloring, if desired. Spread ½ teaspoon filling each on flat side of half of cookies; top with remaining cookies.

KitchenAid®

TEA COOKIES

MAKES 8 TO 9 DOZEN COOKIES

5½ cups all-purpose flour

4 teaspoons cream of tartar

2 teaspoons baking soda

½ teaspoon salt

1 cup finely chopped almonds, walnuts or pecans

3 cups sugar

2 cups shortening

2 teaspoons vanilla

4 eggs

1. Preheat oven to 375°F. Sift flour, cream of tartar, baking soda and salt into separate large bowl. Stir in nuts.

2. Attach flat beater to stand mixer. Beat sugar, shortening and vanilla in mixer bowl on medium speed until creamy. Add eggs, one at a time, beating well after each addition; beat until smooth. Beat in flour mixture on low speed until well blended. Shape dough into 1-inch balls. Place 2 inches apart on ungreased cookie sheets.

3. Bake 8 to 10 minutes. Remove to wire racks; cool completely.

KitchenAid®

MOCHA DOTS

MAKES ABOUT 6 DOZEN COOKIES

1 tablespoon instant coffee granules

2 tablespoons hot water

1½ cups all-purpose flour

¼ cup unsweetened cocoa powder

½ teaspoon salt

½ teaspoon baking soda

½ cup (1 stick) butter, softened

½ cup granulated sugar

¼ cup packed brown sugar

1 egg, lightly beaten

1 teaspoon vanilla

Chocolate nonpareil candies (about 1 inch in diameter)

1. Preheat oven to 350°F. Line cookie sheets with parchment paper. Dissolve coffee granules in hot water in small bowl. Combine flour, cocoa, salt and baking soda in medium bowl.

2. Attach flat beater to stand mixer. Beat butter, granulated sugar and brown sugar in mixer bowl on medium speed until light and fluffy. Add egg, coffee mixture and vanilla; beat until well blended. Add flour mixture; beat on low speed until well blended.

3. Shape level teaspoonfuls of dough into balls; place 2 inches apart on prepared cookie sheets. Gently press one candy into center of each ball. (Do not press candies too far; cookies will spread as they bake.)

4. Bake 7 to 8 minutes or until set and no longer shiny. Cool on cookie sheets 2 minutes. Remove to wire racks; cool completely.

NUTMEG MOLASSES COOKIES

MAKES ABOUT 5 DOZEN COOKIES

3 cups all-purpose flour

2 teaspoons baking soda

1 teaspoon ground nutmeg

1 teaspoon ground cinnamon

½ teaspoon salt

1½ cups sugar

1 cup (2 sticks) butter, softened

⅓ cup molasses

1 teaspoon vanilla

2 eggs

Additional sugar

1. Preheat oven to 350°F. Combine flour, baking soda, nutmeg, cinnamon and salt in medium bowl.

2. Attach flat beater to stand mixer. Beat 1½ cups sugar, butter, molasses and vanilla in mixer bowl on medium speed until creamy. Add eggs, one at a time, beating well after each addition. Gradually add flour mixture on low speed until blended. Beat at medium speed until thick dough forms.

3. Shape dough into 1½-inch balls. Place 3 inches apart on ungreased cookie sheets. Flatten with bottom of glass dipped in additional sugar.

4. Bake 10 minutes or until cookies look dry. Remove to wire racks; cool completely.

KitchenAid®

BLACK AND WHITE HEARTS

MAKES ABOUT 3½ DOZEN COOKIES

1 cup (2 sticks) butter, softened

¾ cup sugar

3 ounces cream cheese, softened

1 egg

1½ teaspoons vanilla

3 cups all-purpose flour

1 cup semisweet chocolate chips

2 tablespoons shortening

1. Attach flat beater to stand mixer. Beat butter, sugar, cream cheese, egg and vanilla in mixer bowl on medium-high speed until light and fluffy. Add flour; beat on low speed until well blended. Divide dough in half; wrap separately in plastic wrap. Refrigerate 2 hours or until firm.

2. Preheat oven to 375°F. Roll out dough to ⅛-inch thickness on lightly floured surface. Cut out dough with lightly floured 2-inch heart-shaped cookie cutter. Place cutouts 1 inch apart on ungreased cookie sheets.

3. Bake 7 to 10 minutes or until edges are lightly browned. Remove immediately to wire racks; cool completely.

4. Melt chocolate chips and shortening in small saucepan over low heat 4 to 6 minutes or until melted. Dip half of each heart into melted chocolate. Refrigerate on cookie sheets or trays lined with waxed paper until chocolate is set. Store covered in refrigerator.

TRIPLE CHIPPER MONSTERS

MAKES ABOUT 22 (4-INCH) COOKIES

2½ cups all-purpose flour

1 teaspoon baking soda

¾ teaspoon salt

1 cup (2 sticks) butter, softened

1 cup packed brown sugar

½ cup granulated sugar

2 eggs

2 teaspoons vanilla

2 cups semisweet chocolate chips

½ cup white chocolate chips

½ cup butterscotch or peanut butter chips

1. Preheat oven to 350°F. Combine flour, baking soda and salt in medium bowl.

2. Attach flat beater to stand mixer. Beat butter, brown sugar and granulated sugar in mixer bowl on medium speed until light and fluffy. Beat in eggs and vanilla until blended. Gradually beat in flour mixture on low speed until well blended. Stir in chips.

3. Drop dough by scant ¼ cupfuls onto ungreased cookie sheets 3 inches apart. Lightly flatten dough with fingertips.

4. Bake 12 to 14 minutes or until edges are set and golden brown. Cool cookies on cookie sheets 1 to 2 minutes. Remove to wire racks; cool completely.

LINZER SANDWICH COOKIES

MAKES ABOUT 2 DOZEN SANDWICH COOKIES

1⅔ cups all-purpose flour

¼ teaspoon baking powder

¼ teaspoon salt

¾ cup granulated sugar

½ cup (1 stick) butter, softened

1 egg

1 teaspoon vanilla

Powdered sugar (optional)

Seedless red raspberry jam

1. Combine flour, baking powder and salt in medium bowl.

2. Attach flat beater to stand mixer. Beat granulated sugar and butter in mixer bowl on medium speed until light and fluffy. Beat in egg and vanilla until blended. Gradually add flour mixture on low speed until dough forms. Divide dough in half; wrap separately in plastic wrap. Refrigerate 2 hours or until firm.

3. Preheat oven to 375°F. Roll out half of dough on lightly floured surface to ¼-inch thickness. Cut out circles with 1½-inch floured scalloped or plain round cookie cutters. (If dough becomes too soft, refrigerate several minutes before continuing.) Place cutouts 2 inches apart on ungreased cookie sheets.

4. Roll out remaining half of dough and cut out same number of circles. Cut 1-inch centers of different shapes from circles. Place 2 inches apart on ungreased cookie sheets.

5. Bake 7 to 9 minutes or until edges are lightly browned. Cool cookies on cookie sheets 2 minutes. Remove to wire racks; cool completely.

6. Sprinkle powdered sugar over cookies with holes. Spread jam on flat sides of whole cookies; top with sugar-dusted cookies. Store tightly covered at room temperature or freeze up to 3 months.

KitchenAid®

CASHEW-LEMON SHORTBREAD COOKIES

MAKES ABOUT 2½ DOZEN COOKIES

½ cup roasted cashew nuts

1 cup (2 sticks) butter, softened

½ cup plus 2 tablespoons sugar, divided

1 tablespoon grated Meyer lemon peel*

1 teaspoon vanilla

2½ cups all-purpose flour

Use regular lemon peel if Meyer lemons are not available.

1. Preheat oven to 325°F.

2. Place cashews in food processor; process until finely ground. Add butter, ½ cup sugar, lemon peel and vanilla; process until well blended. Add flour; pulse until dough begins to form a ball.

3. Shape dough into 1½-inch balls; roll in remaining 2 tablespoons sugar. Place 2 inches apart on ungreased cookie sheets; flatten slightly.

4. Bake 17 to 19 minutes or just until set. Remove to wire racks; cool completely.

KitchenAid®

BASIC OATMEAL COOKIES

MAKES 3 DOZEN COOKIES

2 cups old-fashioned oats

1⅓ cups all-purpose flour

¾ teaspoon baking soda

½ teaspoon baking powder

½ teaspoon salt

1 cup packed brown sugar

¾ cup (1½ sticks) butter, softened

¼ cup granulated sugar

1 egg

1 tablespoon honey

1 teaspoon vanilla

1. Preheat oven to 350°F. Line cookie sheets with parchment paper. Combine oats, flour, baking soda, baking powder and salt in medium bowl.

2. Attach flat beater to stand mixer. Beat brown sugar, butter and granulated sugar in mixer bowl on medium speed until light and fluffy. Add egg, honey and vanilla; beat until well blended. Gradually add flour mixture, about ½ cup at a time; beat on low speed just until blended. Drop dough by tablespoonfuls about 2 inches apart onto prepared cookie sheets.

3. Bake 11 to 15 minutes or until cookies are puffed and golden. *Do not overbake.* Cool on cookie sheets 5 minutes. Remove to wire racks; cool completely.

PISTACHIO COOKIES

MAKES ABOUT 2 DOZEN COOKIES

1 cup (2 sticks) butter, softened

¾ cup granulated sugar

¼ cup packed brown sugar

¼ cup unsweetened cocoa powder (optional)

1 teaspoon baking powder

¼ teaspoon ground nutmeg

1 egg

1½ teaspoons vanilla

2 cups all-purpose flour

1 cup coarsely chopped pistachio nuts

1. Attach flat beater to stand mixer. Beat butter, granulated sugar, brown sugar, cocoa, if desired, baking powder and nutmeg in mixer bowl on medium speed until creamy. Add egg and vanilla; beat until light and fluffy. Stir in flour on low speed just until moist. Fold in pistachios. *Do not overmix.* Cover bowl with plastic wrap or damp cloth; refrigerate 1 hour.

2. Preheat oven to 350°F. Line cookie sheets with parchment paper. Shape tablespoonfuls of dough into balls. Place 4 inches apart on prepared cookie sheets.

3. Bake 10 to 12 minutes or until set. Remove to wire racks; cool completely.

KitchenAid®

Brownies and Bars

MOCHA-CINNAMON BLONDIES

MAKES 36 BARS

1 cup (2 sticks) butter, softened

1¾ cups sugar

4 eggs

1 cup all-purpose flour

2 teaspoons instant coffee granules

1 teaspoon ground cinnamon

¼ teaspoon salt

1 cup chopped pecans

¾ cup semisweet chocolate chips

1. Preheat oven to 350°F. Grease 13×9-inch baking pan.

2. Attach flat beater to stand mixer. Place butter, sugar and eggs in mixer bowl; beat on medium speed until light and fluffy. Add flour, coffee granules, cinnamon and salt; beat on low speed until combined. Stir in pecans and chocolate chips. Spread batter in prepared pan.

3. Bake 30 minutes or until sides begin to pull away from pan. Cool completely in pan on wire rack.

KitchenAid®

GERMAN CHOCOLATE BROWNIES

MAKES 12 BROWNIES

4 ounces German chocolate

1 ounce unsweetened
  chocolate

⅔ cup butter

⅓ cup granulated sugar

2 teaspoons vanilla

3 eggs

1 cup all-purpose flour

⅔ cup chopped pecans

Coconut-Pecan Frosting
  (recipe follows)

Candied Pecans (recipe
  follows)

1. Preheat oven to 350°F. Grease 9-inch square baking pan.

2. Melt German chocolate, unsweetened chocolate and butter in small saucepan over low heat, stirring constantly. Cool slightly.

3. Attach flat beater to stand mixer. Combine granulated sugar, vanilla and eggs in mixer bowl; beat on high speed until well blended. Gradually add chocolate mixture on low speed. Add flour in three additions, beating until combined after each addition. Spread batter in prepared pan.

4. Bake 30 to 40 minutes or until sides begin to pull away from pan and toothpick inserted into center comes out clean. Prepare Coconut-Pecan Frosting and Candied Pecans; spread frosting over brownies; top with pecans.

COCONUT-PECAN FROSTING

2 egg yolks

6 ounces evaporated milk

¾ teaspoon vanilla

¾ cup packed brown sugar

6 tablespoons (¾ stick) butter

1⅓ cups unsweetened coconut

¾ cup chopped pecans

1. Whisk egg yolks, evaporated milk and vanilla in small saucepan. Add brown sugar and butter; cook over low heat 10 to 12 minutes or until thickened, stirring constantly.

2. Remove from heat; stir in coconut and pecans. Cool completely.

CANDIED PECANS

2 tablespoons butter

2 tablespoons packed brown
  sugar

¾ cup whole pecans

1. Melt butter and brown sugar in medium saucepan over medium heat. Stir in whole pecans. Cook and stir just until pecans are coated.

2. Spread on waxed paper; cool completely.

KitchenAid®

WHITE CHOCOLATE PEPPERMINT BROWNIES

MAKES 12 BROWNIES

BROWNIES

1 package (12 ounces) white chocolate chips, divided

¼ cup granulated sugar

3 eggs

1 cup all-purpose flour

½ cup (1 stick) butter

½ teaspoon salt

½ cup chopped peppermint candies

FROSTING

6 tablespoons (¾ stick) butter

3 tablespoons cream cheese

1¼ cups powdered sugar

Crushed peppermint candies

1. Preheat oven to 350°F. Grease 9-inch square baking pan.

2. Melt half of white chocolate chips in small saucepan over low heat, stirring constantly until smooth. Cool slightly.

3. Attach flat beater to stand mixer. Beat granulated sugar and eggs in mixer bowl on medium-high speed 5 minutes. Add melted chocolate, flour, ½ cup butter and salt; beat on low speed until blended. Stir in chopped peppermints. Spread batter in prepared pan.

4. Bake 20 to 25 minutes or until toothpick inserted into center comes out clean. Cool completely in pan on wire rack.

5. Meanwhile, prepare frosting. Melt remaining half of white chocolate chips in small saucepan over low heat, stirring constantly until smooth. Cool slightly.

6. Beat 6 tablespoons butter, cream cheese and powdered sugar in mixer bowl on medium speed until smooth. Beat in melted chocolate. Spread over brownies; sprinkle with crushed peppermint candies.

CARAMEL BACON NUT BROWNIES

MAKES 2 DOZEN BROWNIES

¾ cup (1½ sticks) butter

4 ounces unsweetened chocolate

2 cups sugar

4 eggs

1 cup all-purpose flour

1 package (14 ounces) caramels

¼ cup heavy cream

2 cups pecan halves or coarsely chopped pecans, divided

4 slices bacon, crisp-cooked and crumbled

1 package (12 ounces) chocolate chunks or chips, divided

1. Preheat oven to 350°F. Grease 13×9-inch baking pan.

2. Place butter and chocolate in large microwavable bowl. Microwave on HIGH 1½ to 2 minutes or until melted and smooth. Stir in sugar. Add eggs, one at a time, beating until blended after each addition. Stir in flour. Spread half of batter in prepared pan. Bake 20 minutes.

3. Meanwhile, combine caramels and cream in medium microwavable bowl. Microwave on HIGH 1½ to 2 minutes or until caramels begin to melt; stir until smooth. Stir in 1 cup pecan halves and bacon.

4. Spread caramel mixture over partially baked brownie layer. Sprinkle with half of chocolate chunks. Pour remaining brownie batter over top; sprinkle with remaining 1 cup pecan halves and chocolate chunks. Bake 25 minutes or until set. Cool completely in pan on wire rack. Cut into squares.

KitchenAid®

CHERRY CHEESECAKE SWIRL BARS

MAKES 16 BARS

CRUST

1⅔ cups shortbread cookie crumbs

½ cup (1 stick) butter, melted

¼ cup sugar

CHEESECAKE

2 packages (8 ounces each) cream cheese, softened

½ cup sugar

3 eggs

½ cup sour cream

½ teaspoon almond extract

¼ cup cherry preserves, melted and strained

1. Preheat oven to 325°F.

2. For crust, combine cookie crumbs, ½ cup butter and ¼ cup sugar in medium bowl; mix well. Press mixture into 9-inch square baking pan. Bake 10 minutes or until set but not browned. Cool completely.

3. For cheesecake, attach flat beater to stand mixer. Beat cream cheese in mixer bowl on medium speed until fluffy. Add ½ cup sugar; beat until smooth. Add eggs, one at a time, beating well after each addition. Add sour cream and almond extract; beat until well blended. Spread evenly in prepared crust.

4. Drizzle melted preserves in zigzag pattern over cheesecake batter. Drag tip of knife to swirl.

5. Place pan in 13×9-inch baking dish; add water to come halfway up sides of cheesecake.

6. Bake 45 to 50 minutes or until knife inserted 1 inch from edge comes out clean. Cool completely in pan on wire rack. Cover and refrigerate 2 hours or until ready to serve.

KitchenAid®

TANGY LEMON RASPBERRY BARS

MAKES 12 BARS

¾ cup packed brown sugar

½ cup (1 stick) butter, softened

Grated peel of 1 lemon

1 cup all-purpose flour

1 cup old-fashioned oats

1 teaspoon baking powder

½ teaspoon salt

½ cup raspberry jam

1. Preheat oven to 350°F. Grease 8-inch square baking pan.

2. Attach flat beater to stand mixer. Beat brown sugar, butter and lemon peel in mixer bowl on medium speed until combined. Add flour, oats, baking powder and salt; beat on low speed until combined. Reserve ¼ cup mixture. Press remaining mixture into prepared pan. Spread jam over top; sprinkle with reserved mixture.

3. Bake 25 minutes or until edges are lightly brown. Cool completely in pan on wire rack.

CHEWY PEANUT BUTTER BROWNIES

MAKES 2 DOZEN BROWNIES

¾ cup (1½ sticks) butter, melted

¾ cup creamy peanut butter

1¾ cups sugar

2 teaspoons vanilla

4 eggs

1¼ cups all-purpose flour

½ teaspoon baking powder

¼ teaspoon salt

¼ cup unsweetened cocoa powder

1. Preheat oven to 350°F. Grease 13×9-inch baking pan.

2. Attach flat beater to stand mixer. Beat butter and peanut butter in mixer bowl on low speed 3 minutes or until well blended. Add sugar and vanilla; beat until blended. Add eggs; beat until well blended. Stir in flour, baking powder and salt on low speed just until blended. Reserve 1¾ cups batter. Stir cocoa into remaining batter.

3. Spread chocolate batter in prepared pan. Top with reserved plain batter. Bake 30 minutes or until edges begin to pull away from sides of pan. Cool completely in pan on wire rack.

KitchenAid®

TOFFEE BARS

MAKES ABOUT 3 DOZEN BARS

½ cup (1 stick) butter, softened

½ cup packed brown sugar

1 egg yolk

1 teaspoon vanilla

1 cup all-purpose flour

1 cup milk chocolate chips

½ cup chopped walnuts or
pecans

1. Preheat oven to 350°F. Grease 13×9-inch baking pan.

2. Attach flat beater to stand mixer. Beat butter and brown sugar in mixer bowl on medium speed until creamy. Beat in egg yolk and vanilla. Stir in flour until well blended. Press dough into prepared pan.

3. Bake 15 minutes or until golden. Sprinkle evenly with chocolate chips. Let stand several minutes until chips melt; spread chocolate evenly over bars. Sprinkle with walnuts. Score into 2×1½-inch bars while still warm. Cool completely in pan on wire rack; cut into bars.

KitchenAid®

CHOCOLATE CHIP SOUR CREAM BROWNIES

MAKES ABOUT 30 BROWNIES

½ cup (1 stick) butter, softened

1 cup packed brown sugar

1 cup sour cream

1 egg

1 teaspoon vanilla

½ cup unsweetened cocoa powder

½ teaspoon baking soda

¼ teaspoon salt

2 cups all-purpose flour

1 cup semisweet chocolate chips

Powdered sugar (optional)

1. Preheat oven to 350°F. Grease 13×9-inch baking pan

2. Attach flat beater to stand mixer. Beat butter and brown sugar in mixer bowl on medium-high speed until creamy. Add sour cream, egg and vanilla; beat until light. Add cocoa, baking soda and salt; beat on low speed until smooth. Beat in flour until well blended. Stir in chocolate chips. Spread batter evenly in prepared pan.

3. Bake 25 to 30 minutes or until toothpick inserted into center comes out with moist crumbs. Cool in pan on wire rack. Sprinkle with powdered sugar just before serving, if desired.

KitchenAid

FRUIT AND PECAN BROWNIES

MAKES 12 BROWNIES

2 ounces unsweetened chocolate

1 cup sugar

½ cup (1 stick) butter, softened

2 eggs

1 teaspoon vanilla

½ cup all-purpose flour

1 cup chopped mixed dried fruit

1 cup coarsely chopped pecans, divided

1 cup semisweet chocolate chips, divided

1. Preheat oven to 350°F. Grease 8-inch square pan. Melt unsweetened chocolate in top of double boiler over simmering water. Remove from heat; cool.

2. Attach flat beater to stand mixer. Beat sugar and butter in mixer bowl on medium speed until light and fluffy. Add eggs, one at a time, beating until blended after each addition. Beat in melted chocolate and vanilla. Stir in flour, fruit, ½ cup pecans and ½ cup chocolate chips on low speed. Spread batter evenly in prepared pan. Sprinkle with remaining ½ cup pecans and ½ cup chocolate chips.

3. Bake 25 to 30 minutes or until toothpick inserted into center comes out with moist crumbs. Cover top with waxed paper or foil while still warm. Cool completely in pan on wire rack.

KitchenAid®

APRICOT BARS

MAKES 1½ DOZEN BARS

2 eggs

1 cup apricot fruit spread

½ cup (1 stick) butter, melted

2 teaspoons vanilla

1 cup all-purpose flour

⅔ cup old-fashioned oats

1¼ teaspoons baking powder

¾ teaspoon ground cinnamon

¼ teaspoon salt

¼ teaspoon ground allspice

⅛ teaspoon ground mace

1. Preheat oven to 350°F. Grease 12×8-inch baking dish.

2. Attach flat beater to stand mixer. Beat eggs in mixer bowl on medium speed until blended. Beat in fruit spread, butter and vanilla. Stir in flour, oats, baking powder, cinnamon, salt, allspice and mace on low speed until well blended. Spread batter into prepared baking dish.

3. Bake 18 minutes or until golden brown and firm. Cool completely in baking dish on wire rack.

DULCE DE LECHE BLONDIES

MAKES 2 TO 3 DOZEN BARS

2 cups all-purpose flour

1 teaspoon baking soda

1 teaspoon salt

1 cup (2 sticks) butter, softened

1 cup packed brown sugar

2 eggs

1½ teaspoons vanilla

1 package (14 ounces) caramels

½ cup evaporated milk

1. Preheat oven to 350°F. Grease 13×9-inch baking pan. Whisk flour, baking soda and salt in medium bowl.

2. Attach flat beater to stand mixer. Beat butter and brown sugar in mixer bowl on medium speed until creamy. Add eggs, one at a time, beating well after each addition. Beat in vanilla. Gradually add flour mixture, beating on low speed just until blended. Spread half of batter in prepared pan. Bake 8 minutes. Cool in pan on wire rack 5 minutes.

3. Meanwhile, melt caramels with evaporated milk in small saucepan over low heat; reserve 2 tablespoons. Pour remaining caramel mixture over baked crust. Drop tablespoonfuls of remaining batter over caramel layer; swirl slightly with knife.

4. Bake 25 minutes or until golden brown. Cool completely in pan on wire rack. Cut into squares. Reheat reserved caramel, if necessary; drizzle over bars.

KitchenAid®

CHOCOLATE CARAMEL BARS

MAKES 54 BARS

2 cups all-purpose flour

1½ cups packed brown sugar, divided

1¼ cups (2½ sticks) butter, softened, divided

1 cup chopped pecans

1 cup semisweet chocolate chips

1. Preheat oven to 350°F.

2. Attach flat beater to stand mixer. Combine flour, 1 cup brown sugar and ½ cup butter in mixer bowl; mix on low speed until crumbly. Press firmly into 13×9-inch pan; sprinkle evenly with pecans.

3. Combine remaining ½ cup brown sugar and ¾ cup butter in medium heavy saucepan. Cook over medium heat, stirring constantly, until mixture comes to a boil. Boil 1 minute until blended and smooth, stirring constantly. Pour caramel evenly over pecans and crust.

4. Bake 18 to 20 minutes or until caramel layer bubbles evenly all over. Immediately sprinkle with chocolate chips. Let stand 2 minutes or until chips melt; spread chocolate evenly over bars. Let stand until chocolate is set; cut into 2×1-inch bars.

KitchenAid

HAWAIIAN BARS

MAKES 20 BARS

1⅓ cups all-purpose flour

1 teaspoon baking powder

¼ teaspoon baking soda

¼ teaspoon salt

10 tablespoons (1¼ sticks) butter, cubed

1 teaspoon vanilla

2 eggs

1 cup packed dark brown sugar

¾ cup coarsely chopped salted macadamia nuts

¾ cup sweetened shredded coconut

⅓ cup granulated sugar

1. Preheat oven to 350°F. Grease 9-inch square baking pan. Whisk flour, baking powder, baking soda and salt in medium bowl.

2. Melt butter in large heavy saucepan over low heat. Remove from heat; stir in vanilla. Beat in eggs, one at a time. Add flour mixture, brown sugar, nuts, coconut and granulated sugar; mix well. Spread batter in prepared pan.

3. Bake 30 minutes or until edges begin to pull away from sides of pan. Cool completely in pan on wire rack. Cut into bars. Store in airtight container.

Note: Bars firm up and taste better on second day.

KitchenAid®

SHORTBREAD TURTLE COOKIE BARS

MAKES 2 TO 3 DOZEN BARS

1¼ cups (2½ sticks) butter, softened, divided

1 cup all-purpose flour

1 cup old-fashioned oats

1¼ cups packed brown sugar, divided

1 teaspoon ground cinnamon

¼ teaspoon salt

1½ cups chopped pecans

6 ounces bittersweet or semisweet chocolate, finely chopped

4 ounces white chocolate, finely chopped

1. Preheat oven to 350°F.

2. Attach flat beater to stand mixer. Beat ½ cup butter in mixer bowl on medium speed 2 minutes or until light and fluffy. Add flour, oats, ¾ cup brown sugar, cinnamon and salt; beat on low speed until coarse crumbs form. Press firmly into ungreased 13×9-inch baking pan.

3. Combine remaining ¾ cup butter and ¾ cup brown sugar in heavy medium saucepan. Cook over medium heat until mixture comes to a boil, stirring constantly. Boil 1 minute without stirring. Remove from heat; stir in pecans. Pour evenly over crust.

4. Bake 18 to 22 minutes or until caramel begins to bubble. Immediately sprinkle with bittersweet and white chocolates; swirl (do not spread) with knife after 45 seconds to 1 minute or when slightly softened. Cool completely in pan on wire rack.

KitchenAid®

CHOCOLATE DREAM BARS

MAKES ABOUT 2 TO 3 DOZEN BARS

1½ cups packed brown sugar, divided

½ cup (1 stick) butter, softened

1 egg yolk

1 cup plus 2 tablespoons all-purpose flour, divided

2 eggs

1 cup semisweet chocolate chips

½ cup chopped toasted walnuts*

To toast walnuts, spread in single layer on baking sheet. Bake in preheated 350°F oven 5 to 7 minutes or until golden brown, stirring frequently.

1. Preheat oven to 375°F. Grease 13×9-inch baking pan.

2. Attach flat beater to stand mixer. Beat ½ cup brown sugar, butter and egg yolk in mixer bowl on medium-high speed until light and fluffy. Stir in 1 cup flour on low speed until well blended. Press dough into prepared pan. Bake 12 to 15 minutes or until golden.

3. Meanwhile, beat remaining 1 cup brown sugar, 2 tablespoons flour and whole eggs in mixer bowl on medium-high speed until light and frothy. Spread mixture over partially baked crust.

4. Bake about 15 minutes or until topping is set. Immediately sprinkle with chocolate chips. Let stand until chips are softened; spread evenly over bars. Sprinkle with walnuts. Cool completely in pan on wire rack.

KitchenAid®

Cakes and Cupcakes

ANGEL FOOD CAKE

MAKES 1 (10-INCH) TUBE CAKE

1¼ cups cake flour, sifted

1⅓ cups plus ½ cup sugar, divided

12 egg whites

1¼ teaspoons cream of tartar

¼ teaspoon salt (optional)

1½ teaspoons vanilla

Fresh strawberries (optional)

1. Preheat oven to 350°F. Sift flour and ½ cup sugar two times.

2. Attach wire whip to stand mixer. Whip egg whites, cream of tartar, salt, if desired, and vanilla in large bowl on high speed until soft peaks form.

3. Gradually add remaining 1⅓ cups sugar, beating well after each addition until stiff peaks form. Fold in flour mixture. Pour into *ungreased* 10-inch tube pan.

4. Bake 35 to 40 minutes or until cake springs back when lightly touched.

5. Invert pan; place on top of clean empty bottle. Allow cake to cool completely in pan before removing from pan. Serve with strawberries, if desired.

KitchenAid®

PEANUT BUTTER CUPCAKES

MAKES 2 DOZEN CUPCAKES

2 cups all-purpose flour

2 teaspoons baking powder

½ teaspoon baking soda

½ teaspoon salt

1 cup creamy peanut butter, divided

¼ cup (½ stick) butter, softened

1 cup packed brown sugar

2 eggs

1 cup milk

1½ cups mini semisweet chocolate chips, divided, plus additional for garnish

Peanut Buttery Frosting (recipe follows)

1. Preheat oven to 350°F. Line 24 standard (2½-inch) muffin cups with paper baking cups. Whisk flour, baking powder, baking soda and salt in small bowl.

2. Attach flat beater to stand mixer. Beat ½ cup peanut butter and butter in mixer bowl on medium speed until blended. Add brown sugar; beat until well blended. Add eggs, one at a time, beating well after each addition.

3. Add flour mixture alternately with milk; beat on low speed until well blended. Stir in 1 cup chocolate chips. Spoon batter evenly into prepared muffin cups.

4. Bake 15 minutes or until toothpick inserted into centers comes out clean. Cool completely in pans on wire racks. Meanwhile, prepare Peanut Buttery Frosting.

5. Pipe or spread cupcakes with Peanut Butter Frosting. Place remaining ½ cup peanut butter in small microwavable bowl. Microwave on HIGH 15 seconds or until melted. Place remaining ½ cup chocolate chips in another small microwavable bowl. Microwave on HIGH 15 seconds or until melted. Drizzle peanut butter and chocolate over frosting. Garnish with additional chocolate chips.

Peanut Buttery Frosting: Beat ½ cup (1 stick) softened butter and ½ cup creamy peanut butter in mixer bowl with electric mixer on medium speed until smooth. Gradually add 2 cups sifted powdered sugar and ½ teaspoon vanilla until blended. Add 3 to 6 tablespoons milk, 1 tablespoon at a time, until smooth. Makes about 3 cups.

KitchenAid®

FLOURLESS CHOCOLATE CAKE

MAKES 12 SERVINGS

4 ounces unsweetened chocolate, coarsely chopped

4 ounces semisweet chocolate, coarsely chopped

½ cup heavy cream

3 eggs, at room temperature

½ cup sugar

¼ cup strong brewed coffee

¼ teaspoon salt

½ cup chopped walnuts, divided

Sweetened Whipped Cream (page 11, optional)

1. Preheat oven to 350°F. Grease 8-inch round cake pan.

2. Place unsweetened chocolate, semisweet chocolate and cream in medium heavy saucepan; cook over very low heat, stirring constantly until melted and smooth.

3. Attach flat beater to stand mixer. Beat eggs and sugar in mixer bowl on high speed about 7 minutes or until pale and thick. Add chocolate mixture, coffee and salt to egg mixture; beat on medium speed 1 to 2 minutes or until well blended. Stir in ¼ cup walnuts.

4. Place pan in large baking pan; add enough hot water to baking pan to reach halfway up side of cake pan.

5. Bake 30 to 35 minutes or until set but still soft in center. Loosen edge of cake with knife; place serving plate upside down over pan and invert. Sprinkle with remaining ¼ cup walnuts. Prepare Sweetened Whipped Cream, if desired. Serve with warm cake.

CANNOLI CUPCAKES

MAKES 15 CUPCAKES

2 cups all-purpose flour

½ teaspoon baking soda

½ teaspoon baking powder

½ teaspoon salt

1 cup granulated sugar

½ cup (1 stick) butter, softened

1 cup whole-milk ricotta
cheese

1 teaspoon grated orange
peel

1 egg

2 teaspoons vanilla, divided

1 cup heavy cream

8 ounces mascarpone cheese,
softened

½ cup powdered sugar

Mini semisweet chocolate
chips and chopped
unsalted pistachios

1. Preheat oven to 350°F. Line 15 standard (2½-inch) muffin cups with paper baking cups. Whisk flour, baking soda, baking powder and salt in small bowl.

2. Attach flat beater to stand mixer. Beat granulated sugar and butter in mixer bowl on medium speed until creamy. Add ricotta cheese and orange peel; beat until blended. Add egg and 1 teaspoon vanilla; beat until well blended. Add flour mixture; beat on low speed until blended. Spoon batter evenly into prepared muffin cups.

3. Bake 20 minutes or until toothpick inserted into centers comes out clean. Cool in pans 10 minutes. Remove to wire racks; cool completely.

4. Beat cream in mixer bowl on high speed until stiff peaks form. Combine mascarpone cheese, powdered sugar and remaining 1 teaspoon vanilla in separate medium bowl. Fold whipped cream into mascarpone mixture until blended.

5. Frost cupcakes; sprinkle with chocolate chips and pistachios.

CARROT CAKE

MAKES 10 TO 12 SERVINGS

1 pound carrots, peeled and trimmed

2½ cups all-purpose flour

2 tablespoons ground cinnamon, divided

1 teaspoon salt

1 teaspoon baking soda

½ teaspoon ground ginger

2 cups granulated sugar

1½ cups vegetable oil

1 teaspoon vanilla

4 eggs, beaten

1 cup canned crushed pineapple, drained and juice reserved

¾ cup chopped pecans

½ cup golden raisins

Additional pineapple juice

Cream Cheese Frosting (recipe follows)

1. Preheat oven to 350°F. Grease and flour two 8-inch round cake pans. Assemble Food Processor attachment with shredding disc; attach to stand mixer. Shred carrots into large bowl.

2. Sift flour, 1 tablespoon cinnamon, salt, baking soda and ginger into medium bowl.

3. Remove Food Processor; attach flat beater. Beat granulated sugar, oil and vanilla in mixer bowl on low speed until blended. Add flour mixture alternately with eggs, mixing well on low speed after each addition. Stir in carrots, pineapple, pecans and raisins until well blended. Spread batter evenly in prepared pans.

4. Bake 45 to 50 minutes or until toothpick inserted into centers comes out clean. Combine reserved pineapple juice with enough additional pineapple juice to equal 2 cups. Poke holes in warm cake with wooden skewer; pour 1 cup juice over each cake. Let stand in pans until cool and juice is absorbed.

5. Prepare Cream Cheese Frosting. Invert one cake layer onto serving plate; spread about 1 cup frosting over cake. Top with second cake layer; frost top and side of cake. Sprinkle with remaining 1 tablespoon cinnamon. Store in refrigerator.

CREAM CHEESE FROSTING

1 package (8 ounces) cream cheese, softened

½ cup (1 stick) butter, softened

2 tablespoons vanilla

2 cups powdered sugar

3 to 5 tablespoons milk

1. Attach flat beater to stand mixer. Beat cream cheese, butter and vanilla in mixer bowl on medium speed 2 minutes or until light and fluffy.

2. Beat in powdered sugar on low speed until well blended. Beat on medium speed 3 minutes or until fluffy. If frosting is too thick, add milk, 1 tablespoon at a time, until desired consistency is reached.

MAPLE BACON CUPCAKES

MAKES 12 CUPCAKES

CUPCAKES

1½ cups all-purpose flour

1¾ teaspoons baking powder

¾ cup granulated sugar

½ cup (1 stick) butter, softened

2 eggs

2 tablespoons maple syrup

½ cup milk

8 slices bacon, crisp-cooked
   and finely chopped,
   divided

MAPLE FROSTING

½ cup (1 stick) butter, softened

3 tablespoons maple syrup

2 tablespoons milk

3 cups powdered sugar

1. Preheat oven to 350°F. Line 12 standard (2½-inch) muffin cups with paper baking cups.

2. For cupcakes, whisk flour and baking powder in small bowl. Attach flat beater to stand mixer. Beat granulated sugar and ½ cup butter in mixer bowl on medium speed until light and fluffy. Add eggs and 2 tablespoons maple syrup; beat well. Add flour mixture and ½ cup milk; beat on low speed just until combined. Reserve 2 tablespoons bacon for topping; stir remaining bacon into batter. Spoon batter evenly into prepared muffin cups.

3. Bake 20 minutes or until toothpick inserted into centers comes out clean. Cool in pan 10 minutes. Remove to wire rack; cool completely.

4. For frosting, beat ½ cup butter, 3 tablespoons maple syrup and 2 tablespoons milk in mixer bowl on low speed 1 minute. Add powdered sugar; beat on medium speed until fluffy. Frost cupcakes; top with reserved bacon.

KitchenAid®

GLAZED CHOCOLATE POUND CAKE

MAKES 12 SERVINGS

3 cups all-purpose flour

⅓ cup unsweetened cocoa
    powder

1 tablespoon baking powder

¼ teaspoon salt

½ cup (1 stick) butter, softened

½ cup shortening

3 cups sugar

4 eggs

1 teaspoon vanilla

1 cup milk

   Chocolate Glaze (recipe
   follows)

1. Preheat oven to 325°F. Grease 12-cup bundt pan.

2. Sift flour into medium bowl. Sift again with cocoa, baking powder and salt.

3. Attach flat beater to stand mixer. Beat butter and shortening in mixer bowl on medium-high speed 1 minute or until creamy. Gradually beat in sugar; beat 3 minutes or until light and fluffy. Add eggs, one at a time, beating well after each addition. Beat in vanilla. Add flour mixture alternately with milk, beating well after each addition. Pour into prepared pan.

4. Bake 1 hour 15 minutes or until toothpick inserted near center comes out clean. Cool completely in pan on wire rack.

5. Invert cake onto serving plate. Prepare Chocolate Glaze; pour glaze over cake.

CHOCOLATE GLAZE

¾ cup sweetened condensed
    milk

2 ounces unsweetened
    chocolate, chopped

2 cups sugar

¼ cup (½ stick) butter

¼ teaspoon salt

1 teaspoon vanilla

1. Combine condensed milk and chocolate in medium saucepan. Cook and stir over low heat until slightly thickened. Add sugar; bring to a boil. Boil 9 to 10 minutes, stirring constantly. Remove from heat.

2. Add butter and salt; stir until butter is melted. Stir in vanilla. Cool 20 minutes.

Note: This frosting mixture is very hot. Take care not to splash it on your hands and do not leave it unattended while it is boiling.

KitchenAid®

BUTTER PECAN CUPCAKES

MAKES 30 CUPCAKES

2 cups chopped pecans

3 cups all-purpose flour

2 teaspoons baking powder

½ teaspoon salt

2 cups granulated sugar

1 cup (2 sticks) butter, softened

4 eggs

¾ cup milk

¼ cup canola or vegetable oil

1½ teaspoons vanilla

Browned Butter Frosting (recipe follows)

Whole pecans (optional)

1. Preheat oven to 350°F. Line 30 standard (2½-inch) muffin cups with paper baking cups.

2. Spread chopped pecans in shallow baking pan. Bake 5 minutes or until lightly toasted, stirring occasionally. Transfer to plate; cool completely.

3. Whisk flour, baking powder and salt in medium bowl. Attach flat beater to stand mixer. Beat granulated sugar and butter in mixer bowl on medium speed until creamy. Add eggs, one at a time, beating well after each addition.

4. Combine milk, oil and vanilla in small bowl. Alternately add flour mixture and milk mixture to butter mixture, beating well after each addition. Stir in chopped pecans. Spoon batter evenly into prepared muffin cups.

5. Bake 20 minutes or until toothpick inserted into centers comes out clean. Cool in pans 10 minutes. Remove to wire racks; cool completely.

6. Meanwhile, prepare Browned Butter Frosting. Pipe or spread onto cupcakes. Garnish with whole pecans.

Browned Butter Frosting: Melt 1 cup (2 sticks) butter in small saucepan over medium heat. Cook and stir until light brown. Remove from heat; let stand 10 minutes. Beat browned butter, 5½ cups powdered sugar, ¼ cup milk, 1½ teaspoons vanilla and ⅛ teaspoon salt in mixer bowl on medium speed until smooth. Add additional milk, 1 tablespoon at a time, if frosting is too stiff. Makes about 4 cups.

BANANA NUT CAKE WITH BROWN SUGAR TOPPING

MAKES 12 SERVINGS

CAKE

3 cups all-purpose flour

1½ cups packed brown sugar

3 bananas, mashed

1 cup chopped nuts

½ cup white chocolate chips

½ cup oil

¼ cup milk

1 egg

1 teaspoon baking soda

TOPPING

1⅔ cups packed brown sugar

½ cup (1 stick) butter

½ cup chopped nuts

1. Preheat oven to 350°F. Grease and flour 10-inch round baking pan.

2. Attach flat beater to stand mixer. Beat flour, 1½ cups brown sugar, bananas, 1 cup chopped nuts, white chocolate chips, oil, milk, egg and baking soda in mixer bowl on medium speed 2 minutes or until well blended. Pour into prepared pan.

3. Bake 30 to 35 minutes or until toothpick inserted into center comes out clean. Cool in pan on wire rack.

4. Meanwhile, combine 1⅔ cups brown sugar and butter in medium saucepan; cook and stir over medium heat until smooth. Pour over cooled cake. Sprinkle with ½ cup chopped nuts.

PLUM CAKE WITH STREUSEL TOPPING

MAKES 6 SERVINGS

Streusel Topping (recipe follows)

1 cup plus 2 tablespoons all-purpose flour

½ teaspoon baking powder

¼ teaspoon salt

¼ teaspoon baking soda

6 tablespoons (¾ stick) butter, softened

¼ cup granulated sugar

¼ cup packed brown sugar

1 teaspoon vanilla

2 eggs

¼ cup buttermilk

3 medium plums, pitted and cut into 8 wedges*

Plums should be underripe and slightly soft to the touch.

1. Preheat oven to 350°F. Grease 9-inch springform pan. Line bottom of pan with parchment paper; grease paper. Prepare Streusel Topping.

2. Combine flour, baking powder, salt and baking soda in medium bowl.

3. Attach flat beater to stand mixer. Beat butter in mixer bowl on medium speed 1 minute. Add granulated sugar and brown sugar; beat 1 minute or until light and fluffy. Beat in vanilla. Add eggs, one at a time, beating well after each addition.

4. Alternately add flour mixture and buttermilk, beating well on low speed after each addition. Spread batter in prepared pan. Arrange plum wedges in rings on batter; sprinkle with Streusel Topping.

5. Bake 30 minutes or until cake springs back when lightly touched. Place cake on wire rack. Remove side of pan; cool 20 minutes. Transfer to serving plate. Serve warm or at room temperature.

Streusel Topping: Combine ¼ cup all-purpose flour, 3 tablespoons packed brown sugar and ½ teaspoon ground cinnamon in medium bowl. Mix in 2 tablespoons softened butter with fingers until crumbly.

KitchenAid®

CHOCOLATE HAZELNUT LAYER CAKE

MAKES 16 SERVINGS

CAKE

1 package (2¼ ounces) chopped hazelnuts

2 cups cake flour

½ cup unsweetened cocoa powder

1½ teaspoons baking soda

1 teaspoon baking powder

1 teaspoon salt

1 cup (2 sticks) butter, softened

1 cup packed brown sugar

½ cup granulated sugar

3 eggs

4 ounces unsweetened chocolate, melted

1 teaspoon vanilla

1 cup milk

½ cup warm water

FROSTING

1 cup (2 sticks) butter, softened

4 cups powdered sugar

¼ cup milk

1 teaspoon vanilla

1 jar (13 ounces) chocolate hazelnut spread

16 whole toasted hazelnuts (optional)

1. For cake, preheat oven to 350°F. Grease three 9-inch round cake pans; line bottoms with parchment paper. Spread hazelnuts on baking sheet. Bake 7 minutes or until lightly browned and fragrant. Place on clean kitchen towel; rub hazelnuts with towel to remove skins. Finely chop.

2. Whisk cake flour, cocoa, baking soda, baking powder and salt in medium bowl until well blended. Stir in hazelnuts; set aside.

3. Attach flat beater to stand mixer. Beat 1 cup butter, brown sugar and granulated sugar in mixer bowl on medium speed about 5 minutes or until light and fluffy. Add eggs, one at a time, beating well after each addition. Beat in melted chocolate and 1 teaspoon vanilla. Add flour mixture alternately with milk, beating well after each addition. Beat in warm water. Pour batter evenly into prepared pans.

4. Bake 30 minutes or until toothpick inserted into centers comes out clean. Cool in pans on wire rack 10 minutes. Remove from pans and peel off parchment. Cool completely on wire rack.

5. For frosting, beat 1 cup butter in mixer bowl on medium-high until creamy. Beat in powdered sugar until light and fluffy; beat in ¼ cup milk and 1 teaspoon vanilla. Add hazelnut spread; beat until smooth.

6. Place one layer on serving plate and spread with frosting. Repeat with remaining layers. Frost top and side of cake. Pipe 16 rosettes around cake and top each with one whole hazelnut, if desired.

CHOCOLATE CUPCAKES WITH SPICY CHOCOLATE FROSTING

MAKES 24 CUPCAKES

2½ cups all-purpose flour

1 teaspoon baking soda

1 teaspoon baking powder

1 teaspoon ground cinnamon

½ teaspoon salt

⅛ teaspoon ground nutmeg

1½ cups granulated sugar

¾ cup (1½ sticks) butter, softened

3 eggs

1½ teaspoons vanilla

1 container (7 ounces) plain Greek yogurt

2 tablespoons canola or vegetable oil

Spicy Chocolate Frosting (recipe follows)

Chocolate curls (page 12, optional)

Ancho chile powder or ground red pepper (optional)

1. Preheat oven to 350°F. Line 24 standard (2½-inch) muffin cups with paper baking cups.

2. Whisk flour, baking soda, baking powder, cinnamon, salt and nutmeg in medium bowl.

3. Attach flat beater to stand mixer. Beat granulated sugar and butter in mixer bowl on medium speed until creamy. Add eggs and vanilla, beating until well blended. Alternately add flour mixture, yogurt and oil to butter mixture, beating well after each addition. Spoon batter evenly into prepared muffin cups.

4. Bake 18 minutes or until toothpick inserted into centers comes out clean. Cool in pans 10 minutes. Remove to wire racks; cool completely.

5. Meanwhile, prepare Spicy Chocolate Frosting. Pipe or spread onto cupcakes. Dip chocolate curls in chile powder, if desired; place on cupcakes.

Spicy Chocolate Frosting: Beat 2 cups (4 sticks) softened butter in mixer bowl on medium speed until creamy. Add 4 cups powdered sugar, ¼ cup milk, 1 teaspoon ground cinnamon, 1 teaspoon ancho chile powder, 1 teaspoon vanilla and ½ teaspoon ground red pepper; beat until fluffy. Beat in 10 ounces cooled melted bittersweet (70%) chocolate until blended. Makes about 4 cups.

CHOCOLATE HAZELNUT CUPCAKES

MAKES 18 CUPCAKES

1¾ cups all-purpose flour

1½ teaspoons baking powder

½ teaspoon salt

2 cups chocolate hazelnut
  spread, divided

⅓ cup (⅔ stick) butter, softened

¾ cup sugar

2 eggs

1 teaspoon vanilla

1¼ cups milk

  Chopped hazelnuts
    (optional)

1. Preheat oven to 350°F. Line 18 standard (2½-inch) muffin cups with paper baking cups.

2. Whisk flour, baking powder and salt in medium bowl. Attach flat beater to stand mixer. Beat ⅓ cup chocolate hazelnut spread and butter in mixer bowl on medium speed until smooth. Beat in sugar until well blended. Beat in eggs and vanilla. Add flour mixture alternately with milk, beginning and ending with flour mixture, beating until blended after each addition. Spoon batter evenly into prepared muffin cups.

3. Bake 20 minutes or until toothpick inserted into centers comes out clean. Cool in pans 10 minutes. Remove to wire racks; cool completely.

4. Frost cupcakes with remaining 1⅔ cups chocolate hazelnut spread. Sprinkle with hazelnuts, if desired.

KitchenAid®

STRAWBERRY RHUBARB PIE

MAKES 8 SERVINGS

Double-Crust Pie Pastry
(page 9)

1½ cups sugar

½ cup cornstarch

2 tablespoons quick-cooking
tapioca

1 tablespoon grated lemon
peel

¼ teaspoon ground allspice

4 cups sliced rhubarb (1-inch
pieces)

3 cups sliced fresh
strawberries

1 egg, lightly beaten

1. Prepare pie pastry. Preheat oven to 425°F.

2. Roll half of pastry into 11-inch circle on floured surface. Line 9-inch pie plate with pastry.

3. Combine sugar, cornstarch, tapioca, lemon peel and allspice in large bowl. Add rhubarb and strawberries; toss to coat. Pour into crust.

4. Roll out remaining pastry into 10-inch circle. Cut into ½-inch-wide strips. Arrange in lattice design over fruit. Seal and flute edge. Brush pastry with beaten egg.

5. Bake 50 minutes or until pastry is golden brown and filling is thick and bubbly. Cool on wire rack. Serve warm or at room temperature.

KitchenAid®

FANCY FUDGE PIE

MAKES 8 SERVINGS

1 cup chocolate wafer crumbs

⅓ cup butter, melted

1⅓ cups (8 ounces) semisweet
   chocolate chips

¾ cup packed brown sugar

½ cup (1 stick) butter, softened

3 eggs

1 cup chopped pecans

½ cup all-purpose flour

1 teaspoon vanilla

½ teaspoon instant espresso
   powder

   Sweetened Whipped Cream
   (page 11)

   Melted bittersweet
   chocolate (optional)

1. Preheat oven to 375°F. Combine wafer crumbs and melted butter in small bowl. Press onto bottom and up side of 9-inch pie pan. Bake 5 minutes. Cool completely on wire rack.

2. Place chocolate chips in small microwavable bowl. Microwave on HIGH 1 minute. Stir until smooth. Cool slightly.

3. Attach flat beater to stand mixer. Combine brown sugar and softened butter in mixer bowl; beat on medium speed until light and fluffy. Add eggs, one at a time, beating well after each addition. Stir in melted chocolate, pecans, flour, vanilla and espresso powder. Pour into crust.

4. Bake 30 minutes or until set. Cool completely on wire rack. Cover and refrigerate 2 hours or until ready to serve. Garnish with whipped cream and drizzle with melted bittersweet chocolate, if desired.

APPLE BLACKBERRY CRISP

MAKES 6 SERVINGS

4 cups sliced peeled apples

Juice of ½ lemon

2 tablespoons granulated sugar

2 tablespoons Irish cream liqueur

1 teaspoon ground cinnamon, divided

1 cup old-fashioned oats

6 tablespoons (¾ stick) cold butter, cut into pieces

⅔ cup packed brown sugar

¼ cup all-purpose flour

1 cup fresh blackberries

Irish Whipped Cream (recipe follows, optional)

1. Preheat oven to 375°F. Grease 9-inch oval or 8-inch square baking dish.

2. Place apples in large bowl; drizzle with lemon juice. Add granulated sugar, liqueur and ½ teaspoon cinnamon; toss to coat.

3. Combine oats, butter, brown sugar, flour and remaining ½ teaspoon cinnamon in food processor; pulse until combined, leaving some large pieces.

4. Gently stir blackberries into apple mixture. Spoon into prepared baking dish; sprinkle with oat mixture.

5. Bake 30 to 40 minutes or until filling is bubbly and topping is golden brown. Prepare Irish Whipped Cream, if desired; serve with crisp.

Irish Whipped Cream: Attach wire whip to stand mixer. Whip 1 cup heavy cream and 2 tablespoons Irish cream liqueur in mixer bowl on high speed until slightly thickened. Add 1 to 2 tablespoons powdered sugar; whip until soft peaks form.

Tip: This crisp can also be made without the blackberries; just add an additional 1 cup sliced apples.

KitchenAid®

CRANBERRY APPLE NUT PIE

MAKES 8 SERVINGS

Rich Pie Pastry (page 10)

1 cup sugar

3 tablespoons all-purpose flour

¼ teaspoon salt

4 cups sliced peeled tart
    apples (4 large apples)

2 cups fresh cranberries

½ cup golden raisins

½ cup coarsely chopped
    pecans

1 tablespoon grated lemon
    peel

2 tablespoons butter, cubed

1 egg, beaten

1. Prepare pie pastry. Preheat oven to 425°F.

2. Roll out half of pastry into 11-inch circle on floured surface. Line 9-inch pie plate with pastry.

3. Combine sugar, flour and salt in large bowl. Stir in apples, cranberries, raisins, pecans and lemon peel; toss well. Pour into crust; dot with butter.

4. Roll out remaining pastry on lightly floured surface into 11-inch circle. Place over filling. Trim and seal edge; flute or crimp edge. Cut three slits in center of top crust. Lightly brush top crust with egg.

5. Bake 35 minutes or until apples are tender when pierced with fork and pastry is golden brown. Cool 15 minutes on wire rack. Serve warm or cool completely.

KitchenAid®

PEACH CHERRY PIE

MAKES 8 SERVINGS

Single Crust Pie Pastry
(page 9)

¾ cup granulated sugar

3 tablespoons quick-cooking
tapioca

1 teaspoon grated lemon peel

1¼ teaspoons ground cinnamon,
divided

⅛ teaspoon salt

4 cups peach slices (about
7 medium)

2 cups Bing cherries, pitted

1 tablespoon fresh lemon juice

2 tablespoons butter, cubed

¾ cup old-fashioned oats

⅓ cup all-purpose flour

⅓ cup packed brown sugar

¼ cup (½ stick) butter, melted

¾ teaspoon ground cinnamon

Vanilla ice cream (optional)

1. Prepare pie pastry. Preheat oven to 375°F.

2. Roll out pastry into 11-inch circle on lightly floured surface. Line 9-inch pie plate with pastry. Trim excess crust; flute or crimp edge.

3. Combine granulated sugar, tapioca, lemon peel, ½ teaspoon cinnamon and salt in large bowl. Add peaches, cherries and lemon juice; toss until blended. Spread evenly in crust. Dot with 2 tablespoons cubed butter.

4. Combine oats, flour, brown sugar and remaining ¾ teaspoon cinnamon in medium bowl. Stir in melted butter until mixture resembles coarse crumbs. Sprinkle over pie filling.

5. Bake 40 minutes or until bubbly. Cool on wire rack 15 minutes. Serve warm or at room temperature with ice cream, if desired.

RASPBERRY BUTTERMILK PIE

MAKES 8 SERVINGS

Single Crust Pie Pastry
(page 9)

3 eggs, at room temperature

2 tablespoons all-purpose flour

1 cup buttermilk

¾ cup plus 2 tablespoons sugar

¼ cup (½ stick) butter, melted

¼ cup honey

½ teaspoon vanilla

¼ teaspoon salt

1½ cups fresh raspberries (do
not substitute frozen)

1. Prepare pie pastry. Preheat oven to 425°F.

2. Roll out pastry on lightly floured surface into 11-inch circle. Line 9-inch pie plate with pastry. Trim excess crust; flute or crimp edge. Place crust on baking sheet. Bake 5 minutes. Remove from oven; press down any areas that puff up. *Reduce oven temperature to 350°F.*

3. Attach flat beater to stand mixer. Beat eggs and flour in mixer bowl on medium speed until blended. Beat in buttermilk, sugar, butter, honey, vanilla and salt on low speed until sugar is dissolved. Gently stir in raspberries with spoon. Pour into crust.

4. Bake 30 minutes. If crust browns before filling is set, lightly tent pie with foil. Bake 20 minutes or until knife inserted near center comes out clean. Let stand 30 minutes before slicing.

KitchenAid®

SPICED PUMPKIN PIE

MAKES 8 SERVINGS

Single Crust Pie Pastry (page 9)

1 can (16 ounces) solid-pack pumpkin

¾ cup packed brown sugar

2 teaspoons ground cinnamon

¾ teaspoon ground ginger

½ teaspoon ground nutmeg

¼ teaspoon salt

⅛ teaspoon ground cloves

4 eggs, lightly beaten

1 cup half-and-half

1 teaspoon vanilla

Sweetened Whipped Cream (page 11)

1. Prepare pie pastry. Preheat oven to 400°F.

2. Roll out pastry on lightly floured surface into 11-inch circle. Line 9-inch pie plate with pastry. Trim excess crust; flute or crimp edge.

3. Combine pumpkin and brown sugar in large bowl; mix well. Stir in cinnamon, ginger, nutmeg, salt and cloves. Add eggs; mix well. Gradually stir in half-and-half and vanilla, mixing until combined. Pour into crust.

4. Bake 40 to 45 minutes or until knife inserted near center comes out clean. Cool on wire rack. Serve warm with whipped cream.

LATTICE-TOPPED CHERRY PIE

MAKES 8 SERVINGS

Double-Crust Pie Pastry (page 9)

6 cups pitted sweet Bing cherries

¾ cup sugar

3 tablespoons plus 1 teaspoon cornstarch

2 tablespoons fresh lemon juice

1 tablespoon half-and-half

Additional sugar

1. Prepare pie pastry. Preheat oven to 400°F.

2. Combine cherries, ¾ cup sugar, cornstarch and lemon juice in large bowl; mix well to coat cherries. Let stand 15 minutes or until syrup forms.

3. Roll half of dough into 11-inch circle. Line deep-dish 9-inch pie plate with pastry. Pour cherry filling into crust.

4. Roll out remaining pastry into 10-inch circle. Cut into ½-inch-wide strips. Arrange in lattice design over fruit. Seal and flute edge. Brush crust with half-and-half; sprinkle with additional sugar.

5. Cover crust with foil. Bake 30 minutes. Remove foil; bake 30 minutes or until crust is golden brown and filling is bubbly. Cool on wire rack. Serve warm or cool completely.

CHOCOLATE CHESS PIE

MAKES 8 SERVINGS

Single Crust Pie Pastry
(page 9)

4 ounces unsweetened
chocolate

3 tablespoons butter

3 eggs

1 egg yolk

1¼ cups sugar

½ cup half-and-half

1 to 2 teaspoons instant coffee
granules (see Note)

¼ teaspoon salt

Sweetened Whipped Cream
(page 11)

Chocolate-covered coffee
beans (optional)

1. Prepare pie pastry. Preheat oven to 325°F.

2. Roll out pastry on lightly floured surface into 11-inch circle. Line 9-inch pie plate with pastry. Trim excess crust; flute or crimp edge.

3. Melt chocolate and butter in small heavy saucepan over low heat, stirring constantly.

4. Whisk eggs and egg yolk in medium bowl. Whisk in sugar, half-and-half, coffee granules and salt until blended. Whisk in chocolate mixture until smooth. Pour into crust.

5. Bake 35 minutes or until set. Cool completely on wire rack. Refrigerate 2 hours or until ready to serve. Serve with whipped cream; garnish with chocolate-covered coffee beans.

Note: Use 1 teaspoon coffee granules for a subtle coffee flavor and 2 teaspoons coffee granules for a stronger coffee flavor.

MIXED BERRY CRISP

MAKES 2 SERVINGS

1 tablespoon plus 2 teaspoons
   granulated sugar, divided

1 tablespoon cornstarch*

2 cups mixed berries (thawed if
   frozen)

½ cup old-fashioned oats

¼ cup packed brown sugar

2 tablespoons all-purpose flour

½ teaspoon ground cinnamon

⅛ teaspoon ground ginger

⅛ teaspoon salt

3 tablespoons cold butter

*Increase to 2 tablespoons if using
frozen berries.*

1. Preheat oven to 375°F.

2. Combine 2 teaspoons granulated sugar and
cornstarch in medium bowl. Add berries; toss to coat
evenly. Divide berry mixture between two 5-inch
baking dishes or small pie plates.

3. Combine oats, brown sugar, flour, remaining
1 tablespoon granulated sugar, cinnamon, ginger and
salt in small bowl. Cut in butter with pastry blender
until mixture resembles coarse crumbs. Sprinkle
evenly over berries.

4. Bake 20 to 25 minutes or until topping is golden
brown and filling is bubbly. Serve warm with vanilla
ice cream, if desired.

KitchenAid®

Desserts

PLUM-GINGER BRUSCHETTA

MAKES 9 SERVINGS

1 sheet frozen puff pastry (half of 17¼-ounce package)

2 cups chopped firm ripe plums (about 3 medium)

2 tablespoons sugar

2 tablespoons chopped candied ginger

1 tablespoon all-purpose flour

2 teaspoons fresh lemon juice

⅛ teaspoon ground cinnamon

2 tablespoons apple jelly or apricot preserves

1. Unfold puff pastry and thaw 30 minutes on lightly floured work surface. Preheat oven to 400°F. Line baking sheet with parchment paper.

2. Cut puff pastry sheet lengthwise into three strips. Cut each strip crosswise in thirds to make nine pieces. Place on prepared baking sheet. Bake 10 minutes or until puffed and lightly browned.

3. Meanwhile, combine plums, sugar, ginger, flour, lemon juice and cinnamon in medium bowl.

4. Gently brush each piece of puff pastry with about ½ teaspoon jelly; top with scant ¼ cup plum mixture. Bake about 12 minutes or until fruit is tender.

KitchenAid®

BUTTER ALMOND ICE CREAM WITH AMARETTO CARAMEL SAUCE

MAKES ABOUT 1½ QUARTS ICE CREAM

ICE CREAM

¼ cup (½ stick) butter

1¼ cups (about 5 ounces) sliced natural almonds

3 cups half-and-half

6 egg yolks

1 cup sugar

¾ teaspoon almond extract

½ teaspoon vanilla

SAUCE

1 cup sugar

¼ cup water

1 cup heavy cream, heated

2 tablespoons butter, thinly sliced

2 tablespoons amaretto *or* teaspoon almond extract

Pinch of salt

1. For ice cream, melt ¼ cup butter in small heavy saucepan over medium heat. Bring to a boil and cook 3 minutes or until butter turns light brown. Pour brown butter into small bowl, leaving any browned specks in saucepan.

2. Preheat oven to 350°F. Spread almonds on baking sheet. Bake 10 minutes or until almonds are fragrant and lightly browned, stirring occasionally. Drizzle 2 tablespoons melted brown butter over almonds and toss to coat. Let cool.

3. Place wire sieve over medium bowl. Combine half-and-half and remaining brown butter in medium saucepan and bring to simmer over medium heat, stirring frequently. Remove from heat. Whisk yolks and 1 cup sugar in another medium bowl 1 minute or until pale and thickened. Gradually whisk in hot half-and-half. Pour mixture into saucepan and cook over medium-low heat, stirring constantly with wooden spoon, until custard lightly coats spoon and instant-read thermometer reads 185°F. Immediately pour custard through sieve into bowl. Stir in almond extract and vanilla. Refrigerate several hours or until cold.

4. Attach frozen Ice Cream Maker bowl and dasher to stand mixer. Turn mixer to stir; pour cold mixture into bowl with mixer running. Continue to stir 20 to 30 minutes or until consistency of soft-serve ice cream. Stir in buttered almonds.

5. Transfer ice cream to freezer container. Freeze 2 hours or until firm.

6. For sauce, combine 1 cup sugar sugar and water in heavy medium saucepan. Cook over high heat, stirring until sugar dissolves. Cook without stirring 3 to 5 minutes or until caramel is copper colored and smoking, brushing down crystals that form on inside of pan with pastry brush dipped in cold water and swirling pan occasionally. Remove from heat. Gradually stir in heavy cream (sauce will boil up), and stir until caramel dissolves, returning to medium heat. Add 2 tablespoons butter and stir until melted. Stir in amaretto and salt. Let cool to room temperature.

7. Serve ice cream topped with sauce.

VANILLA BUTTERMILK BISCUITS WITH STRAWBERRIES AND WHIPPED CREAM

MAKES 22 SERVINGS

2 cups all-purpose flour

1 tablespoon baking powder

2 tablespoons granulated sugar

¼ teaspoon salt

½ cup (1 stick) cold butter, cut into pieces

¾ cup buttermilk

2 teaspoons vanilla

1½ pounds strawberries, hulled

2 cups (1 pint) heavy cream

2 tablespoons powdered sugar

½ teaspoon grated lemon peel

1. Preheat oven to 425°F. Line baking sheet with parchment paper.

2. Combine flour, baking powder, granulated sugar and salt in food processor; pulse 5 times. Add butter; process on low about 30 seconds or until mixture resembles coarse crumbs. With motor running, add buttermilk and vanilla through feed tube; process until dough begins to form a ball. Transfer dough to floured surface; roll or pat to ½-inch thickness. Cut circles with 3-inch biscuit cutter. Place on prepared baking sheet. Bake 10 to 15 minutes or until lightly browned. Cool completely.

3. Attach adjustable slicing disc to food processor; slide to sixth notch. Slice strawberries.

4. Remove slicing disc. Combine cream and powdered sugar in clean bowl; process on high speed 1 to 1½ minutes or until thickened. Add lemon peel; pulse 5 times.

5. Slice each biscuit in half. Top bottom half with strawberry slices, whipped cream and top half of biscuit. Garnish as desired.

KitchenAid®

FRESH FRUIT TART WITH VANILLA SHORTBREAD CRUST

MAKES 8 TO 10 SERVINGS

¾ cup (1½ sticks) plus
    1 tablespoon butter,
    softened, divided

⅔ cup sugar, divided

1 teaspoon grated lemon peel

3 teaspoons vanilla, divided

1¾ cups all-purpose flour

⅛ teaspoon salt

3 egg yolks

1½ tablespoons cornstarch

1 cup half-and-half

1 tablespoon milk

½ banana, peeled

1 kiwi, peeled

1 peach or nectarine, pitted
    and cut in half

½ mango, peeled and pitted

3 fresh strawberries, hulled

¼ cup *each* raspberries,
    blueberries and
    blackberries

1. Preheat oven to 350°F. Combine ¾ cup butter, ⅓ cup sugar and lemon peel in food processor; process on low speed about 10 seconds or until well combined. Add 2 teaspoons vanilla; pulse 5 times. Add flour and salt; process about 20 seconds or until dough starts to come together. Turn out dough onto lightly floured surface; shape into disc. Press dough into 10-inch tart pan with removable bottom; cover with circle of parchment paper and fill with dried beans or rice. Bake 20 minutes. Remove beans and parchment; prick bottom of crust all over with fork. Bake 20 minutes or until lightly browned. Cool completely.

2. Meanwhile for filling, combine egg yolks and remaining ⅓ cup sugar in food processor; process on low speed 2 to 3 minutes or until mixture is light yellow and slightly thickened. Add cornstarch and remaining 1 teaspoon vanilla; process 10 seconds. Bring half-and-half to a boil in medium saucepan. With motor running on low speed, pour hot half-and-half through feed tube. Transfer mixture to same saucepan. Cook over medium heat 8 to 10 minutes or until mixture thickens, whisking constantly. Remove from heat; whisk in milk and remaining 1 tablespoon butter. Transfer to medium bowl; cool slightly. Press plastic wrap directly onto surface of filling; refrigerate until cold.

3. Fit food processor with adjustable slicing disc; slide to fifth notch for thick slices. Slice banana, kiwi, peach, mango and strawberries. Spread filling over crust; top with sliced fruit and berries.

MOCHA SEMIFREDDO TERRINE

MAKES 8 TO 12 SERVINGS

1½ teaspoons espresso powder

⅓ cup boiling water

2½ cups (4 ounces) amaretti cookies (about 35 cookies)

1 tablespoon unsweetened cocoa powder

3 tablespoons butter, melted

8 egg yolks

¾ cup plus 2 tablespoons sugar, divided

1 cup heavy cream

Sweetened Whipped Cream (page 11)

1. Dissolve espresso powder in boiling water in small bowl; set aside.

2. Line 9×5-inch loaf pan with plastic wrap. Place cookies and cocoa in food processor. Process until cookies are finely ground. Add butter; process until well combined. Press mixture into bottom of prepared pan. Place in freezer while preparing custard.

3. Whisk egg yolks and ¾ cup sugar in top of double boiler or medium metal bowl. Stir in cooled espresso mixture. Place over simmering water. Cook 4 to 5 minutes or until mixture thickens, whisking constantly. Remove from heat; place bowl in pan of ice water. Whisk 1 minute. Let stand in ice water 5 minutes or until cooled to room temperature, whisking occasionally.

4. Attach wire whip to stand mixer. Whip cream and remaining 2 tablespoons sugar in mixer bowl on high speed until stiff peaks form. Gently fold whipped cream into cooled custard. Spread mixture over crust in pan. Cover tightly; freeze until firm, at least 8 hours or up to 24 hours before serving.

5. To serve, invert terrine onto serving plate; remove plastic wrap. Cut into slices. Serve on chilled plates with whipped cream.

KitchenAid®

CHERRY-ALMOND CLAFOUTI

MAKES 4 SERVINGS

½ cup slivered almonds, toasted*

½ cup powdered sugar

⅔ cup all-purpose flour

⅔ cup granulated sugar

¼ teaspoon salt

½ cup (1 stick) cold butter, cut into pieces

⅔ cup milk

2 eggs

½ teaspoon vanilla

1 cup fresh cherries, pitted and quartered

To toast almonds, spread in single layer on baking sheet. Bake in preheated 350°F oven 8 to 10 minutes or until golden brown, stirring frequently.

1. Preheat oven to 350°F. Grease four 6-ounce ramekins; place on baking sheet.

2. Process almonds in food processor until coarsely ground. Add powdered sugar; pulse until well blended. Add flour, granulated sugar and salt. Pulse until well blended. Gradually add butter through feed tube, pulsing just until blended.

3. Combine milk, eggs and vanilla in small bowl. With food processor running, gradually add milk mixture to almond mixture. Process until blended. Remove blade from food processor; gently stir in cherries. Divide batter among prepared ramekins.

4. Bake about 50 minutes or until tops and sides are puffy and golden. Let cool 5 to 10 minutes before serving.

Note: Clafouti (also spelled clafoutis) is a traditional French dessert made by layering a sweet batter over fresh fruit. The result is a rich dessert with a cakelike topping and a puddinglike center.

KitchenAid®

TRIPLE CHOCOLATE ICE CREAM

MAKES 2 QUARTS ICE CREAM

2 cups heavy cream, divided

2 ounces semisweet chocolate, coarsely chopped

2 ounces unsweetened chocolate, coarsely chopped

2 cups half-and-half

1 cup sugar

⅓ cup unsweetened cocoa powder

8 egg yolks

4 teaspoons vanilla

⅛ teaspoon salt

1½ cups chopped milk chocolate candy bars

1. Combine ½ cup heavy cream, semisweet chocolate and unsweetened chocolate in small saucepan. Heat over medium-low heat until chocolate melts, stirring frequently. Remove from heat; set aside.

2. Heat half-and-half in medium saucepan over medium heat until very hot but not boiling, stirring often. Remove from heat. Combine sugar and cocoa in small bowl.

3. Attach wire whip to stand mixer. Place egg yolks in mixer bowl. With mixer running on medium-low speed, gradually add sugar mixture; mix 30 seconds or until well blended and slightly thickened. Gradually add chocolate mixture and half-and-half on medium-low speed, mixing until well blended.

4. Pour mixture into medium saucepan. Cook over medium heat until small bubbles form around edge and mixture is steamy, stirring constantly. *Do not boil.* Transfer mixture to large bowl; stir in remaining 1½ cups heavy cream, vanilla and salt. Cover and refrigerate 8 hours or until cold.

5. Attach frozen Ice Cream Maker bowl and dasher to stand mixer. Turn mixer to stir; pour cold mixture into bowl with mixer running. Continue to stir 20 to 30 minutes or until consistency of soft-serve ice cream, adding milk chocolate during last 1 to 2 minutes of stirring.

6. Transfer ice cream to freezer container. Freeze 2 hours or until firm.

KitchenAid®

CHOCOLATE CRÈME BRÛLÉE

MAKES 4 SERVINGS

2 cups heavy cream

3 ounces semisweet or
    bittersweet chocolate,
    finely chopped

3 egg yolks

¼ cup granulated sugar

2 teaspoons vanilla

3 tablespoons packed brown
    sugar

1. Preheat oven to 325°F. Heat cream in medium saucepan over medium heat until just beginning to simmer. *Do not boil.* Remove from heat; stir in chocolate until melted and smooth. Set aside to cool slightly.

2. Attach flat beater to stand mixer. Beat egg yolks and granulated sugar in mixer bowl on medium-high speed 5 minutes or until thick and pale yellow. Beat in chocolate mixture and vanilla until blended.

3. Divide mixture among four 6-ounce custard cups or individual baking dishes. Place cups in baking pan; place pan in oven. Pour boiling water into baking pan to reach halfway up sides of custard cups. Cover pan loosely with foil.

4. Bake 30 minutes or until edges are just set. Remove cups from baking pan to wire rack; cool completely. Wrap with plastic wrap and refrigerate 4 hours or up to 3 days.

5. Just before serving, preheat broiler. Spread about 2 teaspoons brown sugar evenly over each cup. Broil 3 to 4 minutes, watching carefully, until sugar bubbles and browns. Serve immediately.

KitchenAid®

PANETTONE BREAD PUDDING WITH CARAMEL SAUCE

MAKES 12 SERVINGS

½ (2-pound) loaf panettone bread, cut into ¾-inch cubes (8 cups)

6 eggs

½ cup granulated sugar

3 cups half-and-half

1 teaspoon vanilla

½ teaspoon ground cinnamon

¾ teaspoon salt, divided

1 cup packed dark brown sugar

½ cup heavy cream

6 tablespoons (¾ stick) butter, cubed

¼ cup light corn syrup

1. Preheat oven to 350°F. Grease 11×7-inch baking dish. Arrange bread cubes in dish.

2. Combine eggs and sugar in large bowl; whisk in half-and-half, vanilla, cinnamon and ¼ teaspoon salt. Pour mixture over bread, pressing down to moisten top. Let stand 15 minutes.

3. Bake 40 to 45 minutes or until puffed and golden.

4. For caramel sauce, whisk brown sugar, cream, butter, corn syrup and remaining ½ teaspoon salt in medium saucepan over medium-high heat until sugar is dissolved. Boil 1 minute without stirring. Cool completely.

5. Serve bread pudding warm with caramel sauce.

KitchenAid®

CREAMY LEMON-ORANGE GELATO

MAKES 1 QUART GELATO

- 2 cups milk
- 4 (2¾-inch) strips orange peel
- 4 (2¾-inch) strips lemon peel
- 6 coffee beans
- 5 egg yolks
- ¾ cup sugar

1. Heat milk, orange peel, lemon peel and coffee beans in heavy medium saucepan over medium heat until bubbles form around edge of pan. *Do not boil.* Remove from heat.

2. Whisk yolks and sugar in medium bowl. Gradually whisk in half of milk mixture. Return mixture to saucepan; whisk in remaining milk. Cook over low heat about 8 minutes or until mixture thickens slightly and coats back of spoon, stirring constantly. Strain through fine mesh sieve into medium bowl. Refrigerate 2 hours or until cold.

3. Attach frozen Ice Cream Maker bowl and dasher to stand mixer. Turn mixer to stir; pour cold mixture into bowl with mixer running. Continue to stir 15 to 20 minutes or until consistency of soft serve ice cream.

4. Transfer to airtight container and freeze several hours or until frozen.

KitchenAid®

RASPBERRY CLAFOUTI

MAKES 8 TO 10 SERVINGS

3 eggs

⅓ cup sugar

1 cup half-and-half

2 tablespoons butter, melted
and slightly cooled

½ teaspoon vanilla

⅔ cup almond flour

Pinch salt

2 containers (6 ounces each)
fresh raspberries

1. Preheat oven to 325°F. Generously grease 9-inch ceramic tart pan or pie plate.

2. Attach wire whip to stand mixer. Whip eggs and sugar in mixer bowl on medium speed 4 minutes or until slightly thickened. Add half-and-half, butter and vanilla; whip until combined. Gradually whip in almond flour and salt on medium-low speed. Pour enough batter into prepared pan to just cover bottom. Bake 10 minutes or until set.

3. Remove pan from oven. Scatter raspberries evenly over baked batter. Stir remaining batter and pour over raspberries.

4. Bake 40 to 45 minutes or until center is set and top is golden. Cool completely on wire rack. Refrigerate leftovers.

Note: The most famous and traditional clafouti is made with cherries (see page 486 for individual cherry clafouti), but berries, plums, peaches and pears are also used.

KitchenAid®

POMEGRANATE ORANGE SHERBET

MAKES ABOUT 1 1/2 QUARTS SHERBET

⅔ cup sugar

2 cups bottled pomegranate juice

1 cup fresh orange juice

2 teaspoons grated orange peel

2 tablespoons grenadine (optional)

1. Bring sugar and ⅔ cup water to a boil in small saucepan over high heat, stirring to dissolve sugar. Boil 5 minutes or until syrup is slightly thickened. Cool slightly.

2. Combine pomegranate juice, orange juice, orange peel and grenadine, if desired in medium bowl. Stir in sugar syrup. Refrigerate at least 2 hours or until cold.

3. Attach frozen Ice Cream Maker bowl and dasher to stand mixer. Turn mixer to stir; pour cold mixture into bowl with mixer running. Continue to stir 15 to 20 minutes or until consistency of soft serve ice cream.

4. Transfer sherbet to freezer containers. Freeze at least 2 hours or until firm.

KitchenAid®

PUMPKIN MOUSSE CUPS

MAKES 8 SERVINGS

1¼ cups heavy cream, divided

1 cup solid-pack pumpkin

⅓ cup sugar

½ teaspoon pumpkin pie spice

⅛ teaspoon salt

½ teaspoon vanilla

½ cup crushed gingersnap cookies (about 8 small gingersnaps)

1. Combine ½ cup cream, pumpkin, sugar, pumpkin pie spice and salt in small saucepan; bring to a simmer over medium heat. Reduce heat to low; simmer 15 minutes, stirring occasionally. Stir in vanilla; set aside to cool to room temperature.

2. Attach wire whip to stand mixer. Whip remaining ¾ cup cream in mixer bowl on high speed until soft peaks form. Gently fold 1 cup whipped cream into pumpkin mixture until well blended. Refrigerate until ready to serve.

3. Spoon heaping ¼ cup pumpkin mousse into each of eight ½-cup glasses or dessert dishes. Top with dollop of remaining whipped cream; sprinkle with crushed cookies.

KitchenAid®

INDIVIDUAL CHOCOLATE SOUFFLÉS

MAKES 2 SOUFFLÉS

1 tablespoon butter, plus additional for greasing

2 tablespoons plus 1 teaspoon sugar, divided

4 ounces bittersweet chocolate, broken into pieces

2 eggs, separated, at room temperature

1. Preheat oven to 375°F. Coat two ¾-cup soufflé dishes or ramekins with butter. Add ½ teaspoon sugar to each dish; shake to coat bottoms and sides.

2. Combine chocolate and 1 tablespoon butter in top of double boiler. Heat over simmering water until chocolate is melted and smooth, stirring occasionally. Remove from heat; stir in egg yolks, one at a time. (Mixture may become grainy, but will smooth out with addition of egg whites.)

3. Attach wire whip to stand mixer. Whip egg whites in mixer bowl on high speed until soft peaks form. Gradually add remaining 2 tablespoons sugar; whip until stiff peaks form and mixture is glossy.

4. Gently fold egg whites into chocolate mixture. Do not overmix; allow some white streaks to remain. Divide batter evenly between dishes.

5. Bake 15 minutes until soufflés rise but remain moist in centers. Serve immediately.

KitchenAid®

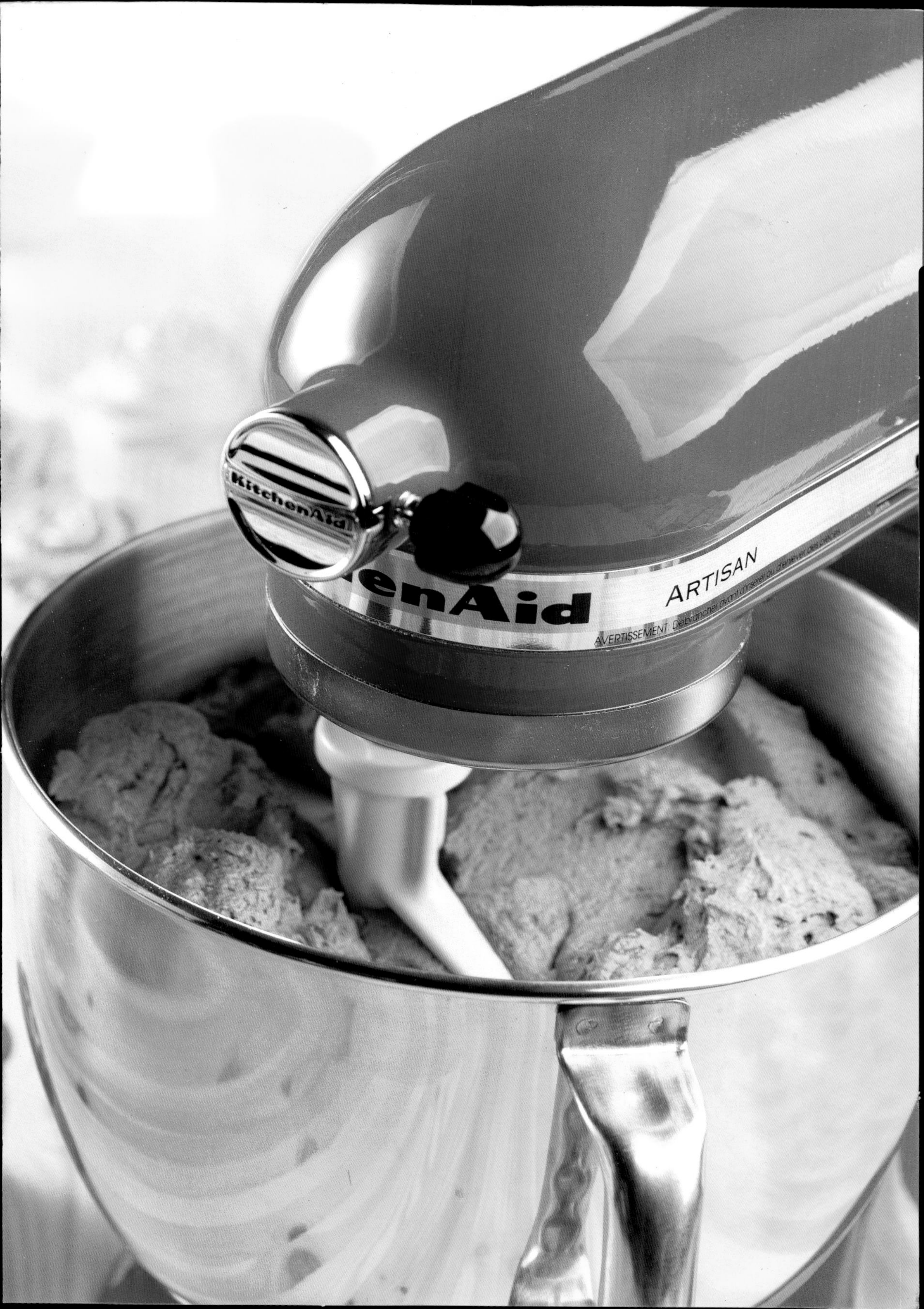
KitchenAid
ARTISAN

KitchenAid®

KitchenAid

KitchenAid

KitchenAid®

KitchenAid®

KitchenAid®

KitchenAid®

KitchenAid®

KitchenAid®

KitchenAid®

KitchenAid®

METRIC CONVERSION CHART

VOLUME MEASUREMENTS (dry)

1/8 teaspoon = 0.5 mL
1/4 teaspoon = 1 mL
1/2 teaspoon = 2 mL
3/4 teaspoon = 4 mL
1 teaspoon = 5 mL
1 tablespoon = 15 mL
2 tablespoons = 30 mL
1/4 cup = 60 mL
1/3 cup = 75 mL
1/2 cup = 125 mL
2/3 cup = 150 mL
3/4 cup = 175 mL
1 cup = 250 mL
2 cups = 1 pint = 500 mL
3 cups = 750 mL
4 cups = 1 quart = 1 L

VOLUME MEASUREMENTS (fluid)

1 fluid ounce (2 tablespoons) = 30 mL
4 fluid ounces (1/2 cup) = 125 mL
8 fluid ounces (1 cup) = 250 mL
12 fluid ounces (1 1/2 cups) = 375 mL
16 fluid ounces (2 cups) = 500 mL

WEIGHTS (mass)

1/2 ounce = 15 g
1 ounce = 30 g
3 ounces = 90 g
4 ounces = 120 g
8 ounces = 225 g
10 ounces = 285 g
12 ounces = 360 g
16 ounces = 1 pound = 450 g

DIMENSIONS

1/16 inch = 2 mm
1/8 inch = 3 mm
1/4 inch = 6 mm
1/2 inch = 1.5 cm
3/4 inch = 2 cm
1 inch = 2.5 cm

OVEN TEMPERATURES

250°F = 120°C
275°F = 140°C
300°F = 150°C
325°F = 160°C
350°F = 180°C
375°F = 190°C
400°F = 200°C
425°F = 220°C
450°F = 230°C

BAKING PAN SIZES

Utensil	Size in Inches/Quarts	Metric Volume	Size in Centimeters
Baking or Cake Pan (square or rectangular)	8×8×2	2 L	20×20×5
	9×9×2	2.5 L	23×23×5
	12×8×2	3 L	30×20×5
	13×9×2	3.5 L	33×23×5
Loaf Pan	8×4×3	1.5 L	20×10×7
	9×5×3	2 L	23×13×7
Round Layer Cake Pan	8×1½	1.2 L	20×4
	9×1½	1.5 L	23×4
Pie Plate	8×1¼	750 mL	20×3
	9×1¼	1 L	23×3
Baking Dish or Casserole	1 quart	1 L	—
	1½ quart	1.5 L	—
	2 quart	2 L	—

KitchenAid®